# The Legal and Ethical Aspects of Telemedicine

# The Legal and Ethical Aspects of Telemedicine

**Ben Stanberry,** LLB (Hons), LLM (Wales), MRIN

*Research Associate & Associate Lecturer*
*Seafarers International Research Centre*
*Cardiff University, UK*

*The* ROYAL
SOCIETY *of*
MEDICINE
PRESS *Limited*

©1998 Royal Society of Medicine Press Ltd
1 Wimpole Street, London W1M 8AE, UK
16 East 69th Street, New York, NY 10021, USA

**British Library Cataloguing in Publication Data**
A catalogue record for this book is available from the British Library

ISBN 1 85315 354 0

Phototypeset by Spot-on design, Leighton Buzzard, Bedfordshire
Printed in Great Britain by Redwood Books, Trowbridge, Wiltshire

*For John and Nicola*

# ▶ Contents

Chapter 5
# Telemedical malpractice     67

Chapter 6
# Standards adopted by the General Medical Council, Royal Colleges and Professional Associations     89

## Chapter 10
# Regulating telemedicine in the future    157

# ▶ Foreword

*by Professor Richard Wootton, Institute of Telemedicine and Telecare, Queen's University, Belfast*

Telemedicine is not new. It has been practised using electronic communication for decades, and using traditional forms of communication for much longer. Despite this historical background, telemedicine appears to have a polarising effect on the healthcare profession. People are rarely neutral about it; they are either enthusiastic proponents or vehement opponents. The proponents believe that telemedicine represents the future. It will lead to higher standards of medical care as well as reduced costs. The opponents believe that it represents a threat to the traditional doctor–patient relationship and is an intrinsically unsafe way to practise medicine. The potential legal and ethical problems associated with telemedicine are often waved as a "shroud" to support the view that the possible complications of telemedicine mean that it could not be used to form the basis of a clinical service.

In comparison with the emerging literature on the technical aspects of telemedicine, including user satisfaction – which seems to be high – comparatively little has been written about the legal and ethical aspects. One of the first papers to appear in a refereed journal made the point that telemedicine didn't raise any new issues of principle. The same paper also predicted that ultimately the issues which are raised would be settled in the courts. In my opinion, one of the major contributions which Ben Stanberry's book makes is to offer an alternative to this rather passive viewpoint. He suggests a rational course of acton with respect to the practice of telemedicine which should minimise the chance of a subsequent legal action, if not prevent it. Another significant contribution he has made is to draw together into a comprehensive and readable account the factors relating to telemedicine and the law.

Ultimately, telemedicine is a vehicle for the delivery of health care. People have the same rights to high quality care as they do with conventional medicine. How does the telemedicine community ensure that this happens in practice? The current fashion is for "evidence-based" medicine (as though medical science had been practised previously without such evidence). It is to be hoped that the launch by the Royal Society of Medicine of a series of textbooks on telemedicine, of which Ben Stanberry's book is the first, will be one mechanism by which we can ensure that as telemedicine comes into mainstream health service use in the future, it is founded on a solid "evidence base" and delivers health care to the highest practicable standards.

# ▶ Preface and acknowledgements

It is common for academic authors to state in the Preface to their books who their work is aimed at: undergraduates, postgraduates, practitioners, other academics or any combination of these. So I shall stick with tradition and state who this book is aimed at. It is for surfers.

Not the blonde, tanned, wetsuit wearing variety, you understand, nor even the young people who stay up well past the time that the rest of us go to bed, exploring the Internet. This book is for a new kind of surfer whose existence I was not aware of until I began my research into telemedicine and unwittingly became one myself. A "surfer" is someone who sees an idea – the wave – and rides it. The surfers that this book is aimed at are a rapidly growing group of men and women in the United Kingdom and beyond whose deep faith in the revolution that telemedicine will undoubtedly bring to the delivery of health care throughout the world motivates them to research, develop, examine, evaluate and ultimately invest in telemedicine and telecare services.

These men and women are doctors, managers and executives in health authorities and NHS trusts, business-people and other professionals working in the growing area where health care and telecommunications meet. But while health care telematics and telemedicine in particular move, with the approach of the millennium, into the mainstream of medical practice, our understanding of the legal, ethical and policy issues that underscore and may even hinder this move is exceptionally limited. This book addresses these issues and is aimed at the people who need to come to grips with them, though I hope that students of medicine, law and ethics as well as lawyers working in-house and in practice will also find it a useful source of reference.

Though many architects of telemedicine describe themselves as surfers, I think a better description of them would be the latest in a long line of pioneers whose dedication has improved medicine and health care over the past century. But as one House of Lords Judge, Lord Edmund-Davies, has put it, in the case of *Independent Broadcasting Authority* v *EMI Electronics*: "the law requires even pioneers to be prudent". With prudence I know that history will judge these "surfers" as having directly brought about one of the most important – if not *the* most important – medical innovations of the twentieth century.

Telemedicine has infinite potential but like so many other medical innovations, the creation of appropriate standards, best practices and legal frameworks lags significantly behind the actual creation of telemedical technology and systems. Consequently, most of the laws governing telemedicine can, at present, be nothing more than the extrapolation of the laws of conventional medical practice. I therefore hope very much that this is the first of many editions of *The Legal and Ethical Aspects of Telemedicine*, and that readers will feel free to make constructive suggestions as to any specific legal and clinical problems they have encountered which are not examined in this book.

The successive drafting and redrafting of chapters and process of deciding on the contents of the book was an uphill struggle and could not have been accomplished without the help and advice of many individuals and organisations. I gratefully acknowledge the assistance of all who made time to speak to me, answer my many questions and send me literature, in particular Neil Marshall at the General Medical Council; Dr Richard Mellish and Dr Susanne Ludgate at the Medical Devices Agency; Dr P K Schutte and Emma Stafford at the Medical

Defence Union; Dr Gerard Ponting at the Medical Protection Society; Lori Bartholemew at the Physicians Insurers Association of America; Suky Overda at the Royal College of Surgeons; Linda Cuthbertson at the Royal College of Physicians and Hazel Beckett at the Royal College of Radiology. The Royal Colleges of General Practitioners, Nursing and Pathology, as well as the British Medical Association, also gave me as much information as they had available.

Without the guidance of my colleagues at Cardiff University I would never have been able to marry the technical and legal aspects of the practice of medicine at a distance. I am grateful to Professor Alastair Couper, Director of the Seafarers International Research Centre for Safety and Occupational Health ("SIRC") at the Department of Maritime Studies and International Transport from 1995 to 1997, and his successor Professor Tony Lane, who have wholeheartedly supported my work. Members of the telemedicine research group at SIRC – Dr Hermantha "Wicks" Wickramatillake and Captain Christopher Walsh – have given me essential advice, guidance and support. Louise Richards, Rhian Morris and Marie-Claire Saranz were a breath of fresh air whenever the going got tough. Dr Peter Clinch and Duncan Montgomery at Cardiff University's Law Library provided invaluable help in locating materials.

At Cardiff Law School, Howard Johnson guided me through the maze of European Union and domestic intellectual property, anti-trust, product liability and private international law.

I owe an enormous debt to Peter Richardson, Miriam Richardson, Tricia Dixon, Georgette Piket and Tanya Thomas at the Royal Society of Medicine Press for their patience and hard work in making the production of this book run so smoothly and to the many people in the fields of health care and telecommunications whose enthusiasm and practical advice have been vital to its completion: Professor Richard Wootton of the Institute of Telemedicine and Telecare at Queen's University, Belfast; Dr Keith Freeman, Director-General of the Global Telemedicine Institute; Daniel Callaghan of Lifesigns; Wyn Evans of Llandough Hospital and Community NHS Trust; John Morgan of the Health Strategy Department at the Welsh Office; Graham Durant and Ken Pyle of BT Health; Terry Dennis of the Institute of Health Services Management; Dr Simon Wallace of World Care UK; Jackie Anne Langelund and Dr Ulrik Kirk of the Institute of Maritime Medicine at South Jutland University, Denmark; Professor Francesco Amenta of the Centro Internationale Radio Medico; Professor Tony Davies of the Electronic Commerce and Innovation Centre at Cardiff University, and last but by no means least, Tessa Shellens and Jane Lang of Bevan Ashford Solicitors. I have tried to state the law as accurately as possible as at 1 January 1998 but any errors or omissions in the finished product are, however, all my own.

Sincere thanks must go to my companion Lisa Davies for proof-reading and general encouragement, to my good friend and colleague Toral Patel for her kindness, support and valuable comments on earlier drafts and to the very lovely Jeya Thiruchelvam for preparing the Guide to Legal Citations. Sincerest gratitude of all, though, to "the Big Guy" and to my dear parents for the sacrifices they have made for me, without which I would never have had the opportunity to write a book like this.

*Ben Stanberry*
*Cardiff University*
*June 1998*

# ▶ Guide to legal citations

*by Jeya Thiruchelvam, LLB (Hons)*

Most of the citations of journal articles and publications that appear in this book are based on the formats used by the US National Library of Medicine in *Index Medicus*. However, legal cases and legislation are cited using the standard conventions described in Raistrick D. *Index to Legal Citations and Abbreviations*. (London: Professional Books, 1981).

## Cases

Cases are referred to by the names of the parties involved, which are usually written in italics or underlined. The name of the plaintiff (the party bringing the action) appears first, followed by a "v" meaning "versus" but which is read as "and" in civil cases, followed by the name of the defendant(s) against whom the action has been brought. For example:

*Bolam* v *Friern Hospital Management Committee*

In criminal actions the name of the plaintiff is replaced by the letter "*R*" which means *Rex* or *Regina* (Latin for "king" or "queen") and indicates the state's role as prosecutor, with the accused person's (the defendant's) name appearing after the "v" which in a criminal case is read as "against". For example:

*R* v *Gold*

Occasionally, the Attorney-General or the Director of Public Prosecutions will bring a prosecution and their name will appear instead of the "*R*". If the action is one of a series of cases involving the same parties then a number may appear in brackets after their names:

*Attorney-General* v *Guardian Newspapers (No. 2)*

*Re* means simply "in the matter of" or "concerning" and is commonly used in family cases or cases involving children and the mentally handicapped. Initials are used to protect their identity and the nature of the case is often indicated in parentheses:

*Re J (a minor) (medical treatment)*

In cases where the court is being asked judicially to review the administrative actions of a government department or a lower court, the name of the party upon whose application the case is being heard usually appears after the Latin phrase "*ex parte*" and the name of the party whose actions are being reviewed appears after the "v", hence:

*R* v *Central Birmingham Health Authority, ex parte Walker*

The citation for a case is abbreviated after the names of the parties and, in this book, appears as an endnote if the case has been cited in the main body of the text, or immediately after the parties' names if the case has been cited only in the endnote. The year in which the case was reported is given in square brackets. Round brackets are used where the date indicates the year the judgment was actually given. The volume number of the publication containing the case report is given next if there has been more than one volume that year. The initials that follow are the abbreviated name of the publication or series of law reports where the case can be found. The most common of which are:

| | |
|---|---|
| AC | Appeal Cases |
| All ER | All England Reports |
| BMLR | Butterworths Medico-Legal Reports |
| Ch | Chancery |
| Crim LR | Criminal Law Review |
| ECR | European Court Reports |
| ER | English Reports |
| FSR | Fleet Street Reports of Patent Cases |
| JP | Justice of the Peace (Law Reports) |
| KB | King's Bench |
| Med LR | Medical Law Reports |
| QB | Queen's Bench |
| RPC | Reports of Patent Design and Trademark Cases |
| Sol Jo | Solicitor's Journal |
| WLR | Weekly Law Reports |

The page number given after this abbreviation refers to the page where the case begins. If attention is drawn to a section of the judgment then it is usually indicated by the name of the judge preceding the case citation proper and the words "at page" (or "at p.") at the end of the citation. For instance:

Per Mr Justice McNair in *Bolam* v *Friern Hospital Management Committee* [1957] 2 All ER 188 at p. 121.

The titles of judges are often abbreviated. For instance, Lord Denning, Master of the Rolls is often "Lord Denning MR". Other common abbreviations include "J" for Justice, "LJ" for Lord Justice, "LCJ" for Lord Chief Justice, "LC" for Lord Chancellor and "VC" for Vice Chancellor. For instance:

See the dicta of Morris LJ in *Hornal* v *Neuberger Products Limited* [1957] 1 QB 247

## Legislation

An Act of Parliament (sometimes referred to as a statute) or a European Union Directive is usually referred to by its short title. Where a section or subsection of an Act is referred to this can be abbreviated as "s" for section or "ss" for sections, with the subsection being written in closed parentheses and sometimes abbreviated "subs." (or "subpara" for subparagraphs). Acts may also contain detailed provisions known as Schedules ("Sch") or may contain paragraphs ("para"). Directives usually contain articles ("art"). Some examples:

s.5(b)(i) of the Wireless Telegraphy Act 1949

section 50(7), Consumer Protection Act 1987

article 1(2) of the software Directive

Statutory Instruments are cited by their short title, followed by the abbreviation "SI", the year and the running number. For instance:

Active Implantable Medical Devices Regulations 1992 (SI 1992 No. 3146)

Further guidance on how to read legal citations is available in Clinch P. *Using a law library: a student's guide to legal research skills*, (London: Blackstone Press, 1992).

# ► Table of legislation

The following legislation is referred to in the main text of this book. References in **bold** type are to pages where extracts from the text of the legislation have been reproduced.

# ▶ Table of cases

The following cases are referred to in the main text of this book. References in **bold** type are to pages where extracts from the cases have been reproduced.

# ▶ 1

# Introduction

Inadequate health care and medical services are a problem afflicting not just third world countries. While it is true to say that the developing world suffers most from a shortage of doctors and other health care professionals, there are also many isolated, rural areas of first world countries that have poor communications networks, making the provision of health care to the communities living and working in these regions extremely difficult. Even within more urbanised and provincial areas with modern communications networks, hospitals may be ill-equipped to deal with certain medical problems while being recognised as centres of excellence in other specialties. Thus hospitals must share their human and medical resources and many are consequently overstretched – both financially and logistically.

For countries with limited resources, telecommunications can provide vital access to medical and health care expertise. Moreover, the advent of digital satellite technology means that such communications are no longer dependent upon the existence of land lines or radio stations. So regardless of geography the many medical specialties can now be accessible to under-served locations to provide regular check-ups, relief after natural disasters or assistance in combating tropical diseases.

In developed countries also, such as the United Kingdom, interest is growing rapidly in the benefits telecommunications can bring both to isolated, rural communities and to urban and sub-urban communities falling within the responsibility of health authorities and NHS trusts, by way of improving patient care and maximising staff skills. The word used to describe this growing area where telecommunications and medicine meet is "telemedicine".

## What is telemedicine?

"Telemedicine", a phrase first coined in the 1970s by Thomas Bird, refers to health care delivery whereby physicians examine distant patients through the use of telecommunications technology. The term derives from the Greek "tele", meaning "at a distance", and of course our existing word "medicine", which itself derieves from the Latin "mederi" meaning "healing". There have been many attempts to provide an all-encompassing definition of "telemedicine". The European Commission's health care telematics programme defines telemedicine as:

> Rapid access to shared and remote medical expertise by means of telecommunications and information technologies, no matter where the patient or relevant information is located.

Other definitions include:

> The practice of medicine at a distance.

The practice of medical care using interactive audiovisual and data communications. This includes medical care delivery, diagnosis, consultation and treatment, as well as education and the transfer of medical data.

The use of telecommunication technology to assist in the delivery of health care.

A system of health care delivery in which physicians examine distant patients through the use of telecommunications technology.

The use of telecommunications and informatics for medical and health purposes.

The interactive transmission of medical images and data to provide patients in remote areas with better care.

Telemedicine is the delivery of medical care to patients anywhere in the world by combining telecommunications and medical expertise.

Hence telecommunications and medical technologies which provide any or all of the following services may be described as "telemedicine":

▶ the data transfer of medical, health care, research and/or educational materials in electronic form;
▶ audiovisual or multimedia communication between health care providers (consultants, physicians, general practitioners, nurses or non-professional medics); and
▶ audiovisual or multimedia communication between a health care provider and their patient.

Related terms such as "telehealth" and "telecare" are also used. "Telehealth" refers to the use of telecommunication technologies to make health and related services more accessible to health care consumers and providers in rural or otherwise under-served areas. It is distinguishable from telemedicine in that it provides a service to those who are not necessarily sick or wounded but who want to stay well and independent – whether through receiving regular check-ups, advice on a healthy lifestyle or counselling. Telecare provides nursing and community support to a patient located at a different site from the nursing staff. The common element in telemedicine, telehealth and telecare therefore, is that telecommunications are used to bring medical and health care services to patients wherever they are. They are all examples of health care telematics. "Telematics for Health" is the name of a division of the European Commission and includes all forms of informatics or information technology aimed at improving the efficiency of health care even within a single hospital or health administration.

## The beginnings of telemedicine

If one were pedantic enough then one could consider the first instance of a patient calling for their doctor by radio or telephone to be the first ever telemedical consultation. Certainly it is true today that the provision of medical advice by telephone and radio is a form of telemedicine, although the latter is more usually known as "radiomedicine". The idea of using telecommunications technology to send and receive more than just sound is by no means new.

As far back as 1940 scientists were experimenting with the radiotelegraphic transmission of pulse, respiration and heartbeat graphs from a long-distance patient.[1] It was Guglielmo Marconi who developed radio-telegraphy in 1897, and the subsequent introduction of radio equipment on board ships which could be used for communication with coastal radio-stations made the provision of medical advice from a distance possible for the first time: "radiomedicine", the forerunner to telemedicine, was born.

## Radiomedicine

Radiomedical advice, which essentially comprises a request for medical help by a layperson responsible for health care on board a ship or airplane, or from someone living in a remote area such as the Australian outback to a centre providing the radiomedical service, represents, in the absence of a qualified physician or surgeon on site, the most realistic way of guaranteeing quality health care for merchant seamen and remote communities, as well as dealing with medical emergencies in the air. The very first organisation to provide radio-medical assistance was probably the Seamen's Church Institute of New York which was granted a commercial radio licence on 18 November 1920. The Church Institute's radio station had a range of about 2,500 miles and had available a team of doctors who could provide round-the-clock medical assistance. It was seven years later that a conference on telecommunications was held in Washington DC and it was there decided to add a medical section to the International Code of Signals. Around this time several other countries also established radiomedical services for their own fleets. The Sahlgrenska University Hospital in Gothenburg, Sweden, began a radiomedical service in 1922, sending signals by morse code. The Seamen Relief Association was set up in Japan six years later in 1928; Radio Scheverningen in Holland soon followed in 1930. In 1931 Germany set up her own radiomedical advice centre, followed by the Italian International Radio Medical Centre in 1935 and Yugoslavia in 1938.

In 1932 the International Telecommunication Union (ITU) published the first list of coastal radio stations providing medical services but it wasn't until 13 May 1958 that the International Labour Office (ILO) published Recommendation No. 106 which represents, thus far, one of the few detailed official documents on medical assistance to ships without a doctor on board. The main principles established by the ILO were that radiomedical advice should be available by radio to ships at sea free of charge at any hour and that this advice should include specialist assistance if necessary. The ILO also required that special manuals or other kinds of medical instructions should be available to help doctors in giving radiomedical assistance and comprehensive lists of radio stations providing radiomedical services should be kept on board every ship. At present more than 200 organisations worldwide provide radiomedical advice to seafarers and it is in the field of medical assistance to seafarers that the development of radiomedicine has clearly been of greatest benefit. Radiomedical services originally established by maritime States to facilitate advice to their domestic fleets have now evolved to include networks of shore based hospitals linked to coastal radio stations (Japan) or the use of hospital ships to support the activities of vessels in fishing areas (Spain). By far the best example of the extension of radiomedical services from the domestic to the truly international is, however, provided by the story of the Italian International Radio Medicine Centre, the Centro Internazionale Radio Medico ("CIRM") which started its activities on 1 March 1935 with the purpose of providing medical assistance by radio to ships of any nationality without a doctor on board, navigating in all seas of the world. This activity was later extended to include aircraft in flight and to those requiring medical care who could not be reached by a doctor (primarily those on the smaller Italian islands). Between 1935 and 1996 the CIRM assisted 42,935 patients, mainly seafarers, which is by far the largest contribution by a single body to the provision of health care from a distance.

The services offered by the CIRM are, at one remove, both unique in their comprehensiveness and very similar to those offered by the many other radiomedical services around the world. Radiomedicine organisations have undoubtedly increased the quality of medical care provided to seafarers and remote communities. Radiomedical advice in the United Kingdom is now provided exclusively through British Telecom and Portishead Radio near Bristol from the accident and emergency unit at the Royal Naval Hospital, Portsmouth (Haslar). The twenty-four hour duty doctors there have access to specialist opinions on a round the clock basis when required. The Marine Safety Agency pay all the telecom charges both for ships and for Haslar.

### The problems of radiomedicine

Manning levels today, with perhaps only thirty seafarers crewing large bulk carriers, mean that although hospital facilities are still provided on board ocean-going vessels in merchant fleets, supplying care to the sick seafarer has become exceedingly difficult. Whilst historically the Chief Steward would have been the designated medical officer, as he would usually have more time to devote to this task than the rest of the crew, it is now more common for the Second or Third Navigation Officer to be the designated medical officer on the basis of a course of on-shore first aid training. The level of skill of a ship's medical officer varies tremendously between countries and between shipping lines. Although there is presently a move towards the worldwide standardisation of medical training, it is sadly still the case that the level of training of a ship's medical officer is often no greater than that of the designated first-aider in a shore-based firm or office. At the same time the courts, particularly those in the United States, now place a very high value on a seafarer's life when they consider his death to have been unnecessary or avoidable. It is therefore imperative to provide seriously injured or sick seafarers with immediate expert medical attention.

Since it is not usually possible to have a qualified doctor on board an ocean-going vessel, medical emergencies can easily evolve into critical situations, especially when managed by inexperienced medical officers. This was recognised by European Union Directive 92/29/EEC which proposed that:

> The use of long distance medical consultation methods constitutes an efficient
> way of contributing to the protection of the safety of health workers.[2]

Additionally, European Union Council Directive 93/103/EC set up minimum safety and health requirements for work on board fishing vessels by extending the applicability of the most important first aid provisions of Council Directive 92/29/EEC.[3] But radiomedicine does not always provide the best solution. In their report *The Navigators' Health Education*, Kirk et al[4] found, in a survey of navigation officers on board Danish registered ships that, many wanted to see their ship's radiomedical link giving them access to a general practitioner as opposed to a specialist. Some felt that, too often, they were instructed through the radiomedical link to proceed to an emergency port to evacuate a casualty when the designated medical officer on board would have been more than able to deal with the casualty himself. Moreover, many of those surveyed also commented that while they always used the radiomedical link when uncertain about the correct diagnosis or treatment, the physicians at the radiomedical centre had too limited a knowledge of the possibilities for giving treatment on board. The majority of those surveyed all agreed that they would use the radiomedical service more often if it were free.

A similar survey of Finnish Ships Officers[5] found that 25% of those officers had difficulties in describing the status and symptoms of the patient using a radiomedical link. Thirty-three per cent felt that they had received good medical advice via radiomedicine even though as many considered that medical doctors on shore did not have enough knowledge about the living, working and treatment conditions on board ship. The extent of medical training of the ship's officer in charge of health care is a decisive factor in successful treatment of a sick or injured person on board ship[6] and it is equally true that insufficiencies in the medical aids available to the ship, such as the medicine chest and the radiomedical service, could also be factors in the fatality rate following an accident on board ship.[7] Hence, while the provision of radiomedical advice has benefited seafarers and remote communities for at least sixty years, clearly there are restrictions on the capabilities of this system and new techniques are required to meet the challenge of providing medical care to sick and injured seafarers and people living in remote areas.

## The evolution of modern telemedicine

Among the earliest examples of telemetry in action would be the monitoring of astronauts' physiological functions by the United States National Aeronautics and Space Administration. The main concerns of scientists and doctors at mission control at this time were the effects of zero gravity so they monitored blood pressure, respiration rate, ECG and temperature. Such a use of telecommunication and telemetry systems was considered highly sophisticated and a medical support team was on constant alert in case they were required to diagnose and treat an in-flight medical emergency. NASA weren't the only ones experimenting with telemedicine in the late 1960s and early 1970s, however.

In 1967 the first telemedicine system in which physicians and patients interacted was installed in Boston between Massachusetts General Hospital and a medical "shop" at Logan Airport. Doctors passing through the airport were invited to bring X-rays to a room on the passenger concourse. These would be illuminated by an ordinary wall-mounted light box and then scanned by a black and white camera before being transmitted to a video monitor in the General Hospital's radiology department. Physicians at the radiology department could then discuss the case with the doctor at the airport shop by telephone.

The first ever truly interactive link was set up in the same year between the Nebraska Psychiatric Institute in Omaha and the Norfolk State Hospital, some 112 miles away. Both this and the Logan Airport experiment showed that interactive television links and the transmission of medical data could be undertaken without any significant loss of clarity or detail and hence a "remote diagnosis" made by a doctor many miles away. Other American programmes such as "STARPAHC" (Space Technology Applied to Rural Papago Advanced Health Care), a 20-year joint co-operation between Lockheed, NASA and the United States Public Health Service in the late 1950s, experimented with providing health care to remote rural communities – in this instance an Indian reservation in Arizona.

The first use of satellite communications took place in Canada in January 1976 when the Communications Technology Satellite *Hermes* was launched by NASA as part of a joint project with Canada's Department of Communications to serve the needs of remote areas of Canada. Hermes was used in three telemedicine experiments. In June 1976 the Ontario Ministry of Health used VHF radio and Hermes to test the feasibility of monitoring vital signs such as heart rate, respiration rate, temperature and ECG when a patient was evacuated from a remote community in northern Ontario. In October of that year the University of Western Ontario used Hermes in five-month trials linking the University Hospital in London, Ontario, the Moose Factory General Hospital and the Kashechewan Nursing Station on James Bay. Medical consultations, transmission of X-rays and heart sounds and some continuing education all took place. The third project took place in 1977 and enabled the Memorial University at St John's, Newfoundland, to broadcast a television programme to Stephenville, St Anthony, Labrador City and Goose Bay.

## Telemedicine today

Twenty years later we stand at what can only be described as the dawn of a new era for health. Indeed, history may well judge telemedicine as having made one of the greatest single contributions to the development of medical and health care this century. Although there are at present only a few commercial, profitable telemedicine services "up and running", the explosion of interest in telemedicine and telecare has led to an exponential growth in the number of research and development projects being undertaken in the United Kingdom and Europe. The telemedicine industry is expanding rapidly – almost every other month a telemedicine conference takes place somewhere in the world. There are several telemedicine web sites on the Internet and a growing number of health authorities and NHS trusts in the United Kingdom are looking at ways of using telemedicine to provide new services and improve existing ones. Alongside the traditional medical journals such as *The Lancet* and the journals of the many Royal Colleges there is now a *Journal of Telemedicine and Telecare* published quarterly by the Royal Society of Medicine Press and edited by Professor Richard Wootton of the Institute of Telemedicine and Telecare at Queen's University Belfast. The *Journal of Telemedicine and Telecare* is the only peer-reviewed journal in this area to be indexed in MEDLINE. In the United States of America, always several years ahead of everyone else, there are at least a dozen such regional and national publications and even a *Telemedicine 200* and a *Who's Who in Telemedicine*, although only one American publication, the *Telemedicine Journal*, is peer-reviewed.

Much of the telemedicine research and development taking place around the world today is dependant upon government subsidies and the goodwill of telecommunications companies and international organisations. The European Commission ran a large number of telemedicine and telehealth projects under its Third Framework Programme – about 45 in all. Under the present Fourth Framework Programme there are almost twice as many projects taking place. In June 1996 the total funding for the eight-year period of the fourth framework stood at 235 million ECUs. The European Commission has its health telematics applications projects aimed squarely at developing a competitive European telemedicine industry in the next millennium, as well as substantially improving the delivery of health care services to European citizens.

## Types of telemedicine

Most telemedicine projects in the United Kingdom are still in the developmental stage but many are now "going live". *NHS Estates' Health Guidance Note on Telemedicine* describes several current projects.[8]

### (a) Teleradiology

Radiology is the scientific study of X-rays and other high-energy radiation used in the medical profession. Strictly speaking, teleradiology refers to the electronic transmission of radiological images from one location to another for the purpose of interpretation or consultation. In reality, the term has grown to include other related types of image transfer including computed tomography (CT), magnetic resonance imaging (MRI) and ultrasound. It could also include nuclear medicine, thermography, fluoroscopy and digital subtraction. Each of these applications can produce an image of the patient's anatomy and/or pathology.

A neurosurgical teleradiology system has been set by the Southern Health Board in Ireland so that referring hospitals can transmit images to the neurosurgical departments at both the University Hospital in Cork and in Dublin. This national teleradiology system serves the entire population of Ireland and is based on PCs interconnected by leased data circuits and ISDN lines.[9]

### (b) Telepathology

Pathology is the area of medical science which deals with the causes and nature of disease and with the bodily changes this brings about. Telepathology requires the rendering of diagnostic opinions on specimens taken at remote locations using computer and telecommunications technologies. In pathology a large amount of information (diagnostic and prognostic) is available from the examination of biopsy material, requiring an extensive knowledge of diseases and their clinical consequences. Hence consultations are an important practice in pathology. Studies are often required of pathology specimens after initial viewing under a microscope. Often these studies cannot be performed at the referring site and hence the pathology material has to be sent. This costs money and may take a great deal of time — time that a patient might not have. There is also the possibility that the special conditions required to keep a pathology specimen "clean" are lacking, and the sample is ruined.

Telepathology can minimise these limiting factors through remote dynamic screening by robotic video microscopy and remote diagnosis from selected still video microscopic images. A one-off demonstration of such a system was performed between Massachusetts General Hospital (MHG) and Riyadh in Saudi Arabia in 1994. A histopathological slide specimen was transmitted from Riyadh to the MGH over normal telephone lines. The images were observed through a high definition monitor. The images were scanned and compressed. Then they were transmitted to the MGH where decompression of the images took place and they were read by pathologists. A telepathology service has been run from Tromsø in Norway since the early 1990s,[9a] and both live and static sections are being transmitted with confidence by the Telemonitoring Research Centre at the John Radcliffe Hospital in Oxford.

### (c) Teledermatology

Dermatology is the study of the skin and its diseases. Teledermatology involves the transfer of images of affected areas of skin in order to make a diagnosis. Teledermatology has been carried out successfully in Wales where teleconsultants diagnose patients' skin problems remotely using videophones. A commercial videophone card and minicamera are attached to each surgery's personal computer and a high definition camcorder is also available if more detailed images are needed. Eight general practice surgeries in Montgomeryshire are involved in this scheme which covers 30 general practitioners and 65,000 patients. In the past patients with a dermatological problem their GP couldn't solve were sent to Bronglais Hospital in Aberystwyth, some 80 miles from Montgomeryshire, with an outpatient appointment waiting list of several months. With the introduction of teledermatology patients need only visit their GP, who operates the videophone and camera as requested by the consultant. Pictures from the camcorder are captured by the computer and sent to the hospital electronically.

Four centres in Belfast, Craigavon, Manchester and New Zealand are presently taking part in a teledermatology trial aiming to determine diagnostic accuracy by comparing the diagnosis obtained via video-link with those obtained via traditional consultation.[10]

### (d) Medical decision support for remote general practitioners

Teleconsultation is a special form of clinical information exchange. The simplest example is a doctor using the telephone to talk to a colleague and obtain a second opinion. These days a doctor can have a consultation with another doctor, perhaps in another country, or a paramedic equipped with a headset containing a camera and microphone can consult via satellite when he or she is dealing with an emergency.

The Accident and Emergency Department of Aberdeen Hospital has established a link with General Practitioners at a remote community hospital and during a one year clinical trial period videoconferencing was used in 63% of the 120 teleconsultations that took place. Teleradiology was used in some 97% of cases, saving the transfer of some 70 patients and making a financial saving of some £65,000.[11]

### (e) Telepsychiatry

A videoconferencing system has been installed at Guy's Hospital, London as part of the European Union's TELEMED Telematics Applications Project. Results indicate that videoconferencing can be used to support many of the communications tasks necessary in a dispersed psychiatric service, and also that telepsychiatry could become a major method of service provision.[12]

### (f) Ultrasound

Telemedicine can be used to overcome the need to refer patients at district hospital maternity units to specialist fetal medicine centres by enabling the transmission of high-resolution ultrasound images generated in the obstetric ultrasound unit at a remote hospital to a consulting expert. Results show that there is almost no loss of picture quality over the link which thus reduces the need for physical referral.[13]

### (g) Telecardiology

Almost 100 general practitioners in North London took part in the trial of telecardiology facilities from their practices or their patients' homes using electrocardiogram transmitters with direct voice access to send standard 12-lead ECGs to a central cardiac monitoring unit staffed by cardiology registrars and consultants. The service is able to identify patients with problems urgent enough to warrant immediate hospitalisation.[14] A more advanced service has been established by paediatric cardiologists at the Royal Belfast Hospital for Sick Children and the Altnagelvin Hospital in Londonderry to transmit real-time ultrasound scans for newborn infants suspected of having congenital heart disease,[15] via the ISDN digital network.

### (h) Tele-education

Effective health care requires not just expertise but the on-going medical education of health care professionals and the public. Education may improve the chances of early detection and reduce subsequent treatment requirements. Tele-education may help reduce many of the demands on the health care system by focusing on prevention – education on diet, hygiene and the many other basic requirements for a physically healthy society. Telemedicine and telehealth services offer the opportunity for training and education.

Nurses in rural Wales requiring training sessions in asthma and travel immunisation have been able to receive this through videoconferencing equipment which substantially reduced the inconvenience of travel. Indeed, half of the programme for the 1995–1996 academic year was delivered using this technique.[16]

### (i) Minor injuries

A low-cost telemedicine link was established between a minor treatment centre run by nurse practitioners in London and an Accident and Emergency department in Belfast. Nursing staff in London were able to transmit video pictures of wounds, rashes and other areas of concern directly to the A&E consultant in Belfast.[17] Telemedicine can also be used to support international disasters by providing relief workers with instant support from health care professionals not located at an emergency site.

### (j) Joint consulting

In northern Norway joint consulting has been trialled satisfactorily in a wide range of specialties including dermatology, endocrinology, ENT, gastroenterology, gynaecology, oncology, orthopaedics, paediatrics, psychiatry and urology.

### (k) The Intranet/Internet

The Internet is both inexpensive and widely available but it is also very insecure, hence the utilisation of the Internet by medical professionals and institutions has thus far been quite low. Research conducted by the National Library of Medicine in the United States during 1995 indicated that 75% of teaching hospitals, but only 25% of community hospitals, had Internet access. Less than 1% of all the hospitals in the world have their own Internet server and hence the Geneva based Health on the Net Foundation has begun a project that will help new hospitals obtain Internet access to a "Global Hospital".

The NHS, however, does have its own secure network called NHSnet, which embraces both voice and data services intended to meet the communication needs of NHS organisations on mainland Britain, which are in turn expected to meet the requirements for external electronic communications through NHS-wide networking.[18]

# What are the benefits of telemedicine?

## (a) Telemedicine at sea

Let us take as a case study a container ship, some 246 miles west of Gibraltar. A 46-year-old seaman on board is experiencing sudden pain in the front of his chest, radiating into his back and left side, neck and upper arm. His facial appearance is normal but he has tachycardia – his heart is beating too quickly and irregularly. His temperature is 37.3 degrees centigrade and his blood pressure is 110/75. These clinical symptoms could describe a number of possible conditions including a heart attack, coronary ischaemia, aggravated ulcer of the duodenum, gastric bleeding pain or some other complaint. Inevitably the seaman expects the worst and is very distressed. The ship's appointed medical officer, a second mate who had passed a five-day course in elementary first aid over six months ago and who has little experience of dealing with sick or injured seafarers, calls up a Portuguese hospital using the ship's radio and describes the seaman's symptoms to the duty doctor via this radiomedical link. However, without seeing the patient and being able to carry out clinical tests the advising doctor, who speaks Portuguese and only very limited English, is in no better a position to provide a diagnosis than the second mate, who speaks Arabic and a little English. The doctor has to anticipate the worst, therefore, and orders the immediate transfer of the seaman to hospital. The ship changes course and docks in Lisbon some twelve hours later, since weather conditions and distance made a helicopter transfer of the seaman impossible. After the patient's transfer to hospital a simple case of myoskeletal pain is diagnosed. A mild pain reliever combined with a day's bed rest would have been enough for the seaman to feel fine – the ship needn't have deviated from its voyage. The delay caused by the diversion cost the shipowner around $135,000 in lost hire under the charterparty.

The shore-based doctor in the situation described above could not see the patient and had to rely upon the verbal description of the patient's symptoms by the second mate. Although they would both have communicated in English, their only common language, neither of them was fluent. Moreover, the vessel took almost a full day to sail into port – if the seaman really had been suffering a heart attack, his chances of survival would have been poor.

But what if a diversion and the delay that this entailed were not necessary? And what if the consulting doctor could actually see and hear the seaman patient and the second mate through a videoconferencing, rather than just a radio link? Better still, what if simple diagnostic tests, such as an ECG, blood pressure, a blood test or even an X-ray, could have been performed on board and the results transmitted directly to the consulting doctor who would have the benefit of this information in deciding whether an emergency evacuation was necessary, or whether instead to instruct the second mate in caring for the seaman? And what if the hospital and ship had the benefit of multimedia computer software which the seafarer could use to describe a colleague's symptoms, and the consulting doctor could use to illustrate the required treatment? Performing all these functions, and more, will become reality through the implementation of telemedicine at sea.

## (b) Telemedicine on board aircraft

Between April 1993 and March 1994 British Airways Health Services dealt with 2,078 medical incidents (1 per 15,000 passengers) occurring on board British Airways flights. The most common medical incidents were diarrhoea, vomiting and fainting and there was a significant number of very serious incidents such as heart attacks, respiratory problems, sudden collapses and hypoglycaemia. There is a British Airways doctor on call twenty-four hours a day with whom a flight can communicate via a high-frequency radio link. But although, like many merchant vessels, British Airways aircraft are equipped with first class medical kits and have well-trained staff on board, such a radiomedical link has obvious limitations. The average cost of an unscheduled diversion of a Boeing 747 is approximately £40,000, and hence British Airways, in common with other airlines, is examining ways of using telemedicine to measure vital signs and hence improve the quality of medical care offered on board their aircraft. This would mean that, in a medical emergency, the duty doctor would not have to rely on the description of symptoms and signs given by the cabin crew or by a doctor or nurse who may have been among the passengers.

The decision as to whether or not an aircraft should divert always rests with the captain who will consider the condition of the sick passenger, the likelihood of their deteriorating, and the availability of medical facilities at the diversion airfield; other considerations are whether the crew will run out of duty time and whether or not a replacement crew can be positioned to continue the flight if necessary. Naturally, though, making this decision will be a good deal simpler if the captain has a clearer idea of what is wrong with the passenger. Only time will tell whether this will lead to more or fewer diversions (and hence cost-benefit savings or increased expenditure), though British Airways is pragmatic enough to insist that they do not measure the value of a passenger's life in terms of the cost of a diversion.[19]

## (c) Telemedicine in developing countries

Of the 51 million people who died in 1993 throughout the world, almost 80% were in the developing world and of these deaths some 99% were caused by communicable diseases such as tuberculosis and respiratory infections, and during childbirth. The World Health Organization strongly believes that poverty is the main reason for much of the world's suffering. Ironically, during the 1980s the number of people living in extreme poverty increased and was estimated at more than 1.1 billion people in 1990 – more than one fifth of humanity. Yearly, some 12.2 million children in developing countries die under the age of five from preventable causes linked to lack of vaccination, poor sanitation and the absence of clean water. Life expectancy in the developed world is 78 years – in the least developed countries it is 43. One of the key factors in the high morbidity and mortality rates in developing countries is the lack of quality health care and the extreme difficulty of accessing the health care that does exist. Integration, therefore, is essential for the effective delivery of health care in the developing world: if there cannot be a hospital in every part of a country then there can, at least, be some form of remote access to that hospital's facilities. Where a relatively inexpensive and affordable telemedicine system can be implemented, with the majority of patients being seen in remote clinics and referred, where necessary, to district and more specialised hospitals, real progress can be made.

## (d) Telemedicine in primary care

An example of telemedicine in primary care in the United Kingdom is provided by a scenario described by Darkins in his paper *The management of clinical risk in telemedicine applications*:

> A young woman with multiple injuries, including a suspected serious head injury, is taken by ambulance to the accident and emergency department of an hospital without neurosurgical facilities on site. The clinical dilemma for the doctors attending the patient is whether she needs urgent transfer to a neurosurgical facility for her head injury. This decision is not straightforward because transferring the patient many miles in an ambulance may mean that she will deteriorate from another, as yet unrecognised, injury, apart from her known head injury, or from the head injury itself. In transit she will not have access to the investigative and/or resuscitation back-up immediately available in an acute hospital.[20]

In this example there are risks associated with both transfer and non-transfer but a simple telephone consultation is less able to communicate clinical information as effectively as a video-consultation combined with teleradiology. Video-consulting would allow the teleconsulting neurosurgeon who has expertise in assessing head-injured patients, to assess the level of the patient's coma remotely. Teleradiology means that skull radiographs and computerised tomography (CT) scans can be viewed by the teleconsultant. Telemedicine helps alleviate not only the inconvenience of time and distance — but the dangers also.

## The legal challenges of telemedicine

The integration of telemedicine into mainstream conventional health care will be one of the greatest challenges facing health authorities and NHS trusts over the coming years. It is a challenge that, if met, will bring about a revolution in health care that years from now may come to be compared with the discovery of penicillin, because it will completely change our whole way of thinking about the delivery of primary and secondary care in the next millennium. The telecommunications industry must find ways of exploiting and expanding its networks in order to provide health care customers with the solutions they need. When telemedicine switches from the mostly experimental to the fully operational phase it will need to be implemented carefully, managed properly and supervised closely. And there is, of course, a legal challenge.

When the author first began his research only one paper had ever been written about the medico-legal implications of consulting in the United Kingdom, which stated that "unforeseen medico-legal implications of telemedicine will be revealed by litigation as it arises".[21] The Health Guidance Note on Telemedicine published by NHS Estates, an executive agency of the Department of Health, states in almost identical terms:

> Medico-legal issues are not fully resolved. Ultimately telemedicine is a vehicle for the delivery of health, and as such, people have the same rights to quality care, and clinicians owe the same duty of care and have the same interprofessional relationships, as with the conventional delivery of health.[22]

So it seems that, while everybody acknowledges that legal and ethical issues in telemedicine exist, no-one has yet seen fit to address them. This, it is submitted, is because of a fundamental misconception about telemedicine – that in revolutionising medicine and health care, telemedicine will also turn the law and medical ethics on their heads. But this is simply not the case. While it is true that telemedicine raises some very new issues that have not had to be addressed before now, most of these can be resolved by reference to conventional medical law. This is, moreover, the approach that the English courts would take if presented with litigation concerning telemedicine. But it should not take litigation, and the consequent wastage of resources, for telemedicine pioneers to find their legal answers. Many of the solutions to their questions are already staring them in the face. We already know which medical practices carry the greatest risks and we know which factors can combine to turn these risks into actual harm. Hence the approach this book takes is to examine the legal and ethical aspects of telemedicine by extrapolating, wherever necessary, the existing law. That said, telemedicine involves a unique marriage of communications, computing and medicine, and hence many questions can only be answered by reference to the legislation governing data protection, telecommunications and computer security. In this book nine legal topics have been selected for detailed treatment.

## (a) Confidentiality and the telepatient's rights of access

There will be both a legal duty and an ethical duty of confidentiality incumbent upon teleconsultants, as for conventional doctors. The exact nature and extent of this duty is unclear however and the circumstances under which the disclosure of confidential information by a teleconsultant will be justified are examined in detail in chapter 2. In the past, the concept of confidentiality meant that health records were kept secret from patients themselves but nowadays there is broad support for openness and frankness between doctor and patient and the recent legislation (examined in chapter 2) gives the telepatient the right to see information about themselves created by telemedical professionals.[23]

## (b) Data protection, security and European law

Data protection is presently an area of high legislative activity, with national governments and international organisations creating legislation that sets out regulations concerning the collection, processing, communication and storage of medical data. Most domestic instruments such as the United Kingdom's Data Protection Act 1984 show some similarity since they are all based, to a greater or lesser extent, on the European Union Directive on the protection of individuals with regard to the processing of personal data and on the free movement of such data, which Member States must implement.[24]

However the trans-border transmission of patient histories and other identifiable material such as scans and biological analyses can be problematic from the point of view of confidentiality since not all countries have developed systems of data protection. Some of the problems arising from protecting the confidentiality of telemedical transmissions have been addressed by efforts within the European Union aimed at providing common standards for the processing of all manual and electronic data, but not all countries have yet adopted the European Directive on data protection.[25] Moreover, telepatients' medical records may be at risk, when stored electronically, from hackers and people intercepting telemedicine transmissions. In chapter 3 we examine these risks and the legal provisions designed to prevent them.

## (c) Agreeing to telemedical treatment

Every competent adult has an inviolable right to determine what is done to his or her own body and hence a telepatient has the right to determine whether or not they are to receive medical treatment. Many of the legal requirements of telemedical practice are far removed from ethical considerations, which make no reference to the law. Consent, however, is an issue which binds the two since failure to seek a sick or injured person's consent to medical treatment is not only a moral failing but may also be an assault.[26] Any professional or non-professional person examining, injecting or operating on a telepatient's body commits a trespass to that person just as if he had come, uninvited, onto that person's land.[27] The crime and tort of battery is committed.

In recent years, however, the courts have tended to move away from the tort of battery to negligence, reflected in the courts' concern less with the issue of whether medical intrusion was consented to at all and more with the quality of the information imparted to obtain the consent. Obviously, the chance to consent to treatment is offset by the accompanying right to refuse it and as a result of some recent cases examined in chapter 4, the possibility of a telepatient positively refusing to consent to medical treatment, rather than simply failing to give a valid consent, must also now be considered.

## (d) Telemedical malpractice

In the United Kingdom, as in most common law jurisdictions, to maintain an action for negligence the telepatient must establish that the teleconsulting doctor or other medical professional owed him or her a duty of care, that the duty was breached (that is, the doctor or other person was careless) and that they suffered harm caused by that carelessness.[28] In a case of alleged medical malpractice such as might be brought against a teleconsulting doctor or other personnel involved in a telemedical consultation, the outcome of the case will depend as much on the facts that are established as upon the law. Indeed, proving medical malpractice on the facts would be by far the greatest hurdle faced by an aggrieved telepatient, whatever the content of the law of the jurisdiction in which the case is brought.[29] Perhaps it is for this reason that extensive research has not yet revealed any reports at all of a malpractice claim being brought by an individual who claims to have suffered harm through negligent medical advice or treatment given during a radiomedical consultation. But whilst the first major malpractice case against a radio- or tele-medical service has yet to arise, it seems entirely sensible to assume that in today's legal climate this is simply a matter of time and that an evaluation of the principles of medical malpractice as they affect doctors and other medical professionals providing telemedical care, and the specific risks peculiar to that care, would be greatly beneficial in avoiding liability. Chapter 5 attempts just such an evaluation.

## (e) Standards adopted by the General Medical Council, Royal Colleges and professional associations

While the General Medical Council, the Royal Colleges and the professional medical associations in the United Kingdom have yet to issue any detailed written advice to their members concerning teleconsulting, it is incorrect to assume that telemedical practice is therefore an unregulated area. The existing legal and ethical guidance and protocols issued to and adhered to by conventional medical practitioners apply to teleconsultancy and indeed are illuminating about the behaviour that should be expected of a teleconsultant as well as of doctors in conventional practice. Chapter 6 of this book examines these guidelines and suggests in which particular areas the professional associations may need to offer specific guidance in the future.

## (f) Telemedicine equipment

The basic principle of product liability is that a plaintiff has a cause of action for any detriment caused by a defective product in either contract or tort, depending on whether they are in a contractual relationship with the defendant(s) or whether the latter owes them a duty of care. Hence, while the health authority or NHS trust that has purchased telemedical equipment will be owed a contractual duty implied under the Sale of Goods Acts, privity of contract will exclude a patient from bringing a contractual claim. Instead, such a claim will be based on negligence in tort. In the Member States of the European Union a great deal of harmonisation of product liability law has been made possible by the European Council Directive on the approximation of the laws, regulations and administrative provisions of the Member States concerning liability for defective products.[30] Over recent years there has been an increasing tendency, particularly in the United States of America, to certify medical devices such as telemedical terminals in particular relation to their safety. The Federal Safe Medical Devices Act 1990 (amended in 1992) aimed to improve the regulation of medical devices and provide US-wide standards for equipment, personnel, quality assurance and control, reporting and record keeping. Similar actions were taken in the European Union with the enactment of Directives relating to medical devices and the creation in the United Kingdom of a Medical Devices Agency as the country's "competent authority" under the Directives. The legal basis of these Directives is Article 100A of the European Union Treaty which stipulates that measures should be adopted for the approximation of the provisions laid down by law, regulation or administrative action in Member States which have as their objective the establishment and functioning of the internal market. Such harmonisation guarantees the free movement of medical devices such as telemedical equipment systems within the internal market. Chapter 7 examines the role of domestic products liability law, the EU Directives and the Medical Devices Agency in regulating the manufacture and distribution of telemedicine equipment.

## (g) Intellectual property rights and competition law

Intellectual property rights can accrue to the creators of telemedical technology. Intellectual property law is that area of the law which concerns legal rights associated with creative effort or commercial reputation and goodwill. The subject matter of intellectual property is very wide and includes the computer programs and databases that run telemedical systems, as well as the "hardware" such as computer terminals and satellite transmitters. Moreover, the law itself is becoming increasingly complex and a proper understanding of the legal position regarding the patents and copyrights arising from the creation of a telemedical system and the tension that exists in English law between the protection of these rights and the commercial exploitation of telemedicine is essential if original concepts and ideas are to be protected. Chapter 8 examines the various methods of protecting the creative and technical originality of new telemedicine equipment and the difficulties involved in reconciling the protection of intellectual property rights with the free movement of goods within the European Community.

## (h) Jurisdictional problems

The forum in which a claim for medical malpractice against a teleconsulting doctor or other medical professional or a claim of negligence against the producers of a telemedical system may be brought is unclear and hence so too are the laws that would apply to such a dispute. The peculiar problem, in relation to telemedicine, is that telemedical advice provided in one jurisdiction will, in many cases, be received in a completely different jurisdiction. Whilst common-sense dictates that, where a tort is committed by a lay person in a remote clinic or by a ship's medical officer alone, then both the negligence and the resultant damage will have occurred within the same jurisdiction, it is less clear what the position will be where the negligent act is the bad advice of a teleconsultant doctor given from a different jurisdiction to that in which the harm to the seafarer or remote patient occurs.[31] Chapter 9 examines the jurisdictional problems that the practice of medicine across borders creates in the light of the experience of the United States in legislating for "out-of-state" physicians.

## (i) Regulating telemedicine in the future

Litigation is a less than satisfactory means of regulating the doctor–patient relationship and dealing with a patient's unhappiness over treatment. Moreover, it would be contrary to the whole spirit with which telemedicine has been conceived to allow it to develop into a health system which is not professionally and ethically regulated to the very highest standards. Moreover, there is a danger that telemedicine might become a "high-risk" specialty, with a comparatively expensive differential insurance premium that acts as a disincentive for doctors and hospitals considering entering the telemedicine field. Chapter 10 concludes by examining the dual challenges facing health authorities, NHS trusts and other telemedicine providers: the medical challenge presented by telemedicine is for doctors to find ways of doing their jobs from a distance; the legal and ethical challenge is to ensure that the very highest standards are met from the outset. This can only be achieved by the legal and medical professions learning to combine their expertise, rather than by the former adopting the adversarial stance that has come to blight its relationship with the latter in recent years.

# Patient attitudes to telemedicine

A survey by Tachakra et al of public attitudes to telemedicine is illuminating – many of the concerns raised mirror the concerns of teleconsultants themselves.[32] Respondents were most concerned over issues of privacy – 56% felt uneasy about consultations being taped, 50% were worried about others hearing the consultation and 65% were concerned about the use of the tapes for teaching purposes and any accompanying breach of confidentiality.

An overwhelming 91% of those questioned felt that there should be central government funding for telemedicine projects and 98% – almost all those surveyed – would not want to have to pay for it themselves. But by far the greatest concerns were raised concerning the clinical risks associated with telemedicine. Some 94% of those surveyed were anxious that a telemedicine monitor would not show a medical condition adequately and 82% were worried that if anything went wrong the doctor might not admit responsibility but would blame the technology. Over 80% of those surveyed thought that there was a real likelihood that doctors would edit tapes in such circumstances in order to avoid liability in civil litigation. It is important to remember, however, that Tachakra's study involved patients who had no experience of telemedicine. A more balanced study of telepatients themselves undertaken in Kentucky showed a fairly high level of confidence in the service they received.[33]

With telemedicine services now ready to be integrated into conventional health care for the first time, and with both professional and public anxiety over the legal and ethical aspects of telemedicine – at least among the uninitiated – running so high, now is the time to examine these issues in detail and dispel some of the myths surrounding the legal and ethical barriers to telemedicine. That, in a nutshell, is what this book aims to do.

## References

1    *Sixty Years of the International Radio Medical Centre*. Rome: CIRM, 1995.
2    See preamble to Council Directive 92/29/EEC of 31 March 1992 on the minimum safety and health requirements for improved medical treatment on board vessels. See Official Journal of 30 April 1992 (L113).
3    Council Directive 93/103/EC of 23 November 1993 concerning the minimum safety and health requirements for work on board fishing vessels. See Official Journal of 13 December 1993 (L 307).
4    Kirk U, Brandt L, Jensen O, Petersen S. *The Navigators' Health Education*. Esberg: Institute of Maritime Medicine, 1992: Note 2/92.
5    Sarrni H, Niemi L, Nylund S. *Postgraduate Medical Training for Deck Officers*. Turku Regional Institute of Occupational Health.
6    Insofar as incorrect diagnosis and/or careless handling of the patient may lead to severe physical disablement or even death.
7    See also Saarni H. *Medical Training for Seafarers*. Hamburg: Proceedings of the 7th European Nautical Medical Meeting, 1989: 176 - 209.
8    See NHS Estates. *Health guidance note on Telemedicine*. London: The Stationery Office, 1997: 4-6.
9    Gray WR, Somers J, Buckley TF. Report of a national neurosurgical teleradiology system. *Journal of Telemedicine and Telecare* 1997; 3 (Suppl. 1): 36-37.
9a   See Nordrum I et al. Remote frozen section service. A telepathology project in northern Norway. *Human Pathology* 1991; 22: 514-518.
10   See Oakley A et al. Diagnostic accuracy of teledermatology: results of a preliminary study in New Zealand. *New Zealand Medical Journal* 1997; 110: 51-53. Loane MA et al. Preliminary results from the Northern Ireland arms of the UK Multicentre Teledermatology Trial: effect of camera performance on diagnostic accuracy. *Journal of Telemedicine and Telecare* 1997; 3 (Suppl. 1): 73-75. Gilmour E et al. Validation of a teledermatology system in the UK Multicentre Teledermatology Trial. *Journal of Telemedicine and Telecare* 1997; 3 (Suppl. 1): 104-105. Jones DH et al. Teledermatology in the Highlands of Scotland. *Journal of Telemedicine and Telecare* 1997; 2 (Suppl. 1): 7-9. Harrison PV. Dermatological diagnosis accuracy by conventional photography: a prelude to digital image interpretation and telemedicine. *Journal of Telemedicine and Telecare* 1997; 3 (Suppl. 1): 105.
11   Armstrong IJ, Haston WS. Medical decision support for remote general practitioners using telemedicine. *Journal of Telemedicine and Telecare* 1997; 3: 27-34.
12   McLaren P et al. An evaluation of the use of interactive television in an acute psychiatric service. *Journal of Telemedicine and Telecare* 1995; 1: 79-85.
13   Fisk NM et al. Fetal telemedicine: six month pilot of real-time ultrasound and video consultation between the Isle of Wight and London. *British Journal of Obstetrics and Gynaecology* 1996; 103: 1092-1095.
14   Shanit D, Cheng A, Greenbaum RA. Telecardiology supporting the decision-making process in general practice. *Journal of Telemedicine and Telecare* 1996: 2; 7-13.
15   Casey F et al. Diagnosis of neonatal congenital heart defects by remote consultation using a low-cost telemedicine link. *Journal of Telemedicine and Telecare* 1996; 2:165-169.
16   Jarrett C, Wainwright P, Lewis L. Education and training of practice nurses. *Journal of Telemedicine and Telecare* 1997; 3 (Suppl. 1): 40-42.
17   Darkins A et al. An evaluation of telemedicine support for a minor treatment centre. *Journal of Telemedicine and Telecare* 1996; 2: 93-99.
18   NHS Executive, Department of Health. *Electronic communications*. Circular EL (94) 53.

19    See Bagshaw M. Telemedicine in British Airways. *Journal of Telemedicine and Telecare* 1996; 2 (Suppl. 1): 36.

20    Darkins A. The management of clinical risk in telemedicine applications. *Journal of Telemedicine and Telecare* 1996; 2: 179-184.

21    Brahams D. The medico-legal implications of teleconsulting in the UK. *Journal of Telemedicine and Telecare* 1995: 1: 196-201.

22    See NHS Estates. *Health guidance note on Telemedicine*. London: The Stationery Office, 1997.

23    See in this respect the Access to Medical Records Act 1988 and the Access to Health Records Act 1990.

24    The time limit for implementation in all Member States is 24 October 1998; i.e. three years after the passing of the Directive. After that time it will be illegal under Article 25 of the Directive to transmit data to a third country which does not provide for adequate levels of protection.

25    Directive 95/46/EC of the European Parliament and of the Council of 24 October 1995 on the protection of individuals with regard to the processing of personal data and on the free movement of such data. For the authoritative text of the Directive reference should be made to the *Official Journal of the European Communities* of 23 November 1995 No. L. 281 at p. 31.

26    See the dicta of the Master of the Rolls, Lord Donaldson in *Re J. (a minor)(medical treatment)* [1992] 4 All ER 614.

27    See Brazier M. *Medicine, patients and the law*. (2nd ed.) London: Penguin Group, 1992: 73.

28    See the dicta of Justice Nield in *Barnett v Chelsea and Kensington HMC* [1968] 1 All ER 1068.

29    Part III of the Private International Law (Miscellaneous Provisions) Act 1995 provides that the applicable law is the law of the country in which the events constituting the tort or delict in question occur. The place where the negligent act is committed will, therefore, become the jurisdiction whose law governs a claim for medical malpractice or product liability.

30    Directive 85/374/EEC of the European Council of 25 July 1985 on the approximation of the laws, regulations and administrative provisions of the Member States concerning liability for defective products. For the authoritative text of the Directive reference should be made to the *Official Journal of the European Communities* of 7 August 1985 No. L. 210 at p. 29.

31    Armstrong IJ, Haston WS. Medical decision support for remote general practitioners using telemedicine. *Journal of Telemedicine and Telecare* 1997; 3: 27-34. See also the Civil Jurisdiction and Judgments Act 1982 which implements the Brussels Convention on Jurisidiction and Judgments. Where the defendant is domiciled in a country party to the Lugano Convention (which governs the former EFTA states) jurisidiction is governed by the Civil Jurisidiction and Judgments Act 1991. The two Acts are, broadly speaking, identical. Under the two Conventions a defendant may be sued either in his country of domicile, known as the "primary jurisdiction" or the country where the "harmful event" (the tort) occurred – the "alternative jurisdiction". The Convention is of limited assistance, however, as in three cases: *Shevill v Press Alliance SA* [1995] 1 All ER 289; *Handdalswekerij Bier* v *Mines de Potasse d'Alsace* [1976] ECR 1735 and *Minister Investments* v *Hyundai* [1988] 2 Lloyd's Rep 621 the European Court of Justice has interpreted "harmful event" to mean either the place where the wrongdoing occurred *or* the place where the resulting damage ensued!

32    Tachakra S, Mullett STH, Freij R, Sivakumar A. Confidentiality and ethics in telemedicine. *Journal of Telemedicine and Telecare* 1996; 2 (Suppl. 1): 68-71.

33    See *Journal of Telemedicine and Telecare*; 3: pp. 205-208.

# ▶2

# Confidentiality and the telepatient's rights of access

The principle of confidentiality has been at the heart of medical ethics since the time of Hippocrates and has been developed by various codes, including the International Code of Medical Ethics which states that a doctor must preserve "absolute confidentiality in all he knows about his patient" even after the patient's death. Hence the ethical obligation owed by a doctor to his patient to respect the confidences of that patient is beyond doubt, but is there an equivalent legal obligation?

## Confidentiality and the law

That the courts of the United Kingdom have developed jurisdiction to protect against and remedy a breach of confidence is beyond doubt. But the jurisdiction is a pragmatic and unique one that has evolved out of the fields of contract, equity and property law with a view not to conceptual neatness but to deal with the problem in hand. Vice-Chancellor Turner is quoted as having said:

> That the court has exercised jurisdiction in cases of this nature does not, I think, admit of any question. Different grounds have indeed been assigned for the exercise of that jurisdiction...but, upon whatever grounds the jurisdiction is founded, the authorities leave no doubt as to the exercise of it.[1]

The courts of the United Kingdom have also been flexible in introducing an obligation of confidence based upon an implied contract where necessary.[2] Their whole policy has been to hold confidences "sacrosanct". Hence the broad notion of trust, in the words of the American realists, represents "a sort of doctrinal bridge" between contract, equity and the law of property.[3] The duty of confidence arises both out of the circumstances in which information has been disclosed and the nature of the information itself. The circumstances of a disclosure may be such that the confider is placing the confidant in a position of trust. If so, either equity or contract will provide a means by which the trust can be honoured. However, a disclosure will not betray a confidence if what has been disclosed is common knowledge. It is only when the information is private or "confidential" – when its general publication would reveal something which the confider wishes to keep secret – that the confidence can be regarded as having been reposed by one person to another. Here the notion of confidence links contract and equity with property, for the courts have recognised that the publication or misuse of confidential information may injure a person either emotionally or materially even though no immediate relationship of trust has been broken.

# The doctor–patient relationship

Although the legal obligation of confidence existing between a teleconsulting doctor and his patient is straightforward and clear, there has been little case law authority directly on this point. In *Attorney-General* v *Guardian Newspapers* (*No. 2*)[4] Lord Goff stated:

> I start with the broad general principle…that a duty of confidence arises when confidential information comes to the knowledge of a person (the confidant) in circumstances where he has notice, or is held to have agreed, that the information is confidential, with the effect that it would be just in all the circumstances that he should be precluded from disclosing the information to others. I have used the word "notice" advisedly, in order to avoid the…question of the extent to which actual knowledge is necessary, though I of course understand knowledge to include circumstances where the confidant has deliberately closed his eyes to the obvious. The existence of this broad general principle reflects the fact that there is such a public interest in the maintenance of confidences that the law will provide clear remedies for their protection…I realise that, in the vast majority of cases, in particular those concerned with trade secrets, the duty of confidence will arise from a transaction or relationship between the parties, often a contract, in which event the duty may arise by reason of either an express or an implied term of that contract. It is in such cases that the expressions "confider" and "confidant" are perhaps most aptly employed. But it is well settled that a duty of confidence may arise in equity independently of such cases.

The cases of *X* v *Y*[5] and *W* v *Egdell*[6] have now put the matter beyond doubt. In the latter case Lord Justice Bingham expressly referred to the advice given by the General Medical Council to the medical profession, pursuant to section 35 of the Medical Act of 1983.[7] Rule 80 of the old "Blue Book" provided that:

> It is a doctor's duty, except in the cases mentioned below, strictly to observe the rule of professional secrecy by refraining from disclosing voluntarily to any third party information about a patient which he has learnt directly or indirectly in his professional capacity as a registered medical practitioner.[8]

But both of the above cases did, perhaps more importantly, categorically hold that the private interest of an individual in the maintenance of secrecy will always be subordinate to the greater public interest served by the disclosure of confidential information.[9] The GMC's new guidelines, contained in a series of four booklets generally entitled *Duties of a Doctor – Guidance from the General Medical Council*[10] state that:

1.  Patients have a right to expect that you will not disclose any personal information which you learn during the course of your professional duties, unless they give permission. Without assurances about confidentiality, patients may be reluctant to give doctors the information they need in order to provide good care:

    ▶ When you are responsible for confidential information you must make sure that information is effectively protected against improper disclosure when it is disposed of, stored, transmitted or received;

    ▶ When patients give consent to disclosure of information about them, you must make sure they understand what will be disclosed, the reasons for disclosure and the likely consequences;

▶ You must make sure that patients are informed whenever information about them is likely to be disclosed to others involved in their health care, and that they have the opportunity to withhold permission;

▶ You must respect requests by patients that information should not be disclosed to third parties, save in exceptional circumstances (for example, where the health or safety of others would otherwise be at serious risk);

▶ If you disclose confidential information you should release only as much information as is necessary for the purpose;

▶ You must make sure that health workers to whom you disclose information understand that it is given to them in confidence which they must respect;

▶ If you decide to disclose confidential information, you must be prepared to explain and justify your decision.

## The scope of the teleconsultant's duty of confidence

A teleconsulting doctor will be under a legal obligation, just as he would be in any other aspect of his professional practice, not to disclose confidential information which he learns in the course of treating a patient through a telemedical link, rather than face to face:

> In common with other professional men, for instance a priest...the doctor is under a duty not to disclose [voluntarily], without the consent of his patient, information which he, the doctor, has gained in his professional capacity.[11]

By analogy with the relationship of trust existing between a banker and client, the teleconsulting doctor will also be under a duty not to disclose information concerning the patient which the teleconsulting doctor learns from other sources such as medical records or medical data taken from the patient by a third party and subsequently transmitted to the doctor. The obligation of secrecy would also extend to reports given to a teleconsulting doctor by other medical and para-medical professionals. Kennedy and Grubb[12] state that where a doctor acquires information from a third party care-provider (for example a missionary in a remote clinic) in circumstances where the third party knows of the doctor–patient relationship, there is no reason to distinguish this from a case where the doctor is in direct contact with a patient. Such an approach assumes that the third party is conducting himself, for all intents and purposes, as a health care "professional" who is aware of the special nature of the doctor–patient relationship and himself acknowledges his own duty to maintain the confidentiality of the medical information and data obtained from the telepatients that he is called upon to treat. It is questionable, though, whether a less professional third party, such as a ship's medical officer, perhaps with only the most rudimentary understanding of the ethical aspects of the relationship between a patient and their care-provider, is under the same duty. Kennedy and Grubb do not subscribe to this view[13] since they believe that in both situations the doctor receives the information as a professional vis-à-vis the third party. Such a distinction is artificial, however, as a court would recognise a duty to respect confidentiality since what lies at the root of the doctor–patient relationship is the patient's trust that the doctor will not reveal any clinical information to another without permission. This would extend to all information no matter what the level of competency of the third party involved.

In *X* v *Y*[14] and *W* v *Egdell*[15] the Court of Appeal accepted that the obligation of confidence was not absolute, however, but is subject to the requirement of disclosure when the same is compelled by law or is in the public interest. Such an obligation, incumbent upon a teleconsulting doctor, can be released without the need to obtain the consent, either express or implied, of their patient. But in every case the overwhelming ethical duty to respect a patient's confidentiality must be balanced against the danger of maintaining silence. For disclosure to be lawful, therefore, there must be genuine and overriding public interest.

For instance, in *X* v *Y* a tabloid newspaper obtained information which identified two general practitioners as continuing to practise despite being HIV positive. The paper argued that there was a public interest and also an interest on the part of patients in reporting that the two doctors concerned were infected when the health authority for whom they worked sought an injunction restraining publication of the doctors' and their patients' names. However, the Judge in that case, Mr Justice Rose, felt otherwise and, granting the injunction, stated:

> In the long run, preservation of confidentiality is the only way of securing public health; otherwise doctors will be discredited as a source of education, for future individual patients will not come forward if doctors are going to squeal on them. Consequently, confidentiality is vital to secure public as well as private health, for unless those infected come forward they cannot be counselled and self-treatment does not provide the best care...[16]

The facts of *W* v *Egdell* are also illustrative. A patient who had been indefinitely detained in a secure hospital having murdered five people and wounded two others applied to a Mental Health Review Tribunal, after he had been detained some ten years, to be discharged or transferred to a less secure unit. The Home Secretary opposed this application and so the patient's solicitors approached Dr Egdell, a psychiatrist, for a report in support of the application. But rather than finding that W was making steady progress sufficient to permit his discharge or movement to a less secure unit, he actually found W still to be suffering from paranoid psychosis. Indeed, W may even have had an underlying psychopathic deviant personality. Hence he strongly opposed the application and W's solicitor's subsequently withdrew it. Dr Egdell had assumed that his report would be placed before the Tribunal, and when he discovered that the application had been withdrawn he forwarded copies of his report, without the consent of W's solicitors (indeed they had expressly refused permission), to the medical director of the hospital who, in turn, forwarded it to the Home Secretary. Upon an application by W for an injunction to restrain the use of the report in tribunal proceedings and for damages against Dr Egdell for breach of confidence Mr Justice Stott, in the High Court, refused both, holding that the duty of confidence owed to W was subordinated, in this instance, to the greater public interest in making sure that his mental condition was accurately assessed.

This decision was upheld in the Court of Appeal where it was made clear that, though Dr Egdell ethically owed W a duty of confidence which would have been breached by, for instance, selling the report to the press, there was a higher duty to ensure public safety. Balancing the competing interests of telepatient and teleconsultant, in the light of the approach to confidentiality that has developed in conventional practice, will be far from easy for teleconsultants. The General Medical Council's advocacy of posters and leaflets explaining to patients what confidential information about them might be disclosed and to whom, when such a need for disclosure might arise and explaining that they have a right to discuss disclosure with their doctor would be greatly beneficial. Such literature could even include, as Sieghart has suggested,[17] examples of situations when the doctor may consider that a breach of the duty of confidentiality would be justified. Although this would give the doctor and patient an opportunity to define their relationship it is, naturally, difficult to envisage every situation in which disclosure might be warranted.

## Consent to disclosure

Consent to disclosure, although usually express, can be implied in certain circumstances, where the patient is in the care of more than one person. In such a case a patient may be assumed to consent to any relevant third party (such as a teleconsulting doctor) being properly informed so as to carry out his or her obligations. The members of the telemedical "team" therefore, which would include all the health care providers *at all stages of the telemedical link*, would be deemed to receive the information in confidence.

The United Kingdom's General Medical Council has stated in its Professional Conduct and Discipline code:[18]

> Most doctors in hospital and general practice are working in health care teams, some of whose members may need access to information, given or obtained in confidence about individuals, in order to perform their duties. It is for doctors who lead such teams to judge when it is appropriate for information to be disclosed for that purpose. They must leave those whom they authorise to receive such information in no doubt that it is given to them in professional confidence. The doctor also has a responsibility to ensure that arrangements exist to inform patients of the circumstances in which information about them is likely to be shared and to give patients the opportunity to state any objection to this.

The newest guidelines state that:

3. Modern medical practice usually involves teams of doctors, other health care workers, and sometimes people from outside the health care professions... To provide patients with the best possible care, it is often essential to pass confidential information between members of the team.
4. You should make sure – through the use of leaflets and posters if necessary – that patients understand why and when information may be shared between team members, and any circumstances in which team members providing non-medical care may be required to disclose information to third parties.
5. Where the disclosure of relevant information between health care professionals is clearly required for treatment to which a patient has agreed, the patient's explicit consent may not be required. For example, explicit consent would not be needed where a general practitioner discloses relevant information to a medical secretary to have a referral letter typed, or a physician makes relevant information available to a radiologist when requesting an X-ray.
6. There will also be circumstances where, because of a medical emergency, a patient's consent cannot be obtained, but relevant information must in the patient's interest be transferred between health care workers.
7. If a patient does not wish you to share particular information with other members of the team, you must respect those wishes. If you and a patient have established a relationship based on trust, the patient may choose to give you discretion to disclose information to other team members, as required.

8.   All medical members of a team have a duty to make sure that other team
     members understand and observe confidentiality.[19]

The GMC believes in express consent where this is possible, and although the law may not go so far there would seem no harm in patients signing a form consenting to the dissemination among members of a telemedical health care team, details of their records, should the need arise. While this would also serve the useful purpose of raising a patient's awareness of the use and provision of telemedical services, it would, legally speaking, be pointless as long as the courts are content to imply consent whenever the circumstances justify doing so.

Although it is difficult to come to a conclusion, as noted above, regarding whether a duty of confidence is incumbent upon non-professional members of a telemedical team who are not subject to a strictly enforced professional code (e.g. the seafaring medical officer or the missionary in a remote area), it is equally difficult to propose any solution beyond making them aware, at the training stage, of the doctor–patient relationship and the duty of confidence. Although such personnel may not be under the same duty of confidentiality, telemedicine cannot work without them. Given that in today's economic climate the ship's medical officer may have woefully little time to dedicate to medical care, it would be difficult in practice to oppose the appointment or continued employment of a seafarer who did not understand (or, we daresay, much care), about the importance of maintaining confidentiality. Indeed, many medical officers are resentful enough of the extra time demanded of them by these duties, without a strict legal framework being imposed upon them.

It is likely therefore that a court would hold that a teleconsulting doctor has a discretion to disclose to all those personnel involved in a telemedical link on a "need to know" basis, such a discretion being exercised with caution. But there is sometimes a fine line between disclosure and non-disclosure, and decisions as to when and how to disclose are among the most difficult ethical dilemmas faced by doctors. This is made all the more difficult by the potential *legal* consequences that might flow from a situation in which the doctor makes an ethical decision in favour of maintaining patient confidentiality which actually results in harm to others. Where there is a reasonably foreseeable risk of harm to others and the doctor does not disclose information about a patient to the appropriate person or authority, he may well be found liable in negligence. Cases such as *Carmarthenshire County Council* v *Lewis*[20] and *Tarasoff* v *Regents of University of California*[21] illustrate this all too clearly.

The former case is a general authority for the proposition that where a public body failed to minimise or avert a known, reasonably foreseeable risk, they could be held liable. In the latter case a young man approached staff at the students' medical centre at the University of California for psychiatric help and said that he had violent intentions towards another student – a girl who had broken off a relationship with him. He also told staff he had a gun. The medical centre, however, did nothing to warn the girl and soon afterwards she was murdered by the patient. In an action against the University for negligence brought by the girl's family, the medical centre was found liable: they were under a duty to breach the patient's confidentiality in order to warn the girl of the danger she was in.

Whether such an approach would be adopted in the English courts is difficult to predict. This jurisdiction has traditionally been far more "doctor friendly" than that of the United States. Professor Brazier believes that an English court would be unlikely to find a doctor negligent on facts similar to the *University of California* case for a plaintiff would have difficulty in convincing the court that the doctor's knowledge of the risk to them was sufficient to make it "just and reasonable" to breach their patient's confidence. She believes that the highest duty that can be required of a medical man or woman is an obligation only to consider and assess the risk to a third party.[22] But, with respect, it is submitted that it is better to take a more defensive approach to the problem, in light of the long line of authorities since 1914 that consider it a doctor's duty to disclose and assist in the investigation of any serious crime or misdemeanour, whether it is merely being contemplated by the patient or has actually been committed.[23] This is not to say, however, that every type of criminal conduct will justify a breach of confidence, but certainly those involving the risk of violence should give rise to immunity from legal consequences.

## When disclosure is permitted

The teleconsulting doctor is responsible to the patient for the confidentiality and security of any information obtained in a telemedical consultation. There must be no use or disclosure of any confidential information gained in the course of the teleconsulting doctor's professional work for any purpose other than the clinical care of the patient to whom it relates. There may, however, be circumstances in which there is a positive duty upon a third party to disclose information that becomes known to him. This would include when it is brought to a ship's medical officer's attention that a crew member is infected with a notifiable disease such as cholera, plague, relapsing fever, smallpox, typhus or venereal disease. The most fragile of circumstances arise with the latter class, and in particular with the stigma that is attached to HIV and AIDS infection. There is a clear conflict of interest between the importance of observing confidentiality in a situation where a seafarer has become or suspects he has become infected with the AIDS virus and the legitimate concern for the interests of others who may be harmed by a carrier of the virus.

# Multimedia components of electronic medical files

The recording of teleconsultations is widespread, both for audit and teaching purposes, but this practice raises particular concerns since it ought, ethically, to be subject to the consent of the patient. There are obvious advantages, both in the context of the creation of audit trails and of an electronic record of the teleconsultation, for clinical risk management and as evidence of good medical practice. However video-recordings and other audio-visual records of a telemedical consultation should still be subject to the same general safeguards as conventional confidential, patient-identifiable material. The teleconsultant should obtain the patient's permission to incorporate illustrative material such as photographs and X-rays into multimedia medical records and further consent should be sought to use this material for teaching purposes or for its dissemination to medical video libraries. In practice, however, it may be very difficult to facilitate such consent except, as has been discussed earlier, if a blanket consent were to be obtained from any patient that might be examined or treated through a telemedical link by means of a standard consent form. Another possible solution might be to "digitise" (i.e. obscure) a patient's identifying features which, though not yet universally possible, would be ethically appropriate where material is used for teaching purposes.

# Access to medical records

Medical records are used for an increasing number of purposes. This point is well made by A F Westin in *Computers, Health Records and Citizen Rights*:

> As to medical records, when these were in fact used only by the physician or the hospital, it may have been only curiosity when patients asked to know their contents. But now that medical records are widely shared with health insurance companies, government payers, law enforcement agencies, welfare departments, schools, researchers, credit grantors, and employers, it is often crucial for the patient to know what is being recorded, and to correct inaccuracies that may affect education, career advancement or government benefits.[24]

There are both legal and ethical considerations to be borne in mind when discussing a patient's rights of ownership, access and control of their medical records. It is ethically appropriate for a telemedical patient to exercise control over how information about them is used, in the same way as any conventional patient. For this, though, they need to have access to it. Generally speaking, the legal provisions for control and access coincide with widely held ethical beliefs. This is less true however, of the question of ownership of medical records.

## "Ownership" and control

Legally speaking the concepts of ownership and control of a patient's medical records in the UK are somewhat underdeveloped. For while confidential details given to a teleconsulting doctor by their patient remain, in one fundamental sense, the property of the patient, control over the record rests largely with the doctor. His or her position is one of both trust and confidence, in that whilst the teleconsulting doctor or his hospital is the owner of the actual tangible record, the information is to be used by him for the benefit of his patient. Hence it could be said that, in the absence of an agreement, the teleconsulting doctor or hospital owns the medical records of the telemedical patient but that they are considered to have a property interest in the medical information contained in the record, with a right of access to it, but not to its possession. Such a sentiment is expressed by the legal writer R D Miller thus:

> The medical record is an unusual type of property because physically it belongs to the hospital and the hospital must exercise considerable control over access, but the patient and others have an interest in the information in the record. One way of viewing this is that the hospital owns the paper or other material on which the information is recorded, but is just a custodian of the information. Thus, as stated in *Cannell v Medical and Surgical Clinic*, 21 Ill. App. 3d 383, 315 NE 2d 278 (1974), the patient and others have a right of access to the information in many circumstances, but they do not have a right to possession of the original records.[25]

In the view of Kennedy and Grubb[26] the above approach has much to commend it, although it would require the English courts essentially to redefine the doctor–patient relationship as a fiduciary one. The existing approach of the common law, that the person who "controls" a patient's medical records is the person who creates them, has however been modified by the Access to Medical Reports Act 1988 and the Access to Health Records Act 1990.

## Access by patients

Until recently the concept of confidentiality was misapplied both legally and, one could argue, ethically, so that the patient was denied access to their own health records. Today however there is a general consensus that openness and frankness between doctor and patient should be encouraged and giving the patient the right to see what a teleconsulting medical team has written about them is one way of accomplishing this. This commendable and enlightened approach to a relationship which has traditionally been unilaterally secretive, in this respect, has been given effect in the United Kingdom by two pieces of legislation: the Access to Medical Reports Act 1988 and the Access to Health Records Act 1990. The latter gives telemedicine patients access to health records made after 1 November 1991 and to information recorded earlier if this is necessary in order for them to make sense of what is written later. The rights of access given by the Act do not require any kind of formal application in order to be exercised, although patient access outside the scope of the Act is at the doctor's discretion. The British Medical Association (BMA) has gone on the record as saying that it encourages doctors to give patients access to all health information held about them:

> ...unless the doctor believes it deleterious to the patient's health to do so or unless the confidentiality of other people might be compromised. These are also the two grounds for withholding information specified in the legislation.[27]

Furthermore, withholding access solely because disclosure would be embarrassing for doctors or might give rise to legal claims against them would, states the BMA, be totally unacceptable. It should be unusual for a teleconsultant to be obliged to refuse a patient access to their records on the grounds that they believe the information would be harmful to them, although circumstances can be envisaged in which a teleconsultant doctor will have to reserve to themselves information which identifies or relates to someone else. In such circumstances information which disclosed the identification of another person (unless that person were a health professional) could not be made available to the patient without the identified person's permission.

## Access by employers

The potential use of telemedicine to provide occupational health services brings with it the danger of sensitive medical information being shared with a patient's employer without their consent. While a teleconsultant would obviously be under a moral duty to make certain findings known to a patient's employer where there is a risk to others, there is also scope for causing severe distress or embarrassment to a patient, as, for example, where a seafarer on board an ocean-going ship is found to be HIV positive. When asked to disclose medical information without a patient's consent, a teleconsultant must compare the harm that might be caused by the social and cultural stigmatisation of his patient with the risk to that patient's colleagues presented by allowing the patient to continue working. A poor working environment may also adversely affect the health of telepatients and a teleconsulting doctor would be under an obligation to bring any conditions which he believes represent serious shortcomings or dangers to a patient's occupational health to the attention of the workplace's management.

## Control

Section 5(2)(d) of the Data Protection Act 1984 provides that a "data user" within the Act shall not "disclose [data held by him] to any other person" who is not listed as a potential recipient under section 4(3) at the time of the data user's registration under the Act. Section 5(5) states that unauthorised disclosure, whether made knowingly or recklessly, is a criminal offence. The Act simultaneously prevents unauthorised disclosure whilst allowing the same to those named in the register as potential recipients. So whilst there is a statutory regime in the United Kingdom which vests control in the patient, there is also a power to disclose under the Act which the patient cannot influence. The Access to Medical Reports Act 1988 gives the patient a limited right to control a medical report created for employment or insurance purposes. Section 3(1) of the Act states that an employer, or insurance company, must obtain an individual patient's consent prior to seeking a medical report upon the patient. The patient may consent to the preparation and dissemination of the report on the condition that he is granted access to it or he may give his consent unconditionally.

## Summary

▶ In the United Kingdom the legal and ethical duty of confidentiality owed by a doctor to their patient is recognised by the General Medical Council, the British Medical Association and the English courts. It is therefore incumbent upon any medical practitioner, including a teleconsultant, to respect the trust placed in them by their patients. Any unwarranted breach of the duty of confidentiality will be viewed as serious professional misconduct and may give rise to civil liability to the telepatient.

▶ Occasionally there may, however, be a positive duty on doctors and teleconsultants to reveal confidential information where there is an overriding public interest in doing so; there is a risk of serious harm to another or the telepatient is contemplating a serious criminal offence.

▶ The duty of confidentiality must be respected by all the members of a health care team, with team members being informed of telepatient details on a "need to know" basis only.

▶ Under the Access to Medical Reports Act 1988 and the Access to Health Records Act 1990 the telepatient has the right to see any information held on him, subject to certain statutory exceptions.

## References

1   *Morison v Moat* (1851) 9 Hare 241 at p. 255, 68 ER 492 at p. 498.
2   *The Nichrotherm case* (1957) RPC 207; *Thomas Marshall (Exporters) Limited v Guinle* [1979] Ch 227.
3   Fuller L. American Legal Realism. *University of Pennsylvania Law Review* 1934; 82: 492.
4   [1988] 3 All ER 545 at p. 658.
5   [1988] 2 All ER 648.
6   [1990] 1 All ER 835, (1989) 4 BMLR 96 (CA).
7   Section 35 of the Medical Act 1983, establishes the General Council's power to advise on conduct or ethics: "The powers of the General Council shall include the power to provide, in such manner as the Council thinks fit, advice for members of the medical profession on standards of professional conduct or on medical ethics".
8   See also the National Health Service (Venereal Diseases) Regulations 1974 (SI 1974 No. 29); Abortion Regulations 1991 (SI 1991 No. 499) and Human Fertilisation and Embryology Act 1990, s.33.

9  See also *AB* v *Scottish Blood Transfusion Service* (1990) SCLR 263 and *D* v *National Society for the Prevention of Cruelty to Children* [1978] AC 171 where it was held that the defendant could not be compelled to reveal the identity of an informant who had falsely accused the plaintiff of child abuse since to do so would discourage members of the public from coming forward with important information.

10  General Medical Council. *Duties of a doctor – confidentiality: guidance from the General Medical Council*. GMC, 1995.

11  Per Mr Justice Boreham in *Hunter* v *Mann* [1974] QB 767 at p. 722.

12  Kennedy I, Grubb A. *Medical law: text with materials*. London: Butterworths, 1994: 639.

13  Ibid, at p. 640.

14  [1988] 2 All ER 648.

15  [1990] 1 All ER 835 per Lord Justice Bingham at page 848.

16  [1988] 2 All ER 648 at p. 653.

17  Sieghart P. Professional ethics – for whose benefit? *Journal of Medical Ethics* 1982; 8: 25.

18  General Medical Council. *Professional conduct and discipline: fitness to practise*. GMC, 1993: 79.

19  General Medical Council. *Duties of a doctor – confidentiality: guidance from the General Medical Council*. GMC, 1995.

20  [1955] AC 549.

21  (1976) 551 P 2d 334.

22  Brazier M. *Medicine, law and society*. (2nd ed.) London: Penguin, 1992: 58, citing *Smith* v *Littlewoods Organisation Ltd* [1987] 1 All ER 710 (HL); *Peabody Donation Fund* v *Parkinson* [1984] 3 All ER 86 (HL) and de Hahn. My patient's keeper. *Professional Negligence* 1982; 2: 86.

23  See the dicta of Lord Denning, Master of the Rolls, in *Initial Services Ltd* v *Putterill* [1968] 1 QB 396 at p. 405 and Mr Justice Avery at Birmingham Assizes (1914) 78 JP 604.

24  Westin AF. *Computers, Health Records and Citizen Rights*. 1976: 27.

25  Miller RD. *Problems in Hospital Law*. (4th ed.) 1983: 276-277.

26  Kennedy I, Grubb A. *Medical law: text with materials* (2nd ed.) London: Butterworths, 1994: 618.

27  British Medical Associaton. *Medical ethics today: its practice and philosophy*. London: BMJ Publishing Group, 1993: 45.

# ▶ 3

# Data protection, security and European law

So far we have considered confidentiality as it affects the human factor in teleconsultancy, that is, the individuals involved in sending and receiving medical information and data via a telemedical link. But the principles so far examined are, in many ways, a mere extrapolation of the principle of confidentiality as it applies to conventional medicine. Teleconsultancy, however, is unique in that it involves a fusion of both health care and telecommunications. The next question we must examine, therefore, is how to ensure that patient confidentiality is protected not only by medical professionals but also by the system through which they are communicating.

## The teleconsultant's professional duty

In October 1995 the General Medical Council replaced the ubiquitous "Blue Book"[1] with a series of four booklets having the general title *The Duties of a Doctor*. The Blue Book had stated that:

> Doctors carry prime responsibility for the protection of information given to them by patients or obtained in confidence about patients. They must therefore take steps to ensure, as far as lies in their control, that the records, manual or computerised, which they keep or which they transmit, are protected by effective security systems with adequate procedures to prevent improper disclosure.

The new guidance on the protection of medical information is contained in the third booklet of the series entitled "Confidentiality" where the GMC states that:

> Patients have a right to expect that you will not disclose any personal information which you learn during the course of your professional duties, unless they give permission. Without assurances about confidentiality patients may be reluctant to give doctors the information they need in order to provide good care. For these reasons:
> ▶ When you are responsible for confidential information you must make sure that the information is effectively protected against improper disclosure when it is disposed of, stored, transmitted or received.[2]

Similar statements have been made elsewhere in Europe, including Belgium (by the National Council of the Order of Physicians), the Netherlands (by the Royal Dutch Society for the Advancement of Medicine), Ireland (by the Irish Medical Council), Italy (by the National Federation of Medical Doctors, Surgeons and Obstetricians) and in Germany (by the German Medical Association). Moreover, the British Medical Association has stated that the management and security of medical records is just one facet of the duty of confidentiality[3] and in October 1996 it issued a joint statement with the Department of Health that:

> Responsibility for the security and privacy of databases of personal health information in practices, trusts, and health authorities resides with an appropriate medical practitioner.

The NHS Executive Information Management Group has issued the *National Health Service Information Management and Technology Security Manual* which sets basic security standards for health authorities and NHS trusts. Where an organisation cannot guarantee security, access to the secure national network developed exclusively for the NHS – NHSnet – will be restricted.[4] It is certainly not difficult to imagine the consequences for a telemedicine patient – be they a seafarer on board a merchant vessel or a patient at a clinic in a remote area – of sensitive medical information about, for example, mental health, sexually transmitted diseases or drug addiction, being inadvertently disclosed. Embarrassment, social ostracism and a distrust of the telemedicine service generally would all follow such a compromise.

But the "leaking" of information is not the only danger that teleconsultants face. There could be catastrophic consequences for the clinical care of a patient where the unauthorised interception of telemedicine transmissions gives rise to "modifications" that produce inaccurate or incomplete data. The transmission and storage of medical records by a telemedical system must hence be carried out in a manner which minimises the potential harm to the patient. Yet information security is a complex and highly technical subject with which even the communications engineers and computer technologists in whose sphere of competence such issues lie are often not fully acquainted. Moreover, very few health care professionals (let alone ships' medical officers or other lay-people) have sufficient understanding of the nature and extent of the legal duty of confidentiality properly to take charge of the security of such information. So if teleconsultants, NHS trusts and health authorities are to assume responsibility for creating and transmitting electronic medical records, then they must also have an appreciation of the most important legal and ethical issues affecting the processing of health care records. Furthermore, the professionals involved in the design, implementation and management of computerised health records systems for telemedical services must have detailed technical knowledge of information security systems.

## Computer records

Each hospital in a telemedicine network will have an obligation relating to the storage and use of patient health information and will be accountable for any breach of confidence resulting from its insecure handling. In the United Kingdom the Data Protection Registrar has warned, for example, that doctors could face criminal charges as well as private actions by patients if they fail to provide adequate protection for computers and software in surgery premises, which are sometimes targeted by burglars and hackers.

The Data Protection Act 1984 requires hospitals in a telemedicine communications network to take "appropriate" security measures when handling computer generated information. Obvious measures, such as using an identification number or some other means rather than the patient's name, may be useful. Common sense would dictate that the telemedicine terminals in networked hospitals and clinics should be in secure private rooms to which general access can be prevented when the terminal is sending or receiving patient-identifiable information. Any person or organisation holding information of a personal nature must be registered with the Data Protection Registrar. Failure to register is a criminal offence, carrying an unlimited fine if tried in the Crown Court or a maximum fine of £5,000 if tried in the magistrates' court. Hence a computer hacker who copies personal information on telepatients from a computer system will not only have committed an offence under the Computer Misuse Act 1990 (discussed below), but will be guilty of the offence of holding personal data without being registered. Even where he is registered, knowingly or recklessly obtaining personal data beyond the scope of his registration will still be an offence.

The Fourth, Fifth and Sixth Data Protection Principles contained in the Data Protection Act all apply to the storage and transmission of a patient's medical records through a telemedical link. These state that the data held must be relevant and not excessive for the purpose for which it is held; personal data must be accurate and up to date and moreover, personal data held for any purpose cannot be kept longer than is necessary for that purpose. The Data Protection Act and the European Directive on Data Protection are examined in detail later in this chapter.

Confidential medical records kept in a locked filing cabinet in a hospital are vulnerable, of course. But their vulnerability runs only to the risk of being stolen by burglars or interfered with by employees. Imagine, however, how this risk would increase if the filing cabinet were kept in the street outside the hospital: for such virtually is the status of medical records, medical databases and other such confidential electronic information stored on a computer network to which a telecommunications system is connected. All that is required is the right key, or password, to fit the lock − and the hacker probably has all the time in the world to discover this. The Audit Commission's Survey of Computer Fraud and Abuse, carried out among local authorities and the National Health Service in 1994, showed several areas of inadequacy in the realm of computer security and recommended the carrying out of frequent risk analysis reviews; the implementation of vigorous security policies; the provision of staff computer awareness training focusing on risks and precautions to be taken; ensuring that internal audit departments have computer audit skills and making the necessary financial commitment to the security aspects of an organisation's computer systems.[5]

While the common law, the Wireless Telegraphy Act 1949 and the Interception of Communications Act 1985 (discussed below) provide for both civil and criminal remedies where telemedical transmissions are interfered with during transmission, it is the Computer Misuse Act 1990 that provides protection against the abuse of electronic information while it is held within a stand-alone or networked computer.[6]

Criminal prosecutions for computer crime are still rare, perhaps because of the difficulty of detecting such crime, and more often than not the perpetrators are employees rather than outsiders gaining illegal access to an organisation. In *Denco Ltd* v *Joinson*[7] an employee who had used an unauthorised password to access information that he knew he wasn't entitled to see was guilty of gross misconduct and failed in an action for unfair dismissal;[8] but where a crime such as the unauthorised "hacking" of a medical database is committed from outside an organisation, dismissal is not an option. Indeed, even where an act is committed by an employee of an NHS trust or health authority it may be felt that mere dismissal is not enough. Where serious enough, therefore, any breach of the security of a medical database or a telemedical consultation should be referred to the police. The Crown Prosecution Service will then consider the strength of the evidence, the likelihood of obtaining a conviction and the public interest before making a decision as to whether or not to prosecute. If they decline to act it is still possible to bring a private prosecution; this should be seen as an extreme action but one which would, it is submitted, be highly appropriate as a deterrent.

A potted history of computer crime shows two classes of perpetrator. The first is the lowly, dissatisfied employee engaged to perform menial tasks such as data preparation and entry who discovers vulnerability in a computer system but whose fraud is detected by careful scrutiny, audit, spot-check or an occasional manual check. Strong, high-profile security measures and codes of discipline that state in no uncertain terms the serious consequences for an employee of abusing computer-held telepatient information either individually or in concert with others, are the key deterrents to such a person.

The second class of computer criminal is the hacker. The hacker presents a special challenge because more often than not hacking does not take place with the intention of actually carrying out a criminal offence, but is viewed as a form of intellectual challenge, usually undertaken by a young computer enthusiast who wishes to prove himself to his peers. Such people are a nuisance but can also unintentionally cause a great deal of damage, particularly to "safety-critical systems" such as hospital records. If nothing else, however, the computer hacker has helped to raise awareness of the deficiencies of computer systems. For while unauthorised access to a bank or commercial organisation's computer network may bring with it the possibility of financial loss, breaking into a hospital's system might bring equally if not more catastrophic consequences. A hospital's system is vulnerable in three respects:

(a)   Confidential medical records may be read, copied or erased;
(b)   Information contained in records may be changed;
(c)   Though the hacker may only leave something as harmless as a boasting message, he could leave something as harmful as a computer virus, a "logic-bomb" or a "time-bomb".

## Computer Misuse Act 1990

Dissatisfaction with the state of the English law illustrated by cases such as *R* v *Gold*,[7] which appeared to view hacking as something other than a criminal activity, led to the Law Commission's Working Paper No. 110 on Computer Misuse in 1988, and this was followed by the very comprehensive Computer Misuse Act 1990, section 1 of which states that notwithstanding that a hacker who has gained access to computer programs or data doesn't intend to carry out any other act he will be guilty of an offence if:

(a)   He causes a computer to perform any function with intent to secure access to any program or data held in any computer;
(b)   The access he intends to secure is unauthorised; and
(c)   He knows at the time when he causes the computer to perform the function that this is the case.

The hacker must know that his access is unauthorised: careless or reckless access will not be sufficient to make out an offence under the Act. This offence can only be tried in a magistrates' court and hence the maximum fine is £5,000 and the maximum term of imprisonment that can be set is six months. Both a fine and a term of imprisonment could, however, be imposed – though it is unusual to set both at the maximum end of the scale.

The Act has been interpreted widely by the courts so that a second computer need not be involved and an offence can be committed under the Act by an employee or ex-employee who makes unauthorised changes to a computer system.[10] Indeed, a computer as such need not be involved, so abusing telecommunications equipment such as a telemedicine terminal which has computer technology built into it will be covered by the Act.

Section 2 of the 1990 Act provides for an ulterior intent offence. Where a hacker obtains unauthorised access to a system with the intention of committing a further offence such as theft, blackmail or obtaining property or services by deception, then a maximum punishment of up to five years' imprisonment is possible, the offence being triable "either way" that is, either in a magistrates' court or before a jury in a Crown Court. The commission of the crime of blackmail will of course usually be tried as such. The offence is provided for in section 21 of the Theft Act 1968 and carries a maximum penalty of 14 years' imprisonment. A person is guilty of blackmail if, with a view to gain for themselves or another or with the intention of causing loss to another, they make any unwarranted demand with menaces. Examples in telemedicine might include threatening to reveal a telepatient is HIV positive or threatening an NHS trust by inserting a "time-bomb" into their computer system and demanding money in return for details of how to disable the bomb. Section 2 of the Act would come into its own where a hacker gained access to confidential information held about a telepatient with the intention of blackmailing them or the organisation that holds it but, for one reason or another, fails to carry that intention out.

Jurisdictional issues are discussed in some detail in chapter 9. But for now it is sufficient to note that sections 4 to 9 the Computer Misuse Act contain complex provisions regarding jurisdiction over computer crimes committed from abroad in this country, or committed by a person in this country but causing harm in another. All that is required for a prosecution to be brought in the United Kingdom is some tangible link with this country – that the crime either originates from a computer in England, Northern Ireland, Scotland or Wales, or is directed towards a computer in one of these provinces. The offence will not, however, lose its criminal potential in another country simply because it is charged in the United Kingdom: so called "double-criminality". Section 3 of the Act states that a person commits an offence if:

> He does any act which causes an unauthorised modification of the contents of any computer; and at a time when he does the act, he has the requisite intent and the requisite knowledge.

The requisite intent is the intention to cause a modification to the contents of any computer in order to impair its operation, prevent or hinder access to any program or data held in the computer or to impair the operation of any program or the reliability of any data and the requisite knowledge is the knowledge that the intended modification is unauthorised. This section is highly useful since it is able to deal with hackers who leave viruses, time-bombs and logic-bombs as well as those who simply make alterations to existing records. This offence, like that in section 2 of the Act, is triable either way and carries a maximum term of imprisonment of five years and/or a fine.

### Minimising the risk

It is well beyond the scope of this work to examine in detail the ways in which computer systems can be made more secure but there are a number of weaknesses that stand out in the computer systems whose abuse has resulted in litigation – the most obvious being complacency on the part of a network system's manager. All too often hacking is the result of a would-be criminal seeking an enjoyable challenge. The scope of access is also a common weakness – different levels of access are appropriate for different levels of staff and passwords need to be made unobvious (e.g., not the user's car registration) and changed regularly. The number of sites allowed to call a particular ISDN (Integrated Services Digital Network) number should be restricted and PSTN (Public Switched Telephone Network) systems could do likewise – requiring the caller to give a password and then hang up. If the password is authentic, the caller can be called back and the connection re-established. A log of access, noting the time and date of each user's logging in and out of the system, is also a common feature in the detection of computer fraud in its early stages. As has already been stated, it needs to be made crystal clear to employees, through leaflets and posters, that breaches of security are viewed seriously and all incidents will be reported to the police, such a system of publicity being reinforced by frequent audits and spot-checks. Variety is the criminal's greatest enemy – even auditing systems need to be changed frequently if the criminal is not to find flaws in an existing one.

Finally, many computer crimes are committed by aggrieved employees shortly after they are dismissed or made redundant. Access to the computer system could prudently be denied and salary in lieu of notice given to such an employee where there is a reasonably foreseeable risk of them exploiting their familiarity with a computer system in order to deal their employer one final "sting". The codes of practice published jointly by the Department of Trade and Industry and the British Standards Institute provide a useful starting point for health authorities and NHS trusts who need to design their own code of practice.[11]

## Unauthorised interception of transmissions

The possibility exists of patient information being intercepted or misdirected during its transmission. This would pose a significant obstacle to maintaining the confidentiality of data and the architects of any telemedical communications network would naturally need to ensure that such data is encrypted prior to transmission and decoded at the recipient node. Telephone tapping is very easy to achieve, ISDN less so but the possibility of the unauthorised interception and decoding of this information might exist so it should be bundled in with other information, making it difficult to retrieve, or made unintelligible through encryption.

Article 23 of the International Telecommunication Union's Radio Regulations provide that the competent regulatory agency or department in each member State agrees to take the necessary measures to prohibit and prevent:

(a)  The unauthorised interception of radiocommunications not intended for the general use of the public;

(b)  The divulgence of the contents, simple disclosure of the existence, publication or any use whatever, without authorisation, of information of any nature whatever obtained via the interception of any radiocommunication not intended for the general use of the public.

In the United Kingdom the Wireless Telegraphy Act 1949, the Interception of Communications Act 1985 and the common law contain provisions which may be used, inter alia, to protect the confidentiality of medical data transmitted via a telemedical link.

## (i) Wireless Telegraphy Act 1949

Under section 5(b) of the Wireless Telegraphy Act there are two possible criminal offences:

> Any person who...
> (a) ...
> (b) otherwise than under the authority of [the Secretary of State] or in the course of his duty as a servant of the Crown either—
>
> (i) uses any wireless telegraphy apparatus with intent to obtain information as to the contents, sender or addressee of any message (whether sent by means of wireless telegraphy or not) which neither the person using the apparatus nor any person on whose behalf he is acting is authorised by the [Secretary of State] to receive;
>
> or
>
> (ii) except in the course of legal proceedings or for the purpose of any report thereof, discloses any information as to the contents, sender or addressee of any such message, being information which would not have come to his knowledge but for the use of wireless telegraphy apparatus by him or by another person.
>
> shall be guilty of an offence.

These provisions are capable of applying to the reception and subsequent use of radio and satellite transmissions of confidential medical records and results. A typical prosecution is *Paul* v *Ministry of Posts and Telecommunications*.[12] In this case the defendant owned a car fitted with an AMF radio receiver and was a member of a society called the Fire Brigade Society, membership being open to anyone on payment of an annual fee but providing no practical privileges or rights. On two occasions the defendant parked opposite the fire station, a distance of some 40 yards or so away, and tuned in to the fire brigade emergency message. This was done in order to facilitate, from time to time, visiting and observing incidents which the fire brigade attended. However, he had no authority to use the receiver for this purpose and was not on duty as a servant of the Crown. He was charged with contravening section 5(b)(i) of the Wireless Telegraphy Act 1949. There was no mischievous intent in what he did, neither was there any suggestion that he would use the information for any improper purpose unless is could be said that it was undesirable for the scene of a fire to be congested by spectators.

The defendant contested that his actions did not amount to an offence under section 5(b)(i) and that he should be acquitted in the absence of *mens rea* (which it was found difficult to formulate appropriately in argument). On appeal to the Queen's Bench Division against his conviction it was held that no intent was necessary to constitute the offence, other than the intent to do the prohibited act. The prohibited act was within the class of acts which were not criminal in any real sense but were prohibited under penalty in the public interest – hence the difficulty in formulating the *mens rea* appropriately in argument. The acts were, however, prohibited and breach of the prohibition constituted commission of the criminal offence.

The outcome of *Paul* is encouraging, therefore, at least from the point of view of discouraging individuals within the English jurisdiction from using their own equipment to "observe" telemedical transmissions via satellite or radio.[13]

## (ii) Interception of Communications Act 1985

The Interception of Communications Act 1985 was passed following the publication of the Home Office's *White Paper on the Interception of Communications in the United Kingdom* (Cmnd 9438), which put forward several proposals for changes in the law relating to telephone tapping following the decision of the European Court of Human Rights in *Malone* v *Metropolitan Police Commissioner.*[14] Section 1(1) of the Act states:

> (1) Subject to the following provisions of this section, a person who intentionally intercepts a communication in the course of its transmission by post or by means of a public telecommunication system shall be guilty of an offence and liable—
>     (a) on summary conviction, to a fine not exceeding the statutory maximum;
>     (b) on conviction on indictment, to imprisonment for a term not exceeding two years or to a fine or to both.

The Act provides protection for the confidentiality of letters, telephone calls and all other communications entrusted to the Post Office, to British Telecom and other public telecommunications systems. It does this in two ways: first, by making it a criminal offence for anyone improperly to intercept communications (i.e. without a warrant from the Secretary of State), and second, by providing an independent Tribunal as a means of redress against any improper use of the Secretary of State's powers to grant such a warrant. It is a defence to show that the person concerned has reasonable grounds for believing that the person to whom or by whom the communication was sent has consented to the interception[15] or to show that the communication was intercepted in obedience to a warrant issued by the Secretary of State.[16] A warrant can only be issued if it is necessary in the interests of national security, for the purpose of preventing or detecting serious crime or for the purpose of safeguarding the economic well-being of the United Kingdom.[17] Section 7 of the Act provides that:

> (1) There shall be a tribunal...in relation to which the provisions of Schedule 1 of this Act shall apply.[18]
> (2) Any person who believes that communications sent to or by him have been intercepted in the course of their transmission by post or by means of a public telecommunication system may apply to the Tribunal for an investigation under this section.
> (3) On such an application, other than one appearing to the Tribunal to be frivolous or vexatious, the Tribunal shall investigate—
>     (a) whether there is or has been a relevant warrant or a relevant certificate;
>     (b) where there is or has been such a warrant or certificate, whether there has been any contravention of sections 2 to 5 above in relation to that warrant or certificate.
> (4) If, on investigation, the Tribunal, applying the principles applicable by a court on an application for judicial review, conclude that there has been a contravention of sections 2 to 5 above in relation to a relevant warrant or a relevant certificate, they shall:
>     (a) give notice to the applicant stating that conclusion;
>     (b) make a report of their findings to the Prime Minister;
>     (c) if they think fit, make an order under subsection (5) below.
> (5) An order under this subsection may do one or more of the following, namely—
>     (a) quash the relevant warrant or the relevant certificate;
>     (b) direct the destruction of copies of the intercepted material or, as the case may be, so much of it as is certified by the relevant certificate;

(c) direct the Secretary of State to pay to the applicant such sum by way of compensation as may be specified in the Order.

For purposes of section 1(1) of the Act, "a communication which is in the course of its transmission otherwise than by a public telecommunication system" is deemed to be in the course of its transmission by means of such a system if its mode of transmission identifies it as a communication which is to be or has been transmitted by such a system and has been sent from or is to be sent to a country or territory outside the United Kingdom.[19] Section 10 of the Act provides that a "telecommunications system" in that statute has the same meaning as in section 4 of the Telecommunications Act 1984:

> 4.  (1)  In this Act "telecommunication system" means a system for the conveyance, through the agency of electric, magnetic, electro-magnetic, electro-chemical or electro-mechanical energy, of—
>     (a)  speech, music and other sounds;
>     (b)  visual images;
>     (c)  signals serving for the impartation (whether as between persons and persons, things and things or persons and things) of any matter otherwise than in the form of sounds or visual images; or
>     (d)  signals serving for the actuation or control of machinery or apparatus.
>     (2)  For the purposes of this Act telecommunication apparatus which is situated in the United Kingdom and—
>     (a)  is connected to but not comprised in a telecommunication system; or
>     (b)  is connected to and comprised in a telecommunication system which extends beyond the United Kingdom,
>     shall be regarded as a telecommunication system and any person who controls the apparatus shall be regarded as running the system.

The Tribunal set up by the Act only provides for examination of the circumstances surrounding the issuing of a warrant. So if a telepatient, a teleconsultant, a health authority or an NHS trust reasonably believes that telemedicine transmissions have been intercepted and no warrant has been issued permitting this, then the matter can be reported to the police for formal criminal investigation. If sufficient evidence is found to substantiate the complainant's suspicions, then this may lead to a criminal prosecution against the person or persons involved. Such prosecutions have been brought, but in the few cases available to illustrate the operation of the Interception of Communications Act 1985 the courts seem to have been more intent on securing convictions than giving clear guidelines on the application of the Act. In *R v Uxbridge Justices, ex parte Offomah*[20] it was held that where a recording of a telephone conversation between two parties was made by listening in at one end then there was not an "interception" within the terms of the 1985 Act. This decision could be restricted to its facts (an unsuccessful attempt for leave to move for judicial review of a decision to alter the date of committal proceedings). However, it might be extrapolated to reduce the scope of the Act to telemedicine transmissions intercepted only when between two telemedicine nodes.

However, where in *R v Effik and Mitchell*[21] the police intercepted incoming and outgoing calls to a cordless phone and a mobile phone using an FM radio there was no difficulty during the trial for the Judge to hold that there had been an interception within the meaning of section 1. It was conceded in that case that no warrant had been issued to the police officers involved permitting them to intercept the calls but that, nonetheless, the evidence obtained by taping these calls would be admissible since section 9 of the Act did not provide that all such unauthorised interceptions were inadmissible, but that:

(1) In any proceedings before any court or tribunal no evidence shall be adduced and no question in cross-examination shall be asked which (in either case) tends to suggest—
(a) that an offence under section 1 above has been or is to be committed by any of the persons mentioned in subsection (2) below; or
(b) that a warrant has been or is to be issued to any of those persons.

The "forbidden territory" as Lord Justice Steyn called it, was a line of questioning designed to establish that none of the four defences was applicable.[22] The reasoning behind this is that such questioning might reveal how a person's criminal activities had come to the attention of the police, Customs and Excise or the security services in the first place. The point of section 9, in relation to telemedicine therefore, would be to ensure that the nature of any "trap" set by a health authority to catch a criminal interceptor of transmissions or any source of information (such as a human informant) as to the crimes, is not compromised or revealed during the course of a criminal trial or a tribunal.

Nonetheless, it could still be argued that the Interception of Communications Act 1985 has been rendered somewhat otiose by the Court of Appeal's insistence that what mattered in this case was the quality and content of the recordings and not their admissibility, and also by the finding of the court below (which the Court of Appeal did not disturb) that a public telecommunications system terminates at the junction box in the customer's premises and that if the telephone attached to that system is cordless then it is a privately run system connected to a public system. It was not necessary for the Court of Appeal to question this finding but it is submitted that common sense should dictate that the court was wrong and that to create such a distinction between a corded and cordless phone (which are, after all, two ways of accomplishing the connection of a telephone handset with the main equipment, albeit that one allows greater mobility) is to import a distinction into the Act which was never intended and which, moreover, substantially reduces its usefulness.

## (iii) Common law and equity

It is as well that the statutory provisions governing the unauthorised interception of transmissions are detailed and comprehensive as it would be extremely difficult to rely successfully on the common law or equity to prevent such interception.[23] Much depends, though, upon the type of transmission. In *BBC Enterprises Limited* v *Hi-Tech Xtravision Limited*[24] Mr Justice Scott rejected an argument that encrypted transmissions containing the BBC TV Europe television service were confidential:

There is no confidentiality in the content of the...programmes as such. They are simply BBC programmes. The broadcasts are encrypted, but it is possible for Hi-Tech, and no doubt others, to decode the encryption. To do this is, in my judgment, no more a breach of confidence than it would be to decode a coded message placed in the columns of *The Times*. If an author chooses to place a coded message in a public medium he cannot, in my judgment, complain if members of the public decode his message. If the content, once decoded, does

> not qualify for protection on confidentiality grounds, the law of confidentiality is not, in my judgment, of any relevance.

In *Malone* v *Metropolitan Police Commissioner*[25] it was held that no confidentiality existed in respect of telephone conversations and that therefore the tapping of telephones did not breach any duty of confidence which might arise (apart from in contract). The court held that since telephone users are aware of the risks of being overheard by reason of extension lines, private switchboards and so called "crossed lines", a person who utters confidential information must "accept the risk of any unknown overhearing which is inherent in the circumstances of the communication".[26] However, *BBC* v *Hi-Tech* can arguably be distinguished from *Malone* on the basis that the unauthorised interception of satellite communications is not "inherent" (i.e. so easily accomplished) in the way that the interception of telephone communications is and, since the information being transmitted over a telemedical link is, unlike BBC programmes, of an obviously confidential nature to anyone receiving it, the possibility of a duty of confidence and a breach of that duty is not ruled out.

In view of this, it is submitted that where a case similar to *BBC* v *Hi-Tech* arose after the unauthorised interception of a telemedical transmission, an action for breach of confidence could be brought where the information can be shown to:

(a) have the necessary quality of confidence about it;

(b) have been conveyed in circumstances importing an obligation of confidence; and

(c) have been used in an unauthorised way to the disadvantage of the person who had communicated it.

The most usual remedy sought is an injunction to restrain any dissemination or further dissemination of confidential information. These are regularly granted but may be limited in duration. Damages may also be sought as a means of putting the plaintiff in the position he would have been in if the defendant had not wrongly obtained and used the plaintiff's confidential information in the first place.[27]

## Data protection and security in the European Union

Data protection is presently an area of high legislative activity within the European Union. National governments and international organisations are creating regulations concerning the collection, processing, communication and storage of medical data. Most of these show some similarity since they are all based, to a greater or lesser extent, on the Council of Europe's Convention No. 108.[28] There is not, however, a common data protection framework throughout Europe at the present time, although the foundations for such a framework have been laid by the European Union Directive on the protection of individuals with regard to the processing of personal data and on the free movement of such data[29] which Member States must implement by 24 October 1998. The following international instruments have been enacted concerning data protection:

(a) OECD Guidelines Governing the Protection of Privacy and Transborder Flows of Personal Data; 23 September 1980.

(b) Council on Personal Data; 28 January 1981.

(c) Council of Europe Recommendation No. (81)1 on Regulations for Automated Medical Data Banks; 23 January 1981.

(d) Council of Europe Recommendation No. (86)1 on the Protection of Personal Data used for Social Security purposes; 23 October 1986.

(e) Council of Europe Recommendation No. (87)23 on Hospital Information Systems; 22 October 1987.

(f) Council of Europe Recommendation No. (89)2 on the Protection of Personal Data used for Employment Purposes; 18 January 1989.

(g) Directive of the European Parliament and of the Council on the Protection of Individuals with Regard to the Processing of Personal Data and on the Free Movement of such Data.

The following national legislation has also been adopted:

(a) Belgium – Data Protection Act 1992.

(b) Denmark – Private Registers Act 1978 (consolidated 1987) and the Public Authorities Registers Act 1979 (consolidated 1987).

(c) Germany – Federal Data Protection Act 1991 (replacing an earlier Act of 1978).

(d) France – Act 78-17 on Data Processing, Data Files and Individual's Liberties 1978.

(e) Ireland – Data Protection Act 1988 and Data Protection (Access Modification) Health Regulations 1989.

(f) Luxembourg – Act concerning the Use of Normative Data in Computer Processing 1979.

(g) Holland – Act Providing for the Protection of Privacy in Connection with Personal Data Files 1988.

(h) Portugal – Law 10/91 for the Protection of Personal Data with Regard to Automatic Processing 1991.

(i) Spain – Organic Law 5/1992 on the Regulation of the Automatic Processing of Personal Data 1992.

(j) United Kingdom – Data Protection Act 1984.

(k) Italy – Law 675 of 31 December 1996 on Data Protection.

(l) Finland – Personal Data File Act 1987, Access to Public Documents Act.

Some states are notable by their absence from the above list. Greece has not, as yet, enacted any national legislation and hence, in theory at least, it is against basic data protection principles to transfer personal data to that country unless appropriate measures are taken to ensure that the data in question will be dealt with in accordance with data protection principles. However, the coming into force of the European Union's data protection directive will to a large extent make the regulation of telemedical data protection legally binding and, for the first time, the laws of all of the European Union Member States will be harmonised.

## Data protection in the United Kingdom

In the United Kingdom the Data Protection Act 1984 at present regulates the use of automatically processed information relating to individuals, and the provision of services in respect of such information, by providing for the registration of those individuals and organisations, such as telemedicine services, NHS trusts and health authorities, who hold personal information on computers as well as the computer bureaux that provide services to such data users. This enables individuals to discover who holds data on them and what the data may contain as well as forcing data users to be open about their activities. There are criminal penalties for failing to register and for those who act beyond the scope of their registration. Moreover, the Act includes a set of eight Data Protection Principles based on the Council of Europe's Convention on Data Protection which must be followed by persons who store or process information. Individual telepatients have right of access to information held on them to ensure that it is accurate: inaccurate records can be corrected or deleted. The Act appointed a Data Protection Registrar to oversee the registration of data users and to deal with complaints, and provides for both criminal penalties and civil remedies such as compensation.

The eight Data Protection Principles, which are contained in Schedule 1 of the Act are:

1. The information to be contained in personal data shall be obtained, and personal data shall be processed, fairly and lawfully.
2. Personal data shall be held only for one or more specified and lawful purposes.
3. Personal data held for any purpose or purposes shall not be used or disclosed in any manner incompatible with that purpose or those purposes.
4. Personal data held for any purpose or purposes shall be adequate, relevant and not excessive in relation to that purpose or those purposes.
5. Personal data shall be accurate and, where necessary, kept up to date.
6. Personal data held for any purpose or purposes shall not be kept for longer than is necessary for that purpose or those purposes.
7. An individual shall be entitled—
    (a) At reasonable intervals and without undue delay or expense—
        (i) To be informed by any data user whether he holds personal data of which that individual is the subject; and
        (ii) Access to any such data held by the data user; and
    (b) Where appropriate, to have such data corrected or erased.
8. Appropriate security measures shall be taken against unauthorised access to, or alteration, disclosure or destruction of, personal data and against accidental loss or destruction of personal data.

The eighth principle is applicable to computer bureaux as well as data users. The Data Protection Registrar is able to enforce these principles through enforcement notices, de-registration notices and transfer prohibition notices as well as through the publication of practical guidelines.[30] An enforcement notice will be preceded by a preliminary notice, with which the data user usually has 28 days to comply. A form of negotiated settlement known as a formal undertaking may be reached between the data user and the Registrar where the latter agrees not to issue an enforcement notice if the former takes proper steps to remedy their breach of the Data Protection Principles. This should not unduly worry health authorities and NHS trusts intending to integrate telemedicine into primary and secondary care, however. Most such groups will already have been required to develop data protection policies in line with the Data Protection Principles contained in the 1984 Act and so no new procedures should be required.

## When does the Act apply?

The Data Protection Act applies only to the processing of personal data. The Act defines "data" widely as any "information recorded in a form in which it can be processed by equipment operating automatically in response to instructions given for that purpose"[31] and "personal data" as "data consisting of information which relates to a living individual who can be identified from that information (or from that and other information in the possession of the data user), including any expression of opinion about the individual but not any indication of the intentions of the data user in respect of that individual".[32] The definitions are hence wide enough to cover situations where some information on a telepatient is stored on computer and some is stored manually, on index cards for instance.

The Act also gives definitions for "data subject" and "data user".[33] A "data subject" is an individual who is the subject of personal data. A telepatient will obviously be a data subject within the meaning of the Act. A "data user" may be a real or legal person, such as a health authority or telemedicine provider and will "hold" data under section 1(5) of the Act where:

(a) the data form part of a collection of data processed or intended to be processed by or on behalf of that person... and

(b) that person (either alone or jointly or in common with other persons) controls the contents and use of the data comprised in the collection; and

(c) the data are in a form in which they have been or are intended to be processed as mentioned in paragraph (a) above or (though not for the time being in that form) in a form into which they have been converted after being so processed and with a view to being further so processed on a subsequent occasion.

The Act defines "processing" widely to mean amending, augmenting, deleting or re-arranging the data or extracting the information constituting the data and in the case of personal data this means performing any of these operations by reference to the data subject.[34] The distinction is a difficult one to draw but essentially processing by reference to the data subject will occur whenever the data user intends to locate and process information *because* it relates to an individual telepatient. So if an NHS trust merely wishes to check how many telepatients it has, it is not processing data by reference to the data subject. Word processing, as such, is excluded from the Act, section 1(8) stating:

Subsection (7) above shall not be construed as applying to any operation performed only for the purpose of preparing the text of documents.

However, in what is commonly known as a "mail merge", that is, the combination of a word processed document such as a letter with a list of individual names and addresses of telepatients to whom it is to be sent, there may in fact be a form of personal data processing taking place where a degree of selectivity is being used (e.g. when choosing only those patients with cardiac problems or over a certain age). If, however, the mail merge is done indiscriminately (i.e. with absolutely all of the addresses held on the computer), then there has not been any processing for the purposes of the Act.

## Individual rights of access

Under the Data Protection Act 1984 an individual telepatient has a right of access to personal data held by a health authority, NHS trust or telemedicine service. He or she can check to see if a telemedicine provider has information about them stored on a computer and can, upon payment of a fee, see a copy of that information. The telemedicine provider cannot charge more than £10 for doing this and must provide sufficient information within 40 days of the request. Where information about joint records is sought (this is usually in the context of bank accounts), a data user may decline to supply all of the requested information unless satisfied that the other person(s) has consented. If they are not so satisfied they must still provide the information, but ensure that references to other individuals are blanked out. If this information is inaccurate there is a right to have it amended or erased and, if the person has suffered damage as a result, there is a right to claim compensation. The individual may make a complaint to the Data Protection Registrar if they reasonably believe that any of the Data Protection Principles or any part of the Act has been breached.[35]

Under section 22(4) of the Act data is inaccurate for compensation purposes if it is incorrect or misleading as to any matter of fact – hence an opinion stated about a telepatient cannot fall within the compensatable definition, although it will nonetheless be "personal data" under section 1(8). However, where the expression of opinion itself is based on inaccurate data, the statement will fall within section 22(4) and its rectification or erasure can be demanded under that section by an application to either a county court or High Court which is bound to issue an order for the same if it is satisfied that the data concerned is inaccurate. The inevitable expense and delay involved in using the English legal system has led some commentators to criticise its lack of accessibility for ordinary people. So if rectification rather than compensation is a telepatient's overwhelming desire, then the better approach would be to make a complaint to the Registrar.

Even if compensation is sought, the data user may not be liable. For instance, if a health authority or NHS trust has received or obtained data from the telepatient himself or from a third party then, providing the data held is clearly recorded as having been so obtained, no liability will accrue. Moreover, where the authority or trust can show that they took reasonable care in the circumstances to ensure the accuracy of the data, regardless of its source, they will also escape liability. A sensible telemedicine provider will therefore ensure that they have a comprehensive set of procedures for validating and verifying data and this should always include the source of the data in the record. Back-up copies should be kept securely and, as highlighted earlier in this chapter, precautions taken against computer hackers and unauthorised interceptors since damages are payable to a telepatient whose personal data is disclosed without their authority.

## Exemptions from the Act

Exemptions from the operation of the whole of the Data Protection Act can be made on the basis of national security; for payrolls and accounts; for private individuals using their personal computers for domestic and other such recreational purposes (such as clubs) and information required by law to be made available to the general public. Refusal by a data user of an individual's access to personal data held on him is possible in a limited number of circumstances relating to crime and taxation; data held for the regulation of financial services;

judicial appointments; legal professional privilege; statistical or research data; legal prohibition; situations where access for that individual is provided for by the Consumer Credit Act; back-up data; situations where compliance would incriminate the data user; examination marks and for health and social work data.[36]

This latter category is governed by section 29 of the Data Protection Act which states that a health professional or any other person holding medical information can withhold access to data where allowing this would be likely to cause serious harm to the physical or mental health of the telepatient data subject or lead the data subject to identify another person (other than the health professional involved in their care) who has not consented to the disclosure of his or her identity. However, the Department of Health has made it clear that these exceptions should only be relied upon in exceptional circumstances. The social work exemption applies to local authorities, education authorities, the probation service and other such bodies and is identical to the health professional exemption, although the first category is expanded to include the physical or mental health of the telepatient or their emotional condition. Again, this exemption can only be invoked in exceptional circumstances.

The third and final form of exemption under the Act is known as the non-disclosure exemption. When a health authority or NHS trust registers with the Data Protection Registrar as a data user, it must specify to whom it may wish to disclose the personal data it holds (i.e. staff, conventional patients and telepatients). Disclosure to any other person would be an offence unless it falls within any of the six exemptions provided: for the protection of national security; for crime and taxation purposes; for legal purposes; with the consent of the data subject; to a servant or agent of the data user or their computer bureaux or in an emergency situation such as where details of a person's blood group are urgently required.

## The new European regime

In the late 1980s the European Commission established a research and development programme called Advanced Informatics in Medicine (AIM) in order to explore within a harmonised European environment what results could be achieved by the application of informatics to the health care environment. Although there were no specific data protection and security projects within the first phase of the AIM programme, the European Parliament expressed a definite interest in these issues and the AIM secretariat participated with the relevant working group of the European Federation for Medical Informatics in a conference. This was to be a landmark event, in that it attracted the participation of lawyers and data protection commissioners from a number of European States.

In the second phase of the AIM programme, the AIM SEISMED (Secure Environment for Information Systems in Medicine) project developed four sets of specific guidelines for security in Health Care Establishments (HCEs), including a legal analysis and guidance. The legal regulations pertaining to health care data processing in the EU Member States were studied and summarised and the resulting analysis used as the basis for the development of a Deontology Code for the use of health care and legal professionals throughout Europe.

So while domestic statute law and case law go some way towards protecting telemedicine patients from the risk of confidential information being intercepted during transmission, it cannot be denied that the law has developed in an *ad hoc* and piecemeal fashion, and still lags many years behind current practice. Moreover, there is not, as yet, any clear legislative relationship between the duty of confidentiality and the patient's right of access to his health records.

But although the AIM SEISMED's Deontology Code will be of practical use in assisting HCEs in Europe to ensure the security of their patient records, it is the comprehensive implementation of the EU Directive on the protection of individuals with regard to the processing of personal data and on the free movement of such data[37] that will bring a really coherent and comprehensive regulatory framework to the protection of the telemedicine patient's rights. The Council of Ministers reached a common position on the European Data Protection Directive on 20 February 1995 and it was subsequently sent to the European Parliament for a second reading. A comprehensive analysis of this directive is contained in the papers presented at a security workshop hosted by the AIM SEISMED project 11 July 1994 in Brussels.[38] The Directive was formally adopted on 24 October 1995 and Member States have until 24 October 1998 to transpose the terms of the Directive into their national law. The United Kingdom's existing legislation, the Data Protection Act 1984, meets many of the requirements of the Directive. But the Directive goes beyond the present law in a number of important respects:

(a)  it defines certain key concepts differently;
(b)  it extends data protection controls to certain manual records;
(c)  it sets tighter and more detailed conditions for processing sensitive personal data;
(d)  it requires certain exemptions for the media;
(e)  it strengthens individuals' rights;
(f)  it strengthens the powers of the supervisory authority;
(g)  it sets new rules for the transfer of personal data outside the European Union; and
(h)  it allows the existing registration scheme to be simplified.

A Bill implementing the Directive was introduced into Parliament in Autumn 1997 and so we can expect the present 1984 Act to be replaced by a Data Protection Act 1998 in due course.[36] Article 1 of the Directive requires Member States to:

> ...protect the fundamental rights and freedoms of natural persons and in particular their right to privacy with respect to the processing of personal data.

This is a natural corollary of Article 8 of the European Convention on Human Rights which establishes an individual's right to respect for their private life. After much prevarication under the UK's previous government, the European Convention on Human Rights will finally be incorporated into law during 1998. The right to privacy will hence become not just a human right but an enforceable legal right, the breach of which can be remedied by the English courts. The government also intends to enact, in due course, a Freedom of Information Act which will complement the Data Protection Act in providing for access to personal information held by the public sector, including health authorities and NHS trusts.

## Definitions

The first most important difference between the new and the old data protection regimes is the superficial, but nonetheless important, differences between the definitions of "personal data" and "processing" found in the 1984 Act and the definitions that will be found in a 1998 Act bringing into force the EU Directive. Under Article 2(a) of the Directive the scope of the new law will be limited to living people and an individual to whom personal data relates will not be considered as being identifiable where information is anonymous. If separate information exists in a different place that might enable the subject of personal data to be identified, then there will have to be a reasonable likelihood of the two pieces of information being capable of being brought together if that information is to be brought within the operation of the Act.

Under Article 2(b), "processing" will be defined much more widely than in the 1984 Act to cover any operation involving personal data from its collection to its destruction, as well as merely holding it, and will also apply to any automated processing of personal data whether or not by reference to the data subject. The exemption of word processing under the 1984 Act will also be ended by the Directive, although the British government intends to continue to exempt word processing from the notification requirements and processing by natural persons in the course of purely personal or household activities. However, manual records consisting of a structured set of personal data which is accessible according to specific criteria will be brought within the operation of the Directive. However the government intends only to apply the minimum protection required by the Directive to these records, i.e. to non-automated records structured by reference to individuals, which allow easy access to the personal data they contain. Card-indexes, microfiches and similar sources will hence come within the new Act, although only to a limited extent.

The Directive refers not to a "data user" but to a "controller" in Article 2(d), but the definitions are identical. Similarly, "computer bureaux" is replaced with "processor" by Article 2(e) and the wider definition of "processing" in Article 2(b) will, by implication, mean that a "controller" includes those collecting data on their behalf. Article 2(f) will exclude employees, agents, contractors and the like, who are working under the direct authority of the controller or the processor, from requiring authorisation to process data.

Any person who will or may have access to the personal data in question is classed as a recipient under Article 2(g) and information about these recipients must be provided by the controller to data subjects under Articles 10 and 11 in order to guarantee fair processing.

## Processing data

The new law will retain the Data Protection Principles found in Schedule 1 of the 1984 Act, which broadly correspond with Articles 6, 12 and 17 of the European Directive, although the latter two articles are somewhat more detailed than the corresponding Principles in the 1984 Act. The 1984 Act requires that the data user provides the data subject with an intelligible copy of relevant data in response to a subject access request. Under the new law this could be in any form requested by the data subject, including electronic form. A hard copy can still be requested unless this would involve disproportionate effort or is unreasonable. The £10 maximum fee and the 40-day time limit for conforming to a request would both remain, although that time limit will only start to run when both the relevant identifying information and the fee have been received by the data user/controller. The purpose of this provision is, of course, to allow people to have access to information held on themselves. Where there is a danger that giving a data user too much information about the processes for which personal data are held will lead to trade secrets or intellectual property rights in processes or systems being given away, a less detailed explanation can be given.

## Confidentiality and security in handling data

With regard to the confidentiality and security of processing of data, Section VIII of the European Directive provides:

### Article 16
#### Confidentiality of Processing

Any person acting under the authority of the controller or of the processor, including the processor himself, who has access to personal data must not process them except on instructions from the controller, unless he is required to do so by law.

### Article 17
#### Security of Processing

1. Member States shall provide that the controller must implement appropriate technical and organisational measures to protect personal data against unlawful destruction or accidental loss, alteration, unauthorised disclosure or access, in particular where the processing involves the transmission over a network, and against all other unlawful forms of processing. Having regard to the state of the art and the cost of their implementation, such measures shall ensure a level of security appropriate to the risks represented by the processing and the nature of the data to be protected.
2. The Member States shall provide that the controller must, where processing is carried out on his behalf, choose a processor providing sufficient guarantees in respect of the technical security measures and organisational measures governing the processing to be carried out, and must ensure compliance with those measures.
3. The carrying out of processing by way of a processor must be governed by a contract or legal act binding the processor to the controller and stipulating in particular that:
   —the processor shall act only on instructions from the controller;
   —the obligations set out in paragraph 1, as defined by the law of the Member State in which the processor is established, shall also be incumbent on the processor.
4. For the purposes of keeping proof, the parts of the contract or legal act relating to data protection and the requirements relating to the measures referred to in paragraph 1 shall be in writing or another equivalent form.

Additionally, the processing of information regarding racial or ethnic origin, political opinions, religious convictions, trade union membership, health or sexual activity is prohibited under the terms of the Directive unless express consent is provided by the telepatient in question or the use of such information is vital for the treatment of a telepatient who is unable to give consent due to his or her incapacity. A telepatient would also retain the residual right to object to the handling of information which concerns them on the basis of "significant and legitimate reasons related to their particular situation".[40] Section 161 of the Criminal Justice and Public Order Act 1994 has added two new offences to the Data Protection Regime: procuring the disclosure of computer-held personal data (s.5(6)) and selling or offering to sell such procured data (s.5(8)).

## Access to records

As under the present regime, the European Union Directive requires Member States to guarantee, for every "data subject" such as a telepatient, the right to know the identity of the controller of personal data, the purposes of the processing for which the data is intended and any further information such as the recipients or categories of the data and the existence of the right of access to data and the right to rectify any inaccuracies in the data concerning him. Moreover, under Article 12 of the Directive, Member States are obliged to guarantee, without constraint, at reasonable intervals and without delay or excessive expense to provide a telepatient with confirmation as to whether or not data relating to him or her is being processed or held and to communicate to them in an intelligible form any data undergoing processing and any information as to the source of that data.

Under Article 14 the telepatient who is a data subject under the European Directive also has the right to object to data being held on them as well as the right to demand rectification of any incorrect information. The Data Protection Act 1984 provides for a number of exceptions from its subject access provisions (described above, under 'Exemptions from the Act') and these are maintained, save for the provisions relating to back-up data, in the new law as far as is consistent with the requirements of the Directive.

## New registration and enforcement arrangements

Notification arrangements under the new law will be much more straightforward than the registration procedures provided for under the 1984 Act. The Data Protection Registrar will still remain the United Kingdom's supervisory authority (though renamed the Data Protection Commissioner, in line with the corresponding title in other European Member States). Registration however will become simpler, more readily understandable and more useful for data controllers, individuals and the supervisory authority. The key features of the new scheme will be:

▶ a range of notification methods, including on-line access;
▶ a greatly simplified format (including the use of standard packages); and
▶ minimising the detail the controller has to provide.

There will still be a fee for notification and this source of revenue will offset the Data Protection Registrar's administrative and running costs. There would remain a number of categories of data user who would be exempt from notification under the new law, comprising:

▶ pay-roll, personnel and work planning administration;
▶ purchase and sales administration;
▶ advertising, marketing and public relations; and
▶ general administration.

Additionally, the following new exemptions will be made:

▶ processing for the purpose of holding registers and other data required by law to be made public;
▶ processing in connection with mailing and membership lists (as in section 33 of the 1984 Act);
▶ processing by certain non-profit-making organisations in accordance with article 8(2)(d);

- ▶ processing of bibliographic data; and
- ▶ word-processing (if not covered by other exemptions).

Article 18(2) of the Directive provides for "in-house" data protection officials and the new law will enable such a scheme to be established by subordinate legislation (i.e. statutory instrument). Under Article 21(2) a degree of transparency is required and hence the new register of controllers will be open for public inspection. The new law will maintain the existing enforcement arrangements but there will be minor changes designed to streamline the system. It will remain an offence for a telemedicine company or public body such as an NHS trust or health authority not to notify the Data Protection Registrar that they are engaged in personal data processing operations and such notification must be kept up to date.

The offence of "knowingly or recklessly" processing data in breach of the register entry will be changed and, in order to meet the requirements of Article 16 of the Directive, it will become an offence for the controller or an employee of the controller to process data knowingly or recklessly otherwise than in accordance with the instructions of the controller, unless there is a requirement in law to do so. It will remain an offence unlawfully to procure or sell data, although the definitions of the offences will be reformulated to take account of the changes to the registration arrangements.

Under the 1984 Act an enforcement notice would be issued where the Data Protection Principles were being breached. The new law will embrace this and other offences such as transmitting data to a third country with inadequate levels of protection and failure to meet the transparency requirements. Enforcement notices issued under the new law will explain the remedial action that it is suggested be taken; any necessary immediate enforcement or remedial action; the right to make representations before any action is taken and the right of appeal. Appeals against enforcement notices will still be made to the Data Protection Tribunal. Processing will lawfully be allowed to begin once an application for registration has been made, except for categories of data processing where the government will require prior checking of the processing system. No decision has yet been made on exactly what operations should be subject to such a check, although the Government has clearly indicated that it believes operations involving data matching, genetic data and private investigation activities should fall within this category.

The new law enacting the European Directive will provide for individual rights, as does the 1984 Act, and a telepatient who believes their rights have been breached will be able to seek a remedy that matches the right that has been denied, such as an order granting them access where this had been improperly refused by the telemedicine provider, and individuals will continue to be able to seek damages directly from the court from any breach of the new law. The Data Protection Commissioner will be able to carry out quality assessments of telemedicine providers' data protection systems and to propose voluntary codes of practice for such providers.

## Transfer of personal data to third countries

As regards the cross-border transmission of data, Articles 25 and 26 in Chapter IV of the European Directive state:

### Article 25
### Principles

1. The Member States shall provide that the transfer to a third country of personal data which are undergoing processing or are intended for processing after transfer may take place only if, without prejudice to compliance with the national provisions adopted pursuant to the other provisions of this Directive, the third country in question ensures an adequate level of protection.

2. The adequacy of the level of protection afforded by a third country shall be assessed in the light of all the circumstances surrounding a data transfer operation or set of data transfer operations; particular consideration shall be given to the nature of the data, the purpose and duration of the proposed processing operation or operations, the country of origin and country of final destination, the rules of law, both general and sectoral, in force in the third country in question and the professional rules and security measures which are complied within that country.

3. The Member States and the Commission shall inform each other of cases where they consider that a third country does not ensure an adequate level of protection within the meaning of paragraph 2.

4. Where the Commission finds, under the procedure provided for in Article 31(2), that a third country does not ensure an adequate level of protection within the meaning of paragraph 2 of this Article, Member States shall take the measures necessary to prevent any transfer of data of the same type to the third country in question.

5. At the appropriate time, the Commission shall enter into negotiations with a view to remedying the situation resulting from the finding made pursuant to paragraph 4.

6. The Commission may find, in accordance with the procedure referred to in Article 31(2), that a third country ensures an adequate level of protection within the meaning of paragraph 2 of this Article, by reason of its domestic law or of the international commitments it has entered into, particularly upon conclusion of the negotiations referred to in paragraph 5, for the protection of the private lives and basic freedoms and rights of individuals.

Member States shall take the measures necessary to comply with the Commission's decision.

### Article 26
### Derogations

1. By way of derogation from Article 25 and save where otherwise provided by domestic law governing particular cases, Member States shall provide that a transfer or a set of transfers of personal data to a third country which does not ensure an adequate level of protection within the meaning of Article 25(2) may take place on condition that:

   (a) the data subject has given his consent unambiguously to the proposed transfer; or

   (b) the transfer is necessary for the performance of a contract between the data subject and the controller or the implementation of precontractual measures taken in response to the data subject's request; or

   (c) the transfer is necessary for the conclusion or performance of a contract concluded in the interest of the data subject between the controller and a third party; or

   (d) the transfer is necessary or legally required on important public interest grounds, or for the establishment, exercise or defence of legal claims; or

(e) the transfer is necessary in order to protect the vital interests of the data subject; or

(f) the transfer is made from a register which according to laws or regulations is intended to provide information to the public and which is open to consultation either by the public in general or by any person who can demonstrate a legitimate interest, to the extent that the conditions laid down in law for consultation are fulfilled in the particular case.

2. Without prejudice to paragraph 1, a Member State may authorise a transfer or a set of transfers of personal data to a third country which does not ensure an adequate level of protection within the meaning of Article 25(2), where the controller adduces adequate safeguards with respect to the protection of the privacy and fundamental rights and freedoms of individuals and as regards the exercise of the corresponding rights; such safeguards may in particular result from appropriate contractual clauses.

3. The Member State shall inform the Commission and the other Member States of the authorisations it grants pursuant to paragraph 2.

If a Member State or the Commission objects on justified grounds involving the protection of the privacy and fundamental rights and freedoms of individuals, the Commission shall take appropriate measures in accordance with the procedure laid down in Article 31(2).

Member States shall take the necessary steps to comply with the Commission's decision.

4. Where the Commission decides, in accordance with the procedure referred to in Article 31(2), that certain standard contractual clauses offer sufficient safeguards as required by paragraph 2, Member States shall take the necessary measures to comply with the Commission's decision.

Hence, transmitting personal data across national borders may only be prohibited on data protection grounds if the importing country does not have equivalent or adequate data protection measures in comparison with the state exporting the data. Furthermore, if a state has included in its domestic data protection legislation specific regulations regarding certain categories of data, such as for example sensitive health related data, this state may refuse to export such data to another state which does not provide equivalent protection for this type of data. Thus for Member States that have basic data protection legislation and special safeguards for sensitive data, the transborder data flow principle offers a double guarantee that such data will be protected following a transfer out of its jurisdiction, since within the European Union some countries (e.g. Greece) lack data protection laws. The United Kingdom's Data Protection Commissioner will be able to issue an enforcement notice against any telemedicine provider attempting or carrying out such a transfer. Indeed, the new law will require the supervisory authority to notify the European Commission and other EU Member States of cases where levels of protection in third countries are believed to be inadequate.

Outside of the legal framework of the EU Directive, though, the problem of the cross-border transmission of medical data has been overcome through contractual provisions which bind the communicating parties to the observation of basic data protection principles that are expressly provided for in the contract. This solution first emerged when the French subsidiary of the car company Fiat was asked to transfer personal employee data to the central data base of Fiat Italy. At that time Italy had not yet enacted data protection laws. On the objections of the French Data Protection Commission, a contract was made between Fiat, France and Fiat, Italy which bound the latter to the same data protection levels as in France in relation to the data received on the Fiat, France employees.

Such an approach by the architects of a telemedicine system to the cross-border transmission of medical data between shore-based hospitals and ocean-going ships or remote clinics in countries lacking adequate data protection laws (or where existing laws are adequate but may need clarification) would seem to comply with the requirements of Articles 25 and 26 of the Directive.

## Summary

▶ Telemedicine providers have a professional duty to protect the confidentiality of medical data with appropriate security arrangements, both while the data is stored in a computer and while it is being transmitted.

▶ The Computer Misuse Act 1990 provides for criminal offences where a person deliberately hacks into a computer system where telepatients' records are stored. Health authorities and NHS trusts carry a responsibility to ensure that their computer systems are secure and their employees properly trained in the confidential handling of patient data.

▶ The Wireless Telegraphy Act 1949, the Interception of Communications Act 1985 and the common law provide for criminal offences and/or civil remedies for the unauthorised interception of telemedical data during its transmission from one place to another.

▶ In the United Kingdom computer records are subject to the Data Protection Act 1984 which gives legal protection to individuals against the misuse of personal information. Where patient data is transmitted from one hospital in a telemedicine communications network to another it should be borne in mind that only necessary information should be shared and the sending hospital should ensure that the receiving hospital has access only to relevant parts, and not the whole, of the patient's file.

▶ The Data Protection Act 1984 and the European Data Protection Directive aim to provide common standards for all processing of manual and electronic data and deal with many of the challenges presented by the internationalisation of telemedical practice.

▶ The cross-border transmission of patient histories and other identifiable material such as scans and biological analyses can be problematic from the point of view of confidentiality since not all countries have developed uniform systems of data protection. International telemedical consultations therefore raise difficult problems for ensuring patient confidentiality.

## References

1   General Medical Council. *Professional conduct and discipline: fitness to practise*. London: GMC, 1993.
2   General Medical Council. *Confidentiality – guidance from the General Medical Council*. London: GMC, 1995.
3   British Medical Association. *Medical ethics today: its practice and philosophy*. London: BMJ Publishing, 1993: 36.
4   BMA and DoH commit to work together to secure privacy of patient information. *British Journal of Healthcare Computing and Information Management* 1996; 13(9): 2.

5   Audit Commission. *Opportunity makes a thief: an analysis of computer abuse*. London: HMSO. 1994. See also National Audit Office. *IT security in Government departments*. London: HMSO, 1995: 17.
6   The Law Commission's Working Paper No. 150 has proposed a new general defence of unlawfully taking confidential information.
7   [1991] IRLR 63.
8   See also *R* v *Brown* (unreported) 4 June 1993, available throught the *Lexis* database.
9   [1988] 2 WLR 984.
10  *Attorney-General's Reference (No.1 of 1991)* [1992] 3 WLR 432.
11  DTI and BSI. *A code of practice for information security*. 1993.
12  [1973] Crim LR 322.
13  See also *Francome* v *Mirror Group Newspapers* [1984] 1 WLR 892.
14  [1979] Ch 344.
15  Interception of Communications Act 1985, s.1(2)(b).
16  Ibid., ss.2-5.
17  Ibid., s.2(2).
18  Schedule 1 of the Act deals with the constitution of the Tribunal and its procedure and such matters as salaries and expenses.
19  Ibid., s.10(2).
20  3 October 1991, unreported. See Queen's Bench Division Crown Office List CO/1369/91.
21  [1992] 156 JP 830 (CA).
22  Ibid., at p. 836.
23  See *Malone* v *Metropolitan Police Commissioner* [1979] Ch 344.
24  [1990] FSR 217; [1991] 2 AC 327 (HL).
25  [1979] Ch 344.
26  See however *Francome* v *Mirror Group Newpapers* (supra).
27  *Dowson* & *Mason Limited* v *Potter* [1986] 1 WLR 1419.
28  Council of Europe Convention No. 108 for the Protection of Individuals with Regard to Automatic Processing of Personal Data; 28 January 1981.
29  Directive 95/46/EC of the European Parliament and of the Council on the Protection of Individuals with Regard to the Processing of Personal Data and on the Free Movement of such Data; Common Position adopted by the Council 20th February 1995, O.J. C93/1 of 13 April 1995.
30  Data Protection Act 1984, ss. 10-12.
31  Ibid., at s. 1(2).
32  Ibid., at s. 1(3).
33  Ibid., at ss. 1(4) and (5).
34  Ibid., at s. 1(7).
35  See Part III of the Data Protection Act 1984.
36  See Part IV of the Data Protection Act 1984.
37  [1992] O.J. C311/30. Indeed, Article 5 of the Directive states that "Member States shall, within the limits of the provisions of this Chapter, determine more precisely the conditions under which the processing of personal data is lawful."
38  See Barber B, Treacher A, Louwerse K. *Towards security in medical telematics: legal and technical aspects*, Ohmsha: I.O.S. Press, 1996.
39  See Home Office. *Consultation paper on the EC data protection directive (95/46/EC)*. March 1996; Home Office. *Data protection: the Government's proposals (Cm 3725)*. London: HMSO, 1997 and Data Protection Bill 1998.
40  See also the Council of Europe, *Project Group on Data Protection, Draft recommendation on the protection of medical data and draft explanatory memorandum*. Strasbourg, 13 October 1994, (CJ-PD894) Misc. 17.

# ▶4

# Agreeing to telemedical treatment

Every competent adult has an inviolable right to determine what is done to his or her own body and hence a telepatient, no less than a conventional patient, has the right to determine whether or not they are to receive medical treatment or health care. In many aspects of telemedicine the legal and ethical requirements are separate and ethical guidance need make no reference to the law. Consent, however, is an issue which binds the two since failure to seek a sick or injured telepatient's consent to medical treatment is not only a moral failing but also a tort.

Any medic examining, injecting or operating on a telepatient without consent commits a trespass against that person's bodily autonomy. The crime and tort of battery is committed – battery being defined as "any non-consensual contact".[1] In recent years, though, the courts have tended to move away from the tort of battery to negligence, reflected in the court's concern less with the issue of whether medical intrusion was consented to at all than with the quality of the information imparted to obtain consent. Obviously, the chance to consent to treatment is offset by the accompanying right to refuse it and as a result of some recent cases[2] the possibility of a telepatient positively refusing to consent to medical treatment, rather than simply failing to give a valid consent, must also now be considered. In this chapter we shall see how respect for the telepatient, and his or her rights, lies at the heart of the issue of consent.

## The nature and purpose of consent

A seafarer or remote clinic patient who is competent to do so should be allowed to decide what happens to their own body. But for consent to be valid, the telepatient must be aware of what options are available and have the ability to choose. So it is not only the teleconsulting doctor but also the medical officer who is caring for a sick or injured telepatient who will carry a moral duty to act in the telepatient's best interests by recognising what they want. Valid consent may be implicit or explicit, oral or written. Consent is assumed by the opening of the mouth for examination or the offering of an arm for taking blood pressure but can only be applied to the procedure in hand. Of great importance in the treatment of the telepatient is that he or she is communicated with in a language which they understand, in a manner which is intelligible to them and at a pace at which they can digest the information being given to them. For a telepatient who does not speak the same language as the teleconsultant the provision of information in order to obtain effective consent may be a problem – another doctor or medic of the same nationality as the telepatient may be required to act as an interpreter. But in such a situation the teleconsultant must be aware of the possibility of the interpreting physician or nurse themselves influencing the patient's consent or refusal. Lord Donaldson MR in *Re J* (*a minor*) (*medical treatment*) has stated:

> There seems to be some confusion in the minds of some as to the purpose of seeking consent from a patient....It has two purposes, the one clinical and the other legal. The clinical purpose stems from the fact that in many instances the co-operation of the patient and the patient's faith or at least confidence in the efficiency of the treatment is a major factor contributing to the treatment's success. Failure to obtain such consent will not only deprive the patient and medical staff of this advantage, but will usually make it much more difficult to administer the treatment. The legal purpose is quite different. It is to provide those concerned in the treatment with a defence to the criminal charge of assault or battery or a civil claim for damages for trespass to the person.[3]

From an ethical viewpoint the telepatient should be given as much information as they want or need. How much or how little is adequate will vary from person to person. Paragraph 11 of the General Medical Council's new guidelines, *The Duties of a Doctor*, states that doctors:

> ...must give patients the information they ask for or need about their condition, its treatment and prognosis; give information to patients in a way they can understand; [and] respect the right of patients to be fully involved in discussions about care.[4]

What is less easily quantified, however, is how much information the *law* requires for there to be a valid consent. The *Bolam* test, which is explained in depth in the next chapter, is recognised in many jurisdictions as the test for establishing medical negligence. The test requires that a doctor should give as much detail as a recognised body of medical opinion considers appropriate. Naturally there would be no difficulty in applying this test where the teleconsulting doctor has had the opportunity of speaking to the patient directly. But as we have noted previously, the teleconsulting doctor might not have any contact with the sick or injured telepatient himself, communicating instead with another physician, a nurse-practitioner or a paramedic. It is doubtful whether the *Bolam* test can be expanded to encompass a seaman acting as a ship's designated medical officer, not least because there exists such a broad range of experience and competence among such officers. The better view, it is submitted, is that the legal standard of care to be reached by a vessel's medical officer would be that of the "reasonable" or "prudent" medical officer acting in similar circumstances. Likewise, the prudent nurse or the prudent paramedic is to be assessed by reference to the standards maintained by those professions' governing bodies.

## Consent forms

The documentation of consent was originally introduced to protect surgeons from allegations of assault by patients who came to regret surgical intervention carried out on them. In the context of the provision of telemedical treatment and advice to seafarers, such forms could profitably serve a similar purpose in providing a clear legal framework in which the personnel involved in providing such treatment and advice could carry out their jobs without fear of reprisal. The great difficulty, however, is in deciding at what point consent forms should be signed. There are two possibilities. First of all, a consent form could be signed upon registering with a telemedicine service or registering with a hospital or practice that uses telemedicine. On the form a patient would indicate in advance that he or she consents to any medical treatment administered by the staff of that institution, which may involve telemedical consultations with a network of shore-based hospitals when these are necessary. But it is always open for a patient to change their mind and it is impossible to envisage, at the time that a patient joins a practice, what kind of treatment they might require. There is always the possibility that, in a clinical situation, a telepatient might express a radically different treatment preference from that expressed several weeks, months or even years ago when the forms were signed. What is also clear is that it is very difficult to give a general consent when the law has evolved to require that when a patient agrees to a particular operation the surgeon is not justified to depart from instructions and perform a different one.[5] The giving of a blanket consent by a telepatient to any and all medical treatment they may require during the course of their employment is inconsistent with established medical thinking.

The second possibility is to require the telepatient to sign consent forms at the beginning of a course of treatment. Although this avoids the problem of the non-specificity of "pre-emptive" consent, in that the consent will clearly be tailored to the specific treatment being administered, it ignores the fact that in a medical emergency, decisions have to be taken quickly. So while this method will be useful in facilitating routine, occupational health advice and treatment for seafarers, or routine health care in remote hospitals and clinics, it does not provide a solution to the problem of obtaining express consent from a telepatient to emergency treatment.

However, the practical scope of the problem is greatly diminished – at least from a legal point of view – by the fact that a medic who is faced with an emergency situation where there is neither the time nor the possibility of gaining the sick or injured telepatient's consent is not only entitled, but may be legally bound, to carry out such treatment as is necessary to safeguard the life and health of the telepatient until such time as the latter recovers and can be consulted about longer term measures. In *Re F*, Lord Justice Butler-Sloss stated:

> Logically the well known exception of emergency or necessity might be difficult to justify. It is, however, well-established by decisions both in the United States and Canada. In *Pratt* v *Davis* (1906) 224 Ill 300, 309, Scott CJ said: Emergencies arise, and when a surgeon is called it is sometimes found that some action must be taken immediately for the preservation of the life or health of the patient, where it is impracticable to obtain the consent of the ailing or injured one or of anyone authorised to speak for him. In such event, the surgeon may lawfully, and it is his duty to, perform such operation as good surgery demands, without such consent.[6]

Consent to operate or act can properly be assumed by the medic and the advising teleconsultant unless there is convincing evidence that the telepatient would have withheld consent. Making a reliable assessment of what the telepatient would wish to be done in circumstances where they are incapacitated, however, may be far from easy. Hence the courts are usually reluctant to expose a surgeon or doctor to legal liability where he has acted honestly to save the life or preserve the health of a patient.[7]

## When the telepatient cannot give consent

The isolation faced by the individual seafarer, as a member of a diverse, multi-race crew with ethnic, religious, cultural or linguistic differences may mean that it is impracticable for a medical officer to approach other crew members about "what he would have wanted" in the same way that shore-based doctors approach the next of kin of a patient unable to give a valid consent. A similar problem may arise in the context of telepatients living in very remote, rural areas. It is impossible to gauge the workings of the mind of a man who has never communicated at length to his friends or colleagues.[8] It is sometimes stated that where a person is unconscious and incapable of consenting to medical treatment, effective consent may be given by his spouse or by some near relative: the "proxy".

There is limited support for this proposition in the dictum of judges in both the United Kingdom and the United States of America,[9] but judges themselves cite no authority for their assumption. However, although in the Canadian case of *Re Eve*[10] the Supreme Court "rediscovered" the Crown's ancient prerogative jurisdiction over "lunatics, idiots and others of unsound mind", the practical problem has, for all intents and purposes, been solved in *Re F*.[11] The practical effect of this was to give the teleconsulting doctor and ship's medical officer the status of a "quasi-proxy", that is, they are recognised as being the persons to whose judgement the incapacitated seafarer would wish decisions about their treatment to be left. Lord Justice Neill in *Re F* stated:

> To the general rule that the patient's consent must be obtained before an operation can be carried out there is one well-recognised exception. Thus, if a patient is unconscious and therefore unable to give or to withhold his consent, emergency medical treatment which may include surgical procedures can be lawfully carried out. Indeed, once the care of the patient has been assumed by, for example, admission into hospital, a failure to give necessary treatment may well be a ground for complaint. The treatment which can be so given, however, is, within broad limits, confined to such treatment as is necessary to meet the emergency and as such needs to be carried out at once and before the patient is likely to be in a position to make a decision for himself...it is in the public interest that an unconscious patient who requires treatment should be able to receive it and that those who give this treatment in an emergency should be free from any threat of an action for trespass to the person.[12]

In any event, even if the next of kin of a seafarer or someone living in a remote area were contactable in the event of a medical emergency (which is unlikely, given the difficulties and delays this would entail), there would appear to be little sense in distressing a family with the knowledge that their relative is seriously ill, perhaps many thousands of miles away, with the family powerless to do anything except await further news. Moreover, it is usually the case that in the event of an emergency where a person is unconscious or has been given strong analgesics, a medic will be justified in proceeding without prior authority when it is necessary to do so to save the life or preserve the health of the patient and it is not possible to obtain his or her consent. The medic, though, must have no convincing evidence that the patient would object.

## Additional aspects of consent

It may, in time, come to be assumed that by consenting to treatment via a telemedical link a patient is also impliedly consenting to a variety of other measures which might accompany a telemedical consultation, particularly those associated with training. But a telepatient may not always be aware of these measures and cannot be assumed to have agreed to them – they must be informed and their explicit consent obtained.

## Presence of others

Medical students or qualified doctors may be present at a telemedical consultation for the purpose of training in long-distance medical advice techniques. In the United Kingdom the *Patient's Charter* emphasises that the patient should have the choice whether or not to allow a student to be present in the consulting room and it is important, particularly in the context of routine occupational health consultations, that the telepatient feels he or she has a genuine choice in the matter. This will be of particular importance in the case of the less educated telepatient, particularly older patients and those from developing countries, who may already be ill at ease discussing what they see as quite intimate medical information with a complete stranger, let alone a stranger with whom they can only communicate via a television screen.

## Recording of consultations

Of even more fundamental concern is the requirement that telemedical consultations be recorded, not only for teaching purposes, but also for the purpose of obtaining a tangible "hard-copy" of the consultation for legal purposes; i.e. as evidence of correct medical practice and to meet audit and quality control requirements. In the context of conventional medical examinations and consultations it is clear that patients must consent to, and have the opportunity to refuse, the recording of a consultation and if they agree, be asked to give a signed consent. But it would need to be made clear to seafarers from the outset that telemedical advice and treatment is recorded, as much for their benefit as for the care-providing hospital, and that this practice will in no way alter the nature of the consultation. Such an assurance, however, may well be false, for there can be little doubt among both lawyers and doctors that when the latter are aware that their every word is being recorded their behaviour *will* be fundamentally altered, one would hope for the better. One positive effect might be to encourage doctors to request or conduct a far more thorough examination than they might otherwise have done, as well as making them more willing to involve other specialists from relevant medical fields. But what of the behaviour of the telepatient, which may be significantly affected by the information given to him about who will see or hear the material, whether it will leave the hospital from which the telemedical consultation is provided, and for how long it will be kept before being destroyed or erased?

In accident and emergency departments, the video-recording of patients undergoing resuscitation is sometimes carried out for teaching or audit purposes. This is obviously done without patient consent even though the patient will be identifiable in the recording. Upon recovery the patient's permission for the keeping and use of such material is sought unless the film is subsequently digitised to obliterate anything that might identify the patient. But with the recording of telemedical consultations being the norm rather than the exception, the better solution might be to ensure that telepatients are informed that consultations are recorded as part of a general introduction to the medical facilities at a clinic or hospital.

## HIV testing

For some time it has been known that those living in the third world are at a much greater than average risk of being infected with HIV. It has been suggested that wide testing for the virus should be encouraged among telepatients living in remote areas, not only to chart and prevent its spread, but also because the early detection of HIV and appropriate treatment has been shown considerably to delay the onset of full-blown AIDS. But both ethically and legally no treatment or diagnostic procedures should be undertaken without the valid consent of the competent telepatient, and the testing for HIV of blood or tissue samples given for some other purpose is therefore unjustified except in the most exceptional circumstances. Moreover, counselling should be regarded as an essential pre-requisite to HIV testing.

# Refusal of treatment

A competent telepatient has the right to refuse medical treatment, though it would clearly be incumbent upon the medical officer and the teleconsulting doctor to seek to explore their reasons for doing so. In the majority of cases one would envisage that correcting any misunderstandings and advising the telepatient of the danger of non-treatment, without pressure and with time to consider the information, will bring about an informed change of mind. In cases where treatment is refused and some consequent harm is caused to the seafarer it may be that the recording of the teleconsultation is necessary as a legal defence for the doctor and medical officer involved, i.e. to show that treatment was validly refused. It may not have been, for instance, if the doctor or medical officer did not give the telepatient adequate information or help. The telepatient might also be asked to sign, again for the same reason, a written declaration that they have refused medical treatment and accept responsibility for any consequential harm.

As has already been noted, however, the danger exists among a multi-lingual community such as a merchant vessel's crew that a telepatient's refusal of medical treatment may stem from a misunderstanding of the procedures involved, or from not appreciating the seriousness of their condition. Such a rejection, since it does not arise from a true understanding, would not be sufficient to absolve the consulting doctor and medical officer from consequent legal liability for any harm which might come to the telepatient. Indeed, in many cases refusal of the treatment recommended by a doctor or medical officer may arise because of a mistrust of strangers and/or foreigners of a particular race or colour or because of the medical personnel's inability to communicate sympathetically with the telepatient in a manner appropriate to that seafarer's racial, ethnic or religious background.

## Refusal of life saving treatment

The refusal of life saving treatment in a medical emergency raises profound moral difficulties. From a purely ethical viewpoint, if a rational telepatient, fully informed of the potential consequences of his or her refusal of essential treatment, persists in their refusal of that treatment, this decision should be respected. In practice however, there are no simple answers and the teleconsulting doctor and medical officer may well try to explore alternatives acceptable to the seriously ill telepatient. The legal position in the United Kingdom was clearly stated by Lord Donaldson MR in *Re T*[13] thus:

> Doctors faced with a refusal of consent have to give very careful and detailed consideration to the patient's capacity to decide at the time when the decision was made. It may not be the simple case of the patient having no capacity because, for example, at that time he had hallucinations. It may be the more difficult case of a

> temporarily reduced capacity which was commensurate with the gravity of the decision which he purported to make. The more serious the decision, the greater the capacity required. If the patient had the requisite capacity, they are bound by his decision. If not, they are free to treat him in what they believe to be his best interests.

The Judge in that case recommended that in cases of uncertainty doctors seek a declaration from the courts as to the lawfulness of treatment – not a very practical solution for a paramedic dealing with an emergency!

Given the great legal and ethical uncertainty in this area, it is essential that training for teleconsulting doctors and paramedics, and for other health care professionals involved in telecare, should include instruction in the legal and ethical aspects, so that if a difficult situation does arise with a telepatient refusing treatment, they are well appraised of the possible consequences of their actions.

Indeed, in this respect, it is suggested that a "Code of Guidance" or similar handbook be prepared for use by teleconsultants and associated non-professional medics, which will include a section detailing the practical steps an officer should take when a teleconsulting doctor advises a course of treatment which the patient refuses, or which the medic knows the patient has refused by way of a valid advance directive.

## Recording a telepatient's refusal of treatment

Refusal forms, which are available in hospitals and should also be available to telepatients, are unambiguous in that they give the patient the opportunity to communicate what treatment they specifically would *not* consent to for personal or religious reasons. Jehovah's Witnesses, for example, have drafted their own form which specifies precisely what measures are unacceptable to them in all circumstances. Such evidence may take the form of an "advance directive". This is a mechanism whereby competent people give instructions about what they wish to be done if they should subsequently lose the capacity to decide for themselves. An advance directive could be used as a means for a seafarer to continue to exercise autonomy after he has become incapable of communicating his wishes. Such an instrument could, for instance, address the particular issue of a Jehovah's Witness' wish to refuse a blood transfusion in all circumstances. Applying the dicta of Lord Donaldson in *Re T*, therefore, where a telepatient has made an anticipatory choice which is "clearly established and applicable in the circumstances,"[14] a teleconsulting doctor or nurse would be bound by it.

It can be queried, however, whether a telepatient's suicide note could be construed as a valid anticipatory refusal of treatment. The law and common sense require that a doctor provide necessary medical treatment unless absolutely convinced of the patient's competence and full appreciation of the facts at the time of drafting such a document. Since doctors are unlikely to have certain knowledge of this, it is assumed that instructions drafted immediately prior to a suicide attempt cannot be accorded the same respect as an informed advance directive. Similarly, a telepatient who refuses lifesaving treatment at a time when their judgement might be seriously impaired – by drugs, alcohol, pain or fatigue for example – would probably fail to meet the test of competence required for such grave decisions.

Hence, in times of doubt as to the telepatient's real intentions, there is both a legal and ethical duty upon a teleconsultant to take all necessary measures to sustain life, rather than to speculate about what the telepatient intended. In an emergency, however, they should not exceed the treatments necessary to sustain life and health. For example, elective measures or procedures such as the use of blood samples for forensic rather than diagnostic purposes could not be condoned.

## Pre-employment and occupational health programmes

In due course, it is more than likely that telemedicine systems will be used to assist in the conducting of pre-employment medical reports where, for instance, seafarers are recruited from a manning agent at a foreign port, or where a large multi-national corporation in a developing country wishes to offer occupational health services to its workers. From a purely ethical point of view employers and prospective employers have no right to medical information about an individual telepatient without that person's consent. They have a right, however, to know whether, in the doctor's opinion, the individual is fit for certain duties. Questions are sometimes raised about the inclusion of HIV testing in pre-employment medical examinations and discriminatory practices arising against applicants who either decline to be tested or test positive. The British Medical Association[15] is opposed to coercive measures being applied to people to oblige them to accept any form of treatment, particularly measures which do not bring benefit to the individual but which might, on the contrary, be extremely disadvantageous. It also condemns employment discrimination based solely on an applicant's HIV status. This practice cannot be justified by reference to the risk of transmission. Nor is it necessarily the case that HIV-positive workers will be incapable of carrying out their jobs solely by reason of their HIV status.

Similarly, telecare services could play an important part in monitoring the effects of working at sea or in remote areas on a telepatient's health, and the effect of that person's health on his or her performance. The objectives of an occupational health service provided by hospitals in a telecare network to men and women at sea and in remote areas would be:

(a)  To promote and maintain their health and safety;
(b)  To promote immediate treatment for the sick and injured;
(c)  To advise on rehabilitation and suitable placement of workers who are temporarily or permanently disabled by illness or injury;
(d)  To promote health and safety conditions by informed assessment of the working environment and by providing advice or educative material; and
(e)  To promote research into causes of occupational diseases and means of prevention.

In some shipping companies for instance, crew members are required by statute or by their contract to undergo medical examinations. It could be inferred from the subject's attendance upon the ship's medical officer that he or she agrees to the examination under the instructions of a teleconsulting doctor *and* to the disclosure of the result. Nevertheless, the teleconsultant must ensure that the seafarer understands the context in which the examination will take place, the nature of the examination and the need for disclosure of the significance of the findings. Could such routine examinations be used to facilitate, for instance, random drug testing, or other testing among applicants for employment or existing crew-members? Although this isn't, as yet, common practice within the shipping industry, it could be justified by the extreme gravity now attached to the endangering of the lives of others, as well as the environment, by officers and crew whose performance is impaired by drugs or alcohol.

## Summary

▶ Every competent adult telepatient has the right, as does the conventional patient, to dictate what is done to his or her own body and informed, freely-given consent to the specific medical treatment proposed is required in every case.

▶ Failure to obtain a valid consent or properly to inform the patient so they can give a valid consent is serious professional misconduct and an assault upon the telepatient. Teleconsultants must be sure that the telepatient has the capacity to consent and has been given all the information necessary for them to make a reasoned decision.

▶ The requirement of consent has, as its corollary, the right to refuse medical treatment. Where treatment is refused, the teleconsultant is obliged to respect the telepatient's wishes. Such refusal must, however, be freely given by a properly informed telepatient who fully understands the consequences of their refusal.

▶ In most cases where an unconscious or incapacitated telepatient is being cared for, or in emergencies, consent can be implied. But it is possible for a telepatient to give relatives, friends or the telemedicine service an "advance directive" stating their wishes should they be unable to make a decision themselves. Alternatively, a consent form could be filled in upon the telepatient "signing-up" with a service provider.

▶ The telepatient's consent will be required for the recording of teleconsultations and their use for teaching or audit purposes, unless the telepatient's identity is properly hidden. Unused recordings of teleconsultations should be destroyed as soon as is reasonably practicable after they have been made.

## References

1   Brazier M. *Medicine, Patients and the Law*. (2nd ed.) Penguin, 1992: p. 73.
2   *Re R (A Minor)* [1991] 4 All ER 177; *Re J (A Minor)(Medical Treatment)* [1992] 4 All ER 614; *Re T* [1992] 4 All ER 649.
3   [1992] 4 All ER 614.
4   General Medical Council. *The duties of a doctor: guidance from the General Medical Council*. London: GMC, 1995: 4.
5   *Allan* v *New Mount Sinai Hospital* (1980) 109 DLR (3d) 536; *Wilson* v *Pringle* [1986] 3 WLR 1 (CA).
6   [1990] 2 AC 1.
7   See the dicta of Chief Justice Chisholm in *Marshall* v *Curry* [1933] 3 DLR 260 at p. 275.
8   Treatment which is contrary to the known wishes of the patient when competent cannot be justified, see the dicta of Lord Goff of Chievely in the House of Lords in *F* v *West Berkshire Health Authority and another* [1989] WLR 1086.
9   *Canterbury* v *Spence* (1972) 464 F 2d 772 at 789 per Robinson J; *Bonner* v *Moran* (1941) 126 F 2d 121 at 122-123; per Lord Justice Croom-Johnson in Wilson v *Pringle* [1987] QB 237.
10  [1987] 2 SCR 388 (Supreme Court of Canada).
11  *Re F (mental patient) (sterilisation)* [1990] 2 AC 1, (1989) 4 BMLR 1 (HL).
12  [1990] 2 AC at p. 30.
13  [1992] 4 A11 ER 649.
14  [1992] 4 A11 ER 649 at p. 663.
15  BMA. *Medical ethics today: its practice and philosophy*. London: BMJ Publishing Group, 1993: 33-35.

# ▶ 5

# Telemedical malpractice

As long ago as 1954 the great Judge Lord Denning directed a jury in a medical negligence case in language as penetratingly accurate today as it was then. He said:

> An action for negligence against a doctor is for him unto a dagger. His professional reputation is as dear to him as his body, perhaps more so, and an action for negligence can wound his reputation as severely as a dagger can his body. You must not, therefore, find him negligent simply because something happens to go wrong; if, for instance, one of the risks inherent in an operation actually takes away the benefits that were hoped for, or if in a matter of opinion he makes an error of judgment. You should only find him guilty of negligence when he falls short of the standard of a reasonably skilful medical man, in short, when he is deserving of censure – for negligence in a medical man is deserving of censure.[1]

Powers and Harris believe that the principal reason for the rise in medical negligence cases over the past forty years is a communications failure on the part of senior medical students and young doctors.[2] The increasing complexity of medical technology and a growing awareness of legal rights and remedies on the part of patients generally have added to the explosion of medical negligence litigation which has come to blight medical practice throughout the developed world. Extensive research by the author has failed to reveal any reports at all of a negligence claim being brought by a radio- or tele-patient who claimed to have suffered harm through negligent medical advice or treatment given during a radio- or tele-medical consultation. So whilst the first major malpractice case against a telemedicine service is probably still on the horizon, history and common sense tell us that this might only be a matter of time.

But do teleconsultants really have to resign themselves to such a fate? It is hoped that they do not. For if Powers and Harris are correct in their submission that "the principal generator of medical negligence litigation is communication failure",[3] and that the incidence of negligence will begin to decline if junior doctors and senior medical students become thoroughly acquainted with the risks inherent in their speciality, then open and frank discussion among practitioners and trainees of the risks in telemedicine might just make a difference. In this chapter, therefore, we examine the principles of medical malpractice affecting doctors and other medical professionals in a telehealthcare system, as well as some of the risks and legal liabilities that may be unique to telemedicine.

## Anatomy of a claim for medical negligence

In the United Kingdom, as in most common law jurisdictions, to maintain an action for negligence the plaintiff must establish:

(a)  that the teleconsultant owed him or her a duty of care;

(b)    that the duty was breached, that is, the teleconsultant was careless; and

(c)    that he or she suffered harm as a consequence of that carelessness.

## (a) Duty of care

In very general terms, the foundation of a teleconsulting doctor's duty to a patient is the same as that which any conventional doctor owes to any conventional patient. It turns upon the nature of the doctor–patient relationship: the teleconsultant may incur liability at any time after he has accepted responsibility for the telepatient. The dicta of Lord Hewitt CJ in the 1925 case of *R* v *Bateman* are, in this respect, extremely helpful:

> If a person holds himself out as possessing special skill and knowledge and he is consulted, as possessing such skill and knowledge, by or on behalf of a patient, he owes a duty to the patient to use due caution in undertaking the treatment. If he accepts the responsibility and undertakes the treatment and the patient submits to his direction and treatment accordingly, he owes a duty to the patient to use diligence, care, knowledge, skill and caution in administering the treatment. No contractual relationship is necessary, nor is it necessary that the service be rendered for reward.[4]

The telepatient who has cause to establish contact with a health care institution through a telemedical system and to be treated through it – either directly or by an instructed health care provider – is to be treated no differently from a conventional patient. There will therefore be a consequent undertaking by the teleconsultant at the hospital to provide these services. Although no case in England or Wales has really touched upon this matter, the correct approach is almost without doubt that used by Mr Justice Nield in *Barnett* v *Chelsea and Kensington HMC*.[5] He stated that, although an undertaking will not in law be held to exist merely because of the coincidence of an emergency and a doctor nearby, where a doctor holds himself out as being available to treat individuals requiring emergency care, as in the case of doctors who are part of a teleconsulting team, he or she will be deemed to have undertaken to provide emergency care once they are aware of the need for it.[6] An alternative and equally valid interpretation of *Barnett* would be that when a ship's medical officer, a paramedic or a nurse in a remote clinic makes contact with a hospital through a telemedicine network, just as when a man walks into the accident and emergency department of a hospital, there immediately arises a duty on the part of the hospital to care for the patient. The clearest expression of this principle is that of Lord Nathan:

> The medical man's duty of care arises...quite independently of any contract with his patient. It is based simply upon the fact that the medical man has undertaken the care and treatment of the patient. It is clear then that the duty of care which is imposed upon the medical man arises quite independently of contract. It is a duty in tort which is based upon the relationship between the medical man and his patient, owing its existence to the fact that the medical man has assumed responsibility for the care, treatment or examination of the patient, as the case may be.[7]

Where the telepatient and health care provider are in a contractual relationship, i.e. telemedicine or telecare is being used in the private sector, the extent of the duty will be practically identical to that imposed in tort. The only area in which a claim in contract, rather than tort, might be of any benefit to an aggrieved telepatient is in the context of the supply of telemedical equipment which – if it can be established that the equipment was not of merchantable quality or not reasonably fit for the purpose for which it was supplied – will do away with the need to prove fault on the part of the supplier.[8] Moreover, if the user of telemedical equipment can be classed as a consumer, properly so called, he may have a remedy under the Consumer Protection Act 1987, subject to certain statutory defences. These issues are examined in detail in chapter 7.

### Non-professional medics

More problematic is establishing whether or not a ship's medical officer, a paramedic or a nurse owes a duty and if so what the precise scope of that duty is. On board most modern merchant vessels, manning is extremely tight. Whilst historically the Chief Steward would have been the designated medical officer, as he would usually have more time to devote to this task than the rest of the crew, it is now more common for the Second or Third Officer to be the designated medical officer on the basis of on-shore first aid training. The standard of such training varies tremendously between shipping lines and from country to country. Very often, however, the level of skill of a ship's medical officer is no greater than that of the designated first-aider in a shore-based firm or office. Hence, although imposing a duty of care upon such an individual (since a ship's medical officer can reasonably foresee that his conduct may cause harm to a sick or injured seafarer) would not present any legal problem, defining the standard of care that they must reach most probably would.

Paramedics and nurses present a similar problem. Whilst it would not be appropriate to expect them to reach the same standard of care as a doctor, they clearly still owe a duty of care to the patients they treat and the Health Authority or NHS trust that employs them will, as with its doctors and surgeons, be vicariously liable for acts and omissions committed in the course of their employment.[9] Moreover, in *Cassidy* v *Ministry of Health* Lord Denning reasoned that a health authority or NHS trust may also be directly responsible for patients:

> Authorities...are in law under the self same duty as the humblest doctor; whenever they accept a patient for treatment, they must use reasonable care and skill to cure him of his ailment. The hospital authorities cannot, of course, do it by themselves: they have no ears to listen through the stethoscope, and no hands to hold the surgeon's knife. They must do it by the staff which they employ; and if their staff are negligent in giving the treatment, they are just as liable for that negligence as is anyone else who employs others to do his duties for him.[10]

### The "operational" and "policy" issue dichotomy

In recent years attention has been drawn to the "cash crisis" that has beset the provision of health care throughout the NHS. Powers and Harris speculate that "with cash-limited budgets, indicative prescribing and the like, it is possible that the courts will shortly be faced with negligence questions of a different order from those which have hitherto been determined."[11] They are referring to the very real possibility that where a medical negligence claim is brought against a hospital, the court will impute what one might call "semi-fictional" negligence to a doctor or team of doctors in order to allow a deserving plaintiff to recover compensation. That is to say, it will make a finding of personal fault against a doctor in order to avoid examining the real cause of the damage – the inadequacies of the hospital's own management practices and economic strategy.

This is a danger that Sir Nicholas Browne-Wilkinson, as he then was, drew attention to in his judgment in the Court of Appeal in *Wilsher* v *Essex Area Health Authority*.[12] His dicta will be of particular interest to the providers of telemedicine and telecare services:

> An health authority which so conducts its hospital that it fails to provide doctors of sufficient skill and experience to give the treatment offered at the hospital may be directly liable in negligence to the patient.[13]

There is no reason why, in principle therefore, a hospital might not be found liable if its organisation is at fault in failing to provide sufficiently skilled and experienced practitioners to administer telemedicine and telecare to the communities with which it is networked. Browne-Wilkinson LJ also identifies the awkward questions that claims against a health authority in the 1990s may raise: should an health authority or NHS trust be liable if it demonstrates that, due to the financial stringency under which it operates, it cannot afford to fill posts (such as teleconsultancy positions) with those possessing the necessary skills, qualifications, training or experience?

> ...in my judgment, the law should not be distorted by making findings of personal fault against individual doctors who are, in truth, not at fault in order to avoid such questions. To do so would be to cloud the real issues which arise. In the modern world with its technological refinements is it sensible to persist in making compensation for those who suffer from shortcomings in technologically advanced treatment depend on proof of fault, a process which the present case illustrates can consume years in time and huge sums of money in costs? Given limited resources, what balance is to be struck in the allocation of such resources between compensating those whose treatment is not wholly successful and the provision of required treatment for the world at large?...I do not think the courts would do society a favour by distorting the existing law so as to conceal the real questions which arise.[14]

So, given that the National Health Service Act 1977 specifically states that the Secretary of State and the regional and area health authorities are under a duty "to continue to promote a comprehensive health service designed to secure improvement in health and the prevention of illness...and to provide accommodation, facilities and services for these purposes", can the judicial process be used to dictate what funds should be made available to health authorities and how those authorities must use them? The answer seems to be no. In *R* v *Secretary of State for Social Services, ex parte Hincks*[15] orthopaedic patients at a Birmingham hospital failed to obtain a declaration that the Secretary of State and the regional and area health authority were in breach of the statutory duties described above where a shortage of facilities arising partly from the authority's decision not to build a new block at the hospital, on the grounds of cost, meant that they had to wait longer than was medically advisable for treatment. A similar result was reached in *R* v *Central Birmingham Health Authority, ex parte Walker*.[16] In both cases the court held that the 1977 Act did no more than give the Secretary of State a broad discretion as to how to dispose of financial resources and endowed him with a duty only to provide services "to such extent as he considers necessary".

It would seem, therefore, that whilst the courts are prepared to consider and adjudicate upon the "operational" powers or duties of an health authority or NHS trust (e.g. the duty of care of a teleconsultant towards the telepatient), they will studiously avoid becoming involved in value judgements as to the "policy" decisions that an health care provider makes, heavily influenced by its budget. Indeed, even Sir Nicholas Browne-Wilkinson, in his very blunt comments regarding courts that might be tempted to distort the existing law "so as to conceal the real social questions", had the pragmatism to conclude that questions of health care policy in the United Kingdom are "for Parliament, not the courts".[17]

Hence, unless the Secretary of State can be shown to have acted so as to frustrate the policy of the 1977 Act or to have acted as no reasonable Minister would have acted, no breach of the Act will have taken place and the decision whether or not a hospital should, as a matter of policy, provide telemedicine and telecare services and the status in economic terms that it should attach to such services (since specialties within an authority or trust must often vigorously compete for resources) is not one which can properly be addressed or challenged by judicial review.

## (b) Standard of Care

The second matter that the plaintiff must prove is that the teleconsultant breached the duty of care that he or she owed to their patient – that they were negligent in the way described by Alderson B in *Blyth* v *Birmingham Waterworks Co*:[18]

> Negligence is the omission to do something which a reasonable man, guided upon those considerations which ordinarily regulate the conduct of human affairs, would do, or doing something which a prudent and reasonable man would not do.

There are two aspects then to considering the question of negligence or breach of duty. First of all, the court must decide upon the appropriate standard to apply. Secondly and more crucially, the court must consider whether or not the teleconsultant fell short of this standard. The onus of proving both aspects will be upon the plaintiff telepatient. The benchmark for what is and is not to be regarded as a reasonable standard of care in a situation which involves the use of some special skill or competence, such as teleconsultancy, will be the same as for every other medical and surgical specialty. It is the standard famously described by Mr Justice McNair in his direction to the jury in *Bolam* v *Friern Hospital Management Committee*.[19] In exercising his skill, a doctor will not be guilty of malpractice, in accordance with the established *Bolam* test of "accepted medical practice" where he acts:

> "...in accordance with a practice accepted as proper by a responsible body of medical men skilled in that particular art...a doctor is not negligent, if he is acting in accordance with such a practice, merely because there is a body of opinion which takes a contrary view."[20]

In applying the *Bolam* test a judge's preference for one body of distinguished medical opinion over another also professionally distinguished is not sufficient to establish negligence in a practitioner.[21] What is required is simply that a practice is rightly accepted as proper by a body of skilled and experienced medical men.[22] But not every aspect of the standard of care is weighted in the doctor's favour. The House of Lords in *Bolitho* v *City and Hackney Health Authority*[23] has stated that in considering the body of professional opinion, that opinion must be able to withstand logical analysis. If it cannot, it may not be considered either reasonable or responsible.

In arriving at the standard of care the United Kingdom courts make no allowance for inexperience – the junior doctor will be required to reach the same standard of competence as the experienced consultant.[24] So all the members of a team of doctors providing telemedical care will be required to exercise the same standard of competency and experience.[25]

"Accepted practice" in the context of the *Bolam* test means "current practice" – new developments must be incorporated into practice and a doctor will be judged according to the general level of awareness of new equipment, techniques and procedures in the medical field within which he practices.[26] Although a doctor who departs from accepted practice will not automatically be negligent, he will have to demonstrate that his deviation from the norm was justified in the circumstances and to show that his revolutionary, or at the very least, novel approach was superior or equal to the established practice. A wrong diagnosis, without more, is not evidence *per se* of negligence – there will be no finding of malpractice just because one doctor comes to a different conclusion from another.[27] But where a teleconsulting doctor has clearly not asked the right questions or requested the relevant tests, such as an X-ray or ECG – both of which can be transmitted through a telemedicine system – then a finding of negligence could be that much more likely. Examples might include failing to diagnose a broken bone in a man who had fallen over 12 ft,[28] failing to diagnose eighteen fractured ribs and extensive lung damage in a drunk man who had been run over by a lorry[29] or failing to test for malaria in a patient who had recently been in East Africa.[30] In terms of treatment, the most common mistakes made by doctors, which teleconsultants need to be particularly wary of, include failing to check what medication a patient is on before prescribing drugs, failing to check that the correct dosage of a drug is administered and in some cases, failing to ensure that the correct drug is in fact given.

In the context of medical practice at a distance, where communication is via a telemedical link, these risks are amplified somewhat and special care needs to be taken.

### The standard of care for non-professional medics

The standard expected of a non-professional medic such as a ship's medical officer, if one is to extrapolate existing case law, would be objectively judged by comparison with an hypothetical "reasonable officer" with the same elementary first aid training, experience and, one would hope, training in the use of a ship board telemedicine terminal, and acting in the same circumstances as the defendant. Hence the standard to be reached would be a question of fact in every case. In *Phillips* v *William Whiteley Ltd*[31] a woman who went to a jeweller to have her ears pierced developed an abscess because the jeweller's instruments were not aseptically sterile. The jeweller had taken all the precautions that any jeweller could be expected to take and so the woman's claim failed. The defendant in this case had done all that a jeweller could reasonably be expected to do. If she wanted the standard of care a surgeon could offer, then she should have consulted a surgeon. A parallel situation might occur in telemedicine, where a telepatient on board ship complains about the standard of care received from a ship's medical officer. If a court found that such care was of a standard reasonable and appropriate to expect of a ship's officer, the complaint would not be upheld.

### The standard of care for teleconsultants

In *Sidaway* v *Governors of the Bethlem Royal Hospital*[32] Lord Bridge stated that:

> The language of the Bolam test clearly requires a different degree of skill from a specialist in his own field than from a general practitioner. In the field of neuro-surgery it would be necessary to substitute for the...phrase "no doctor of ordinary skill", the phrase "no neuro-surgeon of ordinary skill". All this is elementary, and...firmly established law.

So not only must a teleconsultant meet the standard of competence of the ordinary, competent doctor with ordinary skill[33] but also, where he conducts consultations and treatment through a telemedical system, a reasonable level of skill within the "super-specialty" of teleconsulting. The *Bolam* test will be applied to a teleconsultant simply by substituting this title for the word surgeon, dermatologist, cardiologist and so forth. In short, any defendant doctor will be tested against the standard of the reasonably skilled and competent doctor practising in that field of medicine or surgery.[34]

Hence a patient who visits his GP with a skin complaint cannot expect that doctor to have the skill of a consultant dermatologist. But, of course, the beauty of telemedicine is that any doctor in that patient's general practice could, with nothing more sophisticated than a digital camera and a networked computer, take and transmit high quality, digital pictures of their patient's skin to a consultant dermatologist for his or her consideration, rather than simply having to resign themselves to the long wait involved in getting someone seen as an outpatient.

## (c) Cause of damage

The third element of the tort of negligence that an aggrieved telepatient would be required to prove is what lawyers refer to as "causation". This will be, in practice, the most problematic if not impossible aspect of a telepatient's claim, the difficulty being that he or she must convince a court that it was the medical negligence identified that caused them harm and not some other cause. Moreover, the basis of their allegation may not be that they have been harmed, *per se*, but that their recovery from some disease or injury was delayed or prevented by the telecare provider's negligence. In each and every case a telepatient would need to bring sufficient evidence to show that it is more likely than not that the teleconsultant's negligence caused the injury of which they complain. The best way of phrasing this requirement in terms that have been generally accepted by the courts in relation to conventional medical negligence claims is to ask: "but for the negligence of the teleconsultant, would harm to the telepatient have occurred in any event?"

A useful case to illustrate the application of the "but for" test is *Barnett* v *Chelsea and Kensington Hospital Management Committee.*[35] The plaintiff's husband was one of three security guards who presented themselves at the defendant hospital's accident and emergency department complaining of severe vomiting after drinking tea. Unknown to them, the tea had been laced with arsenic. A nurse in the department consulted the duty doctor by telephone who advised that the men should go home and see their own GPs in the morning. Sadly, the plaintiff's husband died later that day of arsenic poisoning.

Although it was held that the doctor was in breach of his duty of care to the watchman in failing to examine him and sending him away, the expert medical evidence showed that, even if he had been immediately admitted to hospital, examined and treated, it was more probable than not that it would already have been too late to save his life. The watchman's widow's claim therefore failed. Not only is this case illustrative of the need to prove that the damage complained of would not have happened "but for" the negligence of the defendant but it should also serve as a warning to teleconsultants of the dangers of dismissing a referring nurse or general practitioner's genuine concerns *vis-à-vis* a patient.

Two further cases, *Kay* v *Ayrshire and Arran Health Board*[36] and *Wilsher* v *Essex Area Health Authority*[36] show the importance for the plaintiff telepatient of adducing expert witnesses of the highest possible calibre who can demonstrate that, at the very least, it is more likely than not that the defendant teleconsultant's negligence either materially contributed to their injury or increased the risk of succumbing to such an injury or disease to a material degree. Moreover, the burden of proving causation rests on the plaintiff alone, and does not move to the defendant even though negligence has been proved or admitted. A telepatient would therefore be required to prove, on the balance of probabilities, that the harm that he or she had suffered was due to the negligence of the teleconsultant.

### Liability of employer of a non-professional medic

What happens if the operative cause of harm to a telepatient on board a vessel, in a remote clinic or in the treatment room of a GP's surgery, is not the negligence of the teleconsultant but of the person the teleconsultant was instructing to carry out a procedure? In English common law an employer is responsible if their negligence results in injury to an employee and moreover, is vicariously liable for the negligent acts or defaults of their employees that similarly cause injury. Returning, therefore, to the dicta in *Gold* v *Essex County Council*,[38] health authorities and NHS trusts clearly owe a vicarious duty of care to patients in respect of the acts and omissions of their staff committed in the course of their employment. Similarly, by the terms and conditions of the contract of employment it is the duty of the shipowner to provide a safe vessel and equipment and to ensure that his seafarer employees are reasonably competent to perform the tasks for which they have been employed. This would naturally include the duty to provide proper medical equipment including, where appropriate, telemedical equipment and a properly trained medical officer to operate it. Furthermore, a shipowner may be in breach of statutory duty by, for instance, not providing specified equipment such as a correctly stocked medicine chest or not providing for the proper training and certification of medical officers.[39]

The personal representatives of any crew member killed in the course of sea duties may bring an action under the Fatal Accidents Act 1976, alleging that his death resulted directly from the negligence of the shipowner or his servants, including the medical officer in failing to treat the seafarer promptly or correctly. Where a ship has radiomedical equipment or a telemedicine terminal then such a claim could also properly cite failure to hold a radio- or tele-medical consultation with a hospital either promptly or at all as *prima facie* evidence of the medical officer's negligence.[40] Indeed, this principle would apply to telemedicine generally and not just in the context of medical care at sea.

Under the Merchant Shipping Act 1995 a shipowner is no longer able to limit his liability for the death or personal injury of one of his crew employed on board under a crew agreement. Moreover, the Health and Safety at Work Act 1974 provides that a shipowner has a duty to ensure, so far as is reasonably practicable, the health, safety and welfare at work of his employees. When they become widely and freely, or at least, inexpensively available therefore, a telemedicine terminal installed in the sick bay of an ocean-going ship can be expected to become a compulsory piece of equipment.

## The burden and standard of proof and the role of the expert witness

It is, of course, well established in English law that there are two "burdens": the "evidential" burden of adducing sufficient evidence to make out a *prima facie* case, and what could be titled "the burden of proof properly so called". The latter is the "persuasive" or "probative" burden that rests upon one party – the person who has brought the claim – throughout the litigation.[41] In the type of "telemedical malpractice" claim we are considering here, this will be the burden of proving to the trial judge that the damage alleged was caused by the negligent act, or omission to act, of the teleconsultant. This burden will rest on the telepatient – "he who asserts must prove". The standard of proof required to discharge that burden will be the balance of probabilities – it must be proved that it is more likely than not that the alleged damage was caused by the defendants – but this balance exists on a sliding scale, commensurate with the nature of the allegations made. So held the court in *Hucks* v *Cole*[42] where it was stated that:

> A charge of professional negligence against a medical man was a serious charge, on a different footing to a charge of negligence against a motorist or an employer. The reason is because the consequences for the professional man are far more grave. A finding of negligence affects his standing and reputation. It impairs the confidence which his clients have in him. The burden of proof is correspondingly greater. The principle applies that "In proportion as the charge is grave, so ought the proof to be clear".[43]

The *Bolam* principle, that a doctor is not negligent if he acts in accordance with a practice accepted at the time as proper by a responsible body of medical opinion, thus indicates that the legal standard framed by the courts is set by the medical profession itself in so far as expert witnesses are called upon to provide factual evidence of the practices of the profession and, therefore, what exactly constitutes acceptable medical practice sufficient to defeat a claim of malpractice. The fundamental question in a case of telemedical malpractice would therefore be: would a reasonable teleconsultant have behaved the way the defendant did? The decision of the court in *Maynard* v *West Midlands Regional Health Authority*[44] makes it clear that simply because one distinguished body of medical opinion might prefer the course of action the defendant took while another differently constituted but equally distinguished body of opinion might prefer another will not be sufficient reason for establishing negligence in a teleconsultant whose course of conduct has received the "seal of approval" from the former. As Lord Scarman stated in that case:

> In the realm of diagnosis and treatment negligence is not established by preferring one respectable body of professional opinion to another. Failure to exercise the ordinary skill of a doctor (in the appropriate specialty, if he be a specialist) is necessary.[45]

In *Clark* v *MacLennan*[46] it was held that once a plaintiff has proved that the defendant departed from accepted practice in the manner of his treatment, the burden of proof shifts to the defendant to justify such a departure. But this approach has been viewed quite critically by the Court of Appeal in *Wilsher* v *Essex Area Health Authority*[47] where Lord Justice Mustill felt that although otherwise unimpeachable, the decision in *Clark* could not be taken to be a broad authority for the proposition that there was a general burden of proof upon the defendants but should be limited to its facts[48] and to situations where the maxim *res ipsa loquitur* (the thing speaks for itself) applies. This Latin maxim describes a fairly restricted class of cases of which *Cassidy* v *Ministry of Health*[49] is typical. Lord Justice Denning summarises the case neatly in his judgment. He states:

> If the plaintiff had to prove that some particular doctor or nurse is negligent, he would not be able to do it. But he was not put to that impossible task: he says, "I went into the hospital to be cured of two stiff fingers [Dupuytren's contracture of the hand]. I have come out with four stiff fingers, and my hand is useless. That should not have happened if due care had been used. Explain it, if you can.

In order to force the defendant to "explain it, if he can" the court must be satisfied that control over the relevant event rested entirely with him and that, according to Lord Justice Swift in *Mahon* v *Osborne*[50], "in the ordinary experience of mankind such an event does not happen unless the person in control has failed to exercise due care." But although such a principle can clearly be applied to medical malpractice – in *Mahon* a swab was allegedly left in a patient's body after an operation – its application in practice has been something of a lottery to say the very least. In *Mahon* two out of the three Lord Justices of Appeal held that the plea of *res ipsa loquitur* should be made available to the plaintiff in order to shift the burden of proof onto the defendant, though Lord Justice Swift himself disagreed.

Yet in two further cases – *Fish* v *Kapur*[51] and *Levenkind* v *Churchill-Davidson*[52] – where damage resulted that was clearly due to some tangible fault on the part of the defendant, the plea was refused. Just where the hypothetical line between cases suitable and unsuitable for the application of the maxim exists is therefore unclear. This uncertainty is particularly unhelpful to teleconsultants, not least because one of the main patterns – one of the *only* patterns – that does emerge from the case law is that the courts tend to allow the maxim to be invoked where the medical treatment in question is particularly complex and hence an understanding of what went wrong, as well as "control over the relevant situation, environment or events" lies exclusively within the knowledge of the defendant.

The better approach from a teleconsultant's point of view would naturally be to put the plaintiff to strict proof of any allegation of malpractice made against him or her. But where a situation arises in which many tangible factors might have come together at the same moment to produce the damage (e.g. poor reproduction of pathological or radiological slides, poor voice reproduction and the possible corruption of transmitted information), then it is clear that responsibility lies somewhere among the designers and users of the telemedicine system. In the context of telemedical malpractice it may often be difficult to divorce professional failing and technical failings. Notwithstanding that fact, however, modern personal injury litigation shows that a properly instructed plaintiff will not hesitate to nominate several defendants, including both the responsible doctors and the manufacturers, installers or servicers of telemedicine equipment in their Particulars of Claim, as a litigation tactic designed to get as many potential sources of compensation into the same court, where their respective liabilities can then be assessed.

The approach of Powers and Harris, therefore, which is to see the raising of the plea as a two-stage process, is perhaps the closest we can get to any kind of guide. They describe the process as consisting of evidence being given on behalf of the telepatient, in general terms, as to:

(a) the normal and hence expected outcome of the treatment;

(b) the exclusive control over the treatment exercised by the teleconsultant(s); and

(c) proof that, in the ordinary course of practice, such an event as befell the telepatient could not happen unless the teleconsultant has failed to exercise due care.[53]

## Limitation of actions

Since as long ago as 1623 the Statute of James I has set a six-year time limit upon the bringing of any legal action in contract or tort. Nelson and Bartlett[54] quote the three reasons given for setting limitations upon the bringing of an action by Lord Edmund-Davies in *Birkett* v *James*:[55]

(1) to protect defendants from being vexed by stale claims relating to long past incidents about which their records may no longer be in existence and as to which their witnesses, even if they are still available, may well have no accurate recollection;

(2) to encourage plaintiffs to institute proceedings as soon as it is reasonably possible for them to do so;

(3) to ensure that a person may with confidence feel that after a given time he may regard as finally closed an incident which might have led to a claim against him.

In general, a medical negligence claim must be brought (that is, a writ or summons issued) three years from the date of the mishap. The principal statute, the Limitations Act 1980, states that time will begin to run against a plaintiff telepatient from the date when his cause of action accrues to him - that is, from the date he suffers the damage complained of. Difficulties do however arise when the date of injury cannot be readily ascertained. In such circumstances the law is not concerned with trivialities - de minimis non curat lex. Thus it is a question of fact in every case at what point the plaintiff has suffered harm by reason of the damage actually manifesting itself upon his or her body. The primary period within which a claim for personal injury must be brought is three years from the accrual of the cause of action or, if later, the "date of knowledge", although the court has the power to override this time limit where it appears equitable, in all the circumstances, to do so. 56 Section 14(1) of the Limitations Act describes the extent of the knowledge required to start time running under the Act. There must be knowledge:

(a) that the injury in question is significant; and

(b) that the injury was attributable in whole or in part to the act or omission which is alleged to constitute negligence or other breach of duty; and

(c) of the identity of the defendant.

Where the claim is based, not on the duty of care, but upon a breach of contract, the cause of action is complete when the contract is broken, irrespective of the date when damage results to the plaintiff.[57] For a child injured before birth – and even before his conception – the Congenital Disabilities (Civil Liability) Act 1976 regards the limitation period as running from the child's date of birth. As with all children the limitation period will run during the child's minority and then for three years – until the child reaches the age of 21. In general, the limitation period for claims not originating from personal injury is six years from the date on which the cause of action accrued.

# Clinical risks in teleconsulting

Having considered the legal nature of the medical negligence action we now move on to some of the practical problems presented by telemedical practice. The NHS Executive's circular on clinical negligence costs[58] states that by the year 2000 NHS trusts will be paying for nearly 80% of the total cost of clinical negligence litigation in the National Health Service – either directly or through contributions to the Clinical Negligence Scheme for Trusts (CNST). There has also been a rapid increase in the total cost of litigation from £80 million in 1991 to some £290 million in 1997. The NHS Executive circular predicts that this figure will rise to £500 million by the year 2000, the increasing cost being a reflection of:

(a)  increases in the volume of NHS activity;

(b)  the increasing tendency for patients to seek redress when incidents occur; and

(c)  continuing upward pressures on the size of negligence awards over and above the general level of litigation.

In his paper "Medical negligence – a manager's view" Dr AJ Davison both asks and attempts to answer the important question: why do patients sue? He states that:

> It is probably true to say, but difficult to quantify, that there is probably a far greater number of dissatisfied patients who could sue but who do not, than the numbers who actually do take legal action. The vast majority of patients treated in the NHS seem satisfied with the care they receive. Numerous surveys show this to be the case. A typical NHS trust dealing with around 200,000 in-patients, out-patients, day cases and accidents and emergencies each year might expect to receive something like 3,000–4,000 letters of appreciation against 300 or 400 letters of complaint leading to perhaps only half a dozen new legal actions. More often than not people whom the NHS have failed are seeking not revenge or financial reward but a clear, unambiguous explanation with apology, if that is appropriate, and some indication that the organisation, the hospital or whatever has taken reasonable steps to put matters right. The patients and their relatives will feel understandable anger and want some form of redress though not necessarily financial. Their anger will more clearly turn into litigation if satisfactory explanations and apologies are not given clearly at an early stage. We owe our patients a duty of care but above all we owe them some explanation of what has happened to them so that they do not feel that someone is trying to pull the wool over their eyes. Often litigation begins because of this continued mistrust and sometimes recourse to the law is seen as a last resort of increasingly desperate patients or relatives.[59]

The best defence to telemedical malpractice, therefore, will be a proactive approach to the medico-legal risks associated with teleconsulting, a proposition with which Dr Davison appears to be in broad agreement:

> If we had a better understanding of the main reasons for failure of service then at least we would be in a position to do something about them.[60]

An analysis of these "failures" in the form of an analysis of claims against health authorities and NHS trusts still unsettled in the summer of 1997 provides a clear illustration of the relative clinical risk among existing medical specialties.

*Contingent liability by speciality*[61]

| Specialty | Value (£m) |
|---|---|
| Obstetrics | 59.1 |
| Anaesthetics | 2.9 |
| Paediatrics | 2.9 |
| Accident and Emergency | 2.3 |
| General Surgery | 2.1 |
| General Medicine | 1.6 |
| Orthopaedics | 1.6 |
| Cardio-surgery | 1.5 |
| Gynaecology | 1.2 |
| Other specialties | 6.0 |

Obstetrics tops the bill with over £59 million of claims waiting to be settled and overshadows all other specialties in terms of clinical risk. Among those other specialities, however, accident and emergency, paediatrics and anaesthetics are among the more "risky" specialties. Where will telemedicine fit into the scheme of things? Our hope must be that it will actually assist in lowering the clinical risk prevalent in many other specialties.

Brahams, in her paper *The medico-legal implications of teleconsulting in the UK* pessimistically stated that many of the questions raised about the medicolegal implications of telemedicine will be determined in the courts.[62] With the very greatest respect it is submitted that a more positive approach is required. As Darkins correctly states, clinical risk management is a proactive process designed to reduce the threat of litigation.[63] What is required therefore is not for teleconsultants to resign themselves to finding out the hard way about the dangers of teleconsultancy (i.e. by being sued) but to adopt a retroactive approach to clinical risk by trying, as Davison says, to understand the potential reasons for failure right now.

This may not be easy, though, since as respects the legal and ethical aspects of telemedicine we are in the peculiar position of needing, not to find reasons for mistakes, but to find solutions to risks that have yet to emerge: to defend ourselves by pre-empting telemedical malpractice. Of course, it is impossible to "vaccinate" against negligence, but there are some specific danger areas that should be highlighted.

## (i) The teleconsultant acting beyond his ability

Craig[64] writes that due to the shortage of posts in clinical radiology and the increasing workload of radiologists, radiographical interpretation is frequently undertaken by doctors who are not trained in diagnostic radiotherapy. While the introduction of teleconsultancy in hospitals should dramatically increase the accessibility of specialists in, *inter alia*, radiography, and it is hoped the habit of releasing films unreported will become a thing of the past, it is important that individual doctors are aware of their own limitations. In 1988 an investigation by Vincent et al[65] of the ability of junior doctors working in accident and emergency departments to detect radiographic abnormalities produced the following somewhat alarming result. When comparing the assessment of a radiograph by a senior house officer with that of a consultant radiologist or registrar, the former showed an error rate of 39% – almost four out of ten cases – for abnormalities which might have clinically significant consequences. There was no improvement shown during the officers' six month tenure of their posts. But the paper observes, candidly, that it would naturally be unrealistic to expect senior house officers in A & E departments to acquire the difficult skills of image interpretation in that short time.

Notwithstanding the important contribution that telemedicine will make, therefore, to the more efficient use of time and energy of senior and middle-grade hospital doctors, to avoid allegations of negligence authorities and NHS trusts will need to ensure that more senior practitioners are available, in person, to deal with problems which are inappropriate for junior doctors. The more general debate concerning the operational and policy arena dichotomy in medical negligence litigation has, of course, already been discussed but prudence dictates that a tendency on the part of the courts to finding hospital policy-makers at least as culpable as the men and women "on the factory floor" should serve as a warning to all hospital managers who think that telemedicine may be a "quick fix" solution to the problems of staff shortage.

## (ii) Quality of reproduction of pathology slides and radiographs

An adjunct to this risk is the further risk of pathology (including haematology, biochemistry, histology and bacteriology) results and radiographs displayed on a teleconsultant's visual display unit being of insufficient clarity and resolution for a firm clinical diagnosis to be made. The degree of digital compression that can be tolerated before an unacceptable loss of information occurs will depend upon the type of teleconsultation. For teleradiology, for instance, the American College of Radiologists has stated that:

> Teleradiology is not appropriate if the available teleradiology system does not provide images of sufficient quality to perform the indicated task. When a teleradiology system is used to produce the official interpretation, there should not be a significant loss of spatial or contrast resolution from image acquisition through transmission to final image display. For transmission of images for display use only, the image quality should be sufficient to satisfy the need of the clinical circumstance.[66]

The ACR has also laid down the following specific equipment guidelines for teleradiological systems used for rendering official interpretations:

1.  Small-matrix systems (computed tomography (CT), magnetic resonance imaging (MRI), ultrasound, nuclear medicine, and digital fluorography):
    a.  Acquisition or Digitization system: These systems require 0.5k x 0.5k x 8 bits array or better.
    b.  Display system: These systems require a 0.5k x 0.48k x 8 bits array or better.
2.  Large-matrix systems (digitized radiographic films and computed radiography):
    a.  Acquisition or Digitization system: These systems should enable spatial resolution of a minimum of 2.5 line pairs/mm and acquisition of 10-bit gray scale.
    b.  Display system: These systems should enable spatial resolution of a minimum of 2.5 line pairs/mm and display of 8-bit gray scale.

Kenyon and Nightingale[67] recommend that teleconferencing should be carried out at full common intermediate format (CIF) – 352 pixels by 288 lines (which is close to broadcast quality) or where lower quality is acceptable, at quarter common intermediate format. NHS

Estates' Health Guidance Note on Telemedicine reports that no standards have yet been set for telepathology.[68]

## (iii) Improper or negligent delegation

The delegation of tasks is necessary in all aspects of medical care. To delegate is to trust or empower a medically or non-medically trained colleague to perform a task. A senior doctor may delegate a task to a junior or, of particular importance for present purposes, a teleconsultant may delegate a task to a non-medically qualified person such as a ship's medical officer. The need to delegate tasks to non-medically qualified personnel is acknowledged by the General Medical Council, though the delegator must be satisfied that the delegatee has sufficient experience, training and skill to perform the delegated task. A medical opinion cannot be given by a non-medically qualified person and to so delegate a task requiring the skill and knowledge of a doctor to a mere lay-person is considered to be serious professional misconduct.

Moreover, such an "improper delegation" would lead to liability being placed upon the doctor – whereas in the case of a "proper delegation", that is, one which was properly made by a qualified doctor to a suitably qualified and experienced medical officer, legal responsibility will ultimately lie with that officer for the consequences of his or her negligence. The delegating teleconsultant should therefore ensure that he or she is aware of the complexity of a particular case or procedure and the need both for close supervision of the non-professional medic and for continuing to monitor the progress of both patient and carer. It will be important, therefore, that the teleconsultant remains contactable. It will also be important for the non-professional medic to make it clear when he or she thinks that the task delegated to them is beyond their competence.

## (iv) Poor training of teleconsultants

Much of the credit for the introduction of telemedicine technology can be placed upon a relatively small group of committed enthusiasts – or "surfers" as they are often called – in the medical profession and within health care management generally. But at present there is no central body dealing with the co-ordination of training in teleconsulting and the use of telemedical equipment, nor is there any standard-setting body in this field. The General Medical Council, British Medical Association and the Royal Colleges are largely unaware at present of the medico-legal implications of teleconsulting in the United Kingdom and few of them have had occasion to give verbal, let alone written, advice to their members. There is therefore no yardstick at present against which the adequacy of training and the appropriateness of the training provider can be assessed.

In time there might perhaps be a Royal College of Teleconsultants (or at the very least an Association of Telemedicine and Telecare Specialists) but in the meantime it is essential for the Royal Colleges or teleconsultants themselves to set up accreditation courses and standards in telemedical practice that can form a proper basis for the development of responsible teleconsulting in the next millennium. Hospitals must ensure that staff using telemedical equipment are assessed and re-assessed at appropriate intervals in the skills necessary for their allotted tasks. Failing to remedy a situation where a member of staff is incompetent or insufficiently skilled to carry out their duties may be *prima facie* evidence of negligence.

## (v) Unclear delineation of responsibility

Just as in conventional medicine it is essential for it to be made clear who is responsible for the overall management of a patient's care, particularly where that patient is passed between departments or hospitals, so in telemedicine it must be clearly understood who is responsible for the telepatient's care. There have been examples of patients in private care being harmed by the involvement of too many consultants, none of whom believed themselves to have final responsibility for the patient and therefore the authority to take appropriate action when clinical problems arose.

## (vi) Lack of telemedical equipment

Many conventional medical negligence claims are made on the basis of a culpable failure on the part of a health authority or NHS trust to provide suitable equipment or facilities and health care managers bear the sometimes heavy burden of ensuring that any equipment necessary for providing good quality care is provided. Notwithstanding, therefore, the failure of the applicants in the *Hincks* and *Walker* cases referred to above, there is growing judicial reluctance to allow failings in the "policy" arena, as opposed to the "operational" arena, immunity from judgment. Indeed, one clear way in which such immunity can be lost is where a report by an external body suggests that the numbers of a particular piece of equipment held need to be increased. Where, therefore, a strong recommendation was made to the management of a telemedicine- or telecare-providing health authority or trust that they should increase funding for the service, any subsequent claim alleging damage caused or contributed to by, *inter alia*, a culpable failure to implement those recommendations, would be almost impossible to defend successfully.

Teleconsultants should also have regard to the advice of the General Medical Council set out at paragraph 33 of *Good Medical Practice*:

> You should always seek to give priority to the investigation and treatment of *patients solely on the basis of clinical need* [emphasis the author's, i.e. Stanberry].

## (vii) Communication problems

Lori Bartholomew, Director of Loss Prevention and Research for the Physician Insurers Association of America, cites communication problems as an important factor in incidents leading to claims for medical negligence.[69] The importance of good communication in teleconsultancy is borne out on two levels.

### (a) Protocols for "live" teleconsultancy

All forms of communication carry the danger of misunderstandings through lack of clarity, interference and poor voice or picture reproduction. It will be essential in teleconsultancy, therefore, to ensure that doctors make themselves clearly understood to each other and to their patients and that they listen carefully to telepatients regarding their symptoms, as well as eliciting all the background medical information necessary for the teleconsultant to make an informed diagnosis. This is a recurrent problem in conventional medicine, particularly with deaf, elderly patients and doctors for whom English is not the mother tongue, or who speak with heavy accents or dialects. Such problems tend to be exaggerated in radio and telephone communications.

Where, therefore, parties to a telemedical consultation do not hear or see each other clearly for whatever reason, clarification must be sought and the parties should not be afraid to reconvene a session if this is necessary to sort out technical problems with the telemedical link. The instructing teleconsultant should ask the telepatient or referring physician to read back their recommendations or diagnosis to confirm that these have been correctly recorded. Teleconsultants should be particularly diligent to confirm that:

(a)  where drugs have been prescribed or a prescription changed, the correct dosage and strength has been noted, along with any contra-indications;

(b)  where appointments have been made or altered, the new time and date is correctly recorded;

(c)  a telepatient has clearly understood the therapy or course of treatment that has been recommended; and

(d)  the teleconsultant does not inadvertently "hang-up" before the telepatient or referring physician has finished speaking or transmitting, and vice versa.

It will also, naturally, be extremely important to ensure, particularly in the provision of telecare to patients in rural communities, that follow-up teleconsultations are arranged at appropriate intervals and that the telepatient is aware of the correct times and dates to be available to take part in the teleconsultation. Although this sounds rather obvious, the care staff responsible for running existing audio-communication systems with elderly and disabled people are well aware of the unnecessary panic caused when a patient goes away on holiday without informing them and repeated intercom calls to their home fail to elicit any response.

### (b) Post-incident management

The second level of communication involves the proper reporting and management of mistakes and combines both the preventative aims of the first level with the need to mitigate the impact of errors in medical practice upon the health care provider, an approach which Davison[70] describes as "spotting the litigant":

> Many but not all cases of litigation start with an innocent complaint or a request for information. It is important to head off the potential threat of litigation by ensuring that patients are given adequate explanations. This cannot be stressed enough. When the more usual series of letters has failed to produce a satisfied customer then it is essential that a face-to-face dialogue be held with the patient or his or her relatives on the one hand, and the hospital consultant and hospital manager on the other.

Davison believes that many doctors and managers assume that litigation arises only where they have been negligent. His experience suggests that many claims are begun that have little or no chance of success but which have been catalysed by the health care provider's inability to provide explanations and, where appropriate, apologies, when things have gone wrong. He concludes that:

> All claims must be handled professionally and diligently...management [should not] assume that it is only the articulate well-off who will pursue a claim. Many who do not have the financial resources to sue may be eligible for legal aid and because they are less persistent in seeking explanations may find recourse to the law as the only route to satisfaction.

Moreover, the growing enthusiasm for *pro bono* work and the acceptance of clients on a contingency fee basis by many solicitors' firms specialising in plaintiff personal injury work will exacerbate this danger. Since June 1995 the Lord Chancellor has been permitted under Section 58 of the Courts and Legal Services Act 1990, to authorise conditional fee arrangements. For prospective plaintiffs this will remove much of the worry from commencing a civil action against a telemedicine provider or teleconsultant and for that plaintiff's lawyer there will be the security of knowing that they will receive no fee if they lose such a case but a generous uplift if they win it.

Hence the importance of a comprehensive and efficient reporting system whereby telemedical staff are not operating in a climate of fear – terrified to report errors for fear of reprisals such as disciplinary action. If full blown legal claims arising from errors in telemedicine are to be avoided, the aggrieved telepatient must be satisfied that something has been done and the same mistake cannot happen again. The operation of such a system will require:

(a)   the reporting of incidents immediately after they have taken place, to the teleconsultant in charge, while events are still fresh in the minds of the staff involved;

(b)   the making of accurate and detailed notes concerning the events and the saving of any and all relevant evidence, including any simultaneous recording that might have been made of the transmission or dialogue; and

(c)   the use of disciplinary action only as a very last resort and the open acknowledgement by management and senior consultants that mistakes committed in good faith will be treated as such.

The last point, in particular, is as vital to all aspects of conventional medical practice as it is to telemedicine. However, if young gifted doctors are not to be scared away from using telematics as a means of consulting colleagues and treating patients, then a culture needs to exist in which mistakes are viewed in context and lead not to stigmatisation but to learning and progression for all concerned. Thankfully, the General Medical Council (GMC) is now attempting to steer medical practice this way, having both replaced the old "Blue Book" with new publications presenting a more positive image of the doctor's duties and responsibilities, and widened the options available to the GMC by the enactment of a Medical (Professional Performance) Act 1995. These changes bring their own problems, however, which are examined further in chapter 6.

## (viii) "Telecomplacency"

Telemedicine should not be allowed, with the passage of time, to be developed in a piecemeal fashion by the small group of committed enthusiasts who currently use it in the course of their day to day practice. Health authorities and NHS trusts need to ensure that a central standard setting agency is created that will develop uniform guidelines and training for teleconsultants. Darkins notes that:

> As videoconferencing facilities become ubiquitous, teleconsultations may develop ad hoc, in the manner of an extension of the current use of the telephone, in which event there will be risks.[63]

Telemedicine should never be seen as being an off-the-shelf product you can simply "plug and play", but a process of medical consultation and diagnosis which requires strict protocols and codes of practice to be followed.

## (ix) Malfunctioning of telemedical equipment

The use of telemedical equipment presents its own unique hazards. Where there is a breakdown during use, a loss of contact during a transmission or indeed telemedical equipment does not come up to standard, harm to the telepatient may result. Moreover, one of these factors, while not being the sole cause of a teleconsulting mishap, may still be a significant contributory factor and hence a telecommunications company or telemedical equipment manufacturer may find that its "deep pockets" make it an attractive party to name as a joint defendant to a telemedical malpractice claim. It is the issue of liability for defective telemedical equipment that we examine in chapter 7.

## Summary

▶ A teleconsultant, in common with a doctor engaged in conventional medical consultation and treatment, will owe their patient a duty to exercise reasonable care in undertaking that treatment. A teleconsultant will be negligent if he fails to act in accordance with a practice accepted as proper by a responsible body of teleconsultants skilled in that particular art and, if harm occurs to the telepatient as a result of that negligence, he or she will be liable to the patient for tortious or contractual damages.

▶ A non-professional or paramedic will also owe a duty of care but the standard of care to which they must conform will be judged in relation to their skills and ability or the standards prevailing in their paramedical profession.

▶ Although the courts are traditionally reluctant to find health authorities or NHS trusts negligent in the way in which they manage their financial resources, there is growing judicial unease with allowing hospitals to escape liability where failure to provide adequate medical equipment, staff or services results in harm to a patient. There may therefore be a positive duty, in certain circumstances, to provide telemedical services.

▶ It would be incumbent upon a plaintiff telepatient to prove every element of a claim of negligence against a teleconsultant and to bring their claim within the appropriate limitation period after they allege to have suffered harm or to have discovered that harm. There are special provisions in this respect for patients harmed in utero.

▶ Independent research has shown that poor communication is a major cause of medical malpractice litigation. The utmost care should be taken in responding promptly and sympathetically to patient complaints. Health authorities and NHS trusts should adopt a positive, retroactive approach to clinical risk rather than allowing the commencement of litigation to be a barometer for the quality of telemedical care.

▶ Telemedicine will bring with it some specific medico-legal risks which should be guarded against by teleconsultants and telemedicine providing bodies. These include the risk of the teleconsultant acting beyond his ability; unclear reproduction of pathology slides and radiographs; improper or negligent delegation; poor training of teleconsultants; unclear delineation of responsibility; lack of telemedical equipment; malfunctioning of telemedical equipment; misunderstandings in communication between teleconsultants and telepatients and complacency on the part of teleconsultants.

# References

1 *Hatcher* v *Black* (1954) unreported, though quoted in Lord Denning's own book *The Discipline of Law*. London: Butterworths, 1979.
2 Powers MJ, Harris NH. *Medical negligence*. (2nd ed.) London: Butterworths, 1994: ix.
3 Ibid.
4 (1925) 94 LJKB 791 at p. 794.
5 [1968] 1 All ER 1068.
6 Moreover, as we have seen in chapter 4, where an adult is unconscious and unable to request medical treatment himself the courts will imply the necessary request for treatment, unless there has already been some valid, express statement to the contrary by the patient (*Re F* (*a mental patient*: *sterilisation*) [1990] 2 AC 1, [1989] All ER 545 (HL)).
7 Nathan HL, Barraclough AR. *Medical negligence*. London: Butterworths, 1957.
8 See the Sale of Goods Act 1979, s.14 and of the Supply of Goods and Services Act 1982, s.9.
9 *Gold* v *Essex County Council* [1942] 2 All ER 237.
10 [1951] 2 KB 343 at p. 356.
11 Supra, note 2 at p. 4.
12 [1986] 3 All ER 801.
13 Ibid., at p. 833.
14 Ibid., at p. 834.
15 (1979) 123 s.436.
16 (1987) 3 BMLR 32, CA.
17 [1986] 3 All ER 801 at p. 833.
18 (1856) 11 Ex Ch 781 at p. 783.
19 [1957] 1 WLR 582.
20 Ibid., at p. 587-588.
21 *Maynard* v *West Midlands* R.H.A. [1984] 1 WLR 634 at p. 639.
22 Per Lord Bridge, expressly approving the dicta of Sir John Donaldson, the Master of the Rolls in the Court of Appeal in *Sidaway* v *Board of Governors of the Bethlehem and the Maudsley Hospital* [1985] 2 WLR 480 at p. 505.
23 [1997] 4 All ER 771.
24 *Nettleship* v *Weston* [1971] 2 QB 691 and *Wilsher* v *Essex Area Health Authority* [1986] 3 All ER 801.
25 Query, though, whether a junior doctor who seeks advice from the supervising consultant has discharged his duty, see *Jones* v *Manchester Corporation* [1952] 2 QB 852 at page 871 and *Wilsher* v *Essex Area Health Authority* (supra).
26 *Whiteford* v *Hunter* (1950) 94 SJ 758 (HL); *Crawford* v *Board of Governors of Charing Cross Hospital* [1953] *The Times*, 8 December (CA).
27 *Hunter* v *Hanley* (1955) SLT 213 at p. 217.
28 *Newton* v *Newton's New Model Laundry* [1959] The Times, 3 November.
29 *Wood* v *Thurston* (1951) *The Times*, 25 May.
30 *Langley* v *Campbell* (1975) *The Times*, 6 November; see also *Tuffil* v *East Surrey Area Health Authority* (1978) *The Times*, 15 March where doctors failed to test for amoebic dysentry in a patient who had spent many years in the tropics.
31 [1938] 1 All ER 566.
32 [1985] 1 All ER 643 at p. 660.
33 *Bolam* v *Friern Hospital Management Committee* [1957] 1 WLR 582 at p. 586.
34 *Maynard* v *West Midlands* RHA [1984] 1 WLR 634 at p. 638.
35 [1969] 1 QB 428.
36 [1987] 2 All ER 417.
37 [1988] 1 All ER 871 (HL).
38 [1942] 2 All ER 237. See also *Razzel* v *Snowball* [1954] 3 All ER 429.
39 Section 53 of the Merchant Shipping Act 1995 provides that "Where a United Kingdom ship does not carry a doctor among the seamen employed in it the master shall make arrangements for securing that any medical attention on board the ship is given either by him or under his supervision by a person

appointed by him for the purpose." The global standards (which define the levels of training and first-aid) set by the IMO/ILO joint training recommendations, the revised STCW 95 and ILO Convention 164 on Health Protection and Medical Care (Seafarers) 1987 are useful (even though they are general requirements) in helping to set a definition of a common set of training standards which can be improved and then incorporated into appropriate training manuals and courses for ship's officers. The European Council Directive 92/29/EEC of 31 March 1992 on the minimum safety and health requirements for improved medical treatment on board vessels gives instructions on the required range of drugs and medical instruments on board, the standard of first-aid skills of seafarers and their medical training and on the regulations on advice given by radio. See further on this topic Patel T. *Review of Current Medical Training Procedures and Practices*. Cardiff: Seafarers International Research Centre, 1997.

40    [1966] 1 Lloyd's Rep 335.
41    See *Woolmington* v *DPP* [1935] AC 462 (HL).
42    (1968) 112 SJ 483.
43    Ibid., at p. 484. See also the dicta of Morris LJ in *Hornal* v *Neuberger Products Limited* [1957] 1 QB 247 at p. 266 where he states: "In some civil cases the issues may involve questions of reputation which can transcend in importance even questions of personal liberty. Good name in a man or woman is "the immediate jewel of their souls"...though no court...would give less careful attention to issues lacking gravity than to those marked by it, the very elements of gravity become a part of the whole range of circumstances which have to be weighed in the scale when deciding as to the balance of probabilities."
44    [1984] 1 WLR 634.
45    Ibid., at p. 639.
46    [1983] 1 All ER 416.
47    [1986] 3 All ER 801.
48    Ibid., at p. 815.
49    [1951] 2 KB 343
50    [1939] 2 KB 14.
51    [1948] 2 All ER 176.
52    (1983) 1 *The Lancet* 1452.
53    See further Powers MJ, Harris NH. *Medical Negligence*. (2nd ed.) London: Butterworths, 1994: 19.
54    Nelson RF, Bartlett AVB. "Limitation of actions." Chapter 13 in Powers MJ, Harris NH, *Medical negligence*. (2nd ed.) London: Butterworths, 1994.
55    [1978] AC 297 at p 331 (HL).
56    See Limitation Act 1980, ss.11 and 12 and *Scuriaga* v *Powell* (1979) 123 SJ 406 where the plaintiff had an operation to terminate her pregnancy, but the operation was unsuccessful and she subsequently gave birth. The defendant doctor falsely told her that the lack of success was due to a physical defect in her. More than three years later she discovered, as a result of further medical advice, that the lack of success of the operation was attributable to the manner in which the doctor had performed the operation. The court held that her date of knowledge, from which time ran, was the date on which she received the further advice. While the plaintiff must have knowledge of the essence of the act or omission to which the injury is attributable, it is not necessary for them to know the precise terms in which negligence or breach of duty would be alleged. See also *Nash* v *Eli Lilly & Co* [1992] 3 Med LR 353, 368; *Wilkinson* v *Ancliff (BLT) Ltd* [1986] 1 WLR 1352 (CA); *Driscoll-Varley* v *Parkside Health Authority* [1991] 2 Med LR 346; *Dobbie* v *Medway Health Authority* [1992] 3 Med LR 217; *Broadley* v *Guy Clapham & Co* (1993) The Times, 6 July (CA).
57    *Howell* v *Young* (1826) 5 B & C 259.
58    NHS Executive. *Clinical Negligence Costs*. Circular FDL (96) 39.
59    Davison AJ. "*Medical negligence – a manager's view.*" Chapter 2 in Powers MJ, Harris NH. *Medical Negligence*. (2nd ed.) London: Butterworths, 1994: 23.
60    Ibid., at p. 23.
61    Source: Clinical Negligence Scheme for Trusts Review, Issue 9, Summer 1997.
62    Brahams D. Medicolegal implications of teleconsulting in the UK. *Journal of Telemedicine and Telecare* 1995: 1: 196-201.
63    Darkins A. Managing clinical risk in telemedicine. *Journal of Telemedicine and Telecare* 1996; 2: 179-184.
64    Craig JOMC. "*Litigation concerning clinical radiology.*" Chaper 41 in Powers MJ, Harris NH. *Medical Negligence*. (2nd ed.) London: Butterworths, 1994.
65    Vincent CF, Driscoll PA, et al. Accuracy of Detection of Radiographic Abnormalities by Junior Doctors. *Archives of Emergency Medicine* 1988; 5: 101-109.

66    American College of Radiology. *ACR Standard for Teleradiology*. 1994 (Res. 21), Revised 1996 (Res. 26).

67    Kenyon ND, Nightingale C (eds.) *Audiovisual telecommunications*. London: Chapman and Hall, 1992.

68    NHS Estates. *Health guidance note on telemedicine*. London: The Stationery Office, 1997: 6.

69    Bartholomew LA, *The Legal Environment of Telemedicine*, Physician Insurers Association of America, 15 September 1997.

70    Davison AJ. *"Medical neglicence – a manager's view."* Chapter 2 in Powers MJ, Harris NH. *Medical Negligence* (2nd ed.) London: Butterworths, 1994.

# ▶ 6

# Standards adopted by the General Medical Council, Royal Colleges and Professional Associations

In the United Kingdom the medical profession has, by and large, avoided the interference of an external regulatory body by setting and maintaining its own high standards from within the profession. In chapter 5 we noted that the benchmark for what is and what is not to be regarded as a reasonable standard of care in a situation which involves the use of some special skill or competence is set by reference to the standard of the ordinary skilled man exercising and professing to have that special skill.[1] This is the famous *Bolam* principle which Lord Scarman in *Sidaway* v *Bethlehem and Maudsley Hospitals* described thus:

> The *Bolam* principle may be formulated as a rule that a doctor is not negligent if he acts in accordance with a practice accepted at the time as proper by a responsible body of medical opinion even though other doctors adopt a different practice. In short, the law imposes the duty of care; but the standard of care is a matter of medical judgement.[2]

The responsible body of medical opinion which presently sets the legal standard is the medical profession itself and doctors are closely involved not only in offering factual expert evidence of what is good practice for the purposes of litigation,[3] but also in handling complaints, principally through the General Medical Council. Though some commentators, such as Christopher Newdick[4], have identified recent decisions in which the courts have emphasised their role as the final arbiters in matters of negligence, judges remain reluctant, on the whole, to condemn medical opinion which has the support of even a small minority of doctors.[5]

## The General Medical Council

The General Medical Council (GMC) is the independent statutory body[6] charged with maintaining a register of doctors,[7] overseeing medical education, investigating allegations of serious professional misconduct or serious deficiency in medical practice and handling disciplinary matters. A Preliminary Proceedings Committee, which consists of 11 members elected annually, sits in private and decides on the basis of written evidence and submissions which complaints made against medical practitioners it will refer to the Professional Conduct Committee. It may also refer cases to the Health Committee, which considers cases of doctors whose fitness to practice is impaired by physical or mental illness.

In most cases the Preliminary Committee concludes, after careful consideration of a complaint, that no serious misconduct has taken place and so either sends the doctor a warning letter or letter of advice, or takes no further action. However, about five per cent of the cases reviewed by the Preliminary Committee are referred on to the GMC's Professional Conduct Committee which operates like a court with the power to impose a range of penalties including striking off a doctor. Rosenthal, in his 1987 study *Dealing with Medicine* states that, in comparison with Sweden and the United States, the General Medical Council exercises "an extraordinary degree of control" over professional conduct.

## The GMC and telemedicine

Although the General Medical Council presently deals with a number of enquiries from both general practitioners and hospital doctors involved in telemedicine,[8] no guidelines have yet been issued regarding telemedicine and good telemedical practice. The ad hoc advice that is presently given is, not surprisingly, based upon the application of the existing guidelines on inter alia, advertising and conventional medical practice, to telemedicine. Whether the Council will find it necessary to publish detailed guidelines or regulations concerning telemedical practice, like so many other legal issues surrounding telemedicine, has yet to be seen.

Meanwhile therefore, the teleconsultant's first point of reference will be the General Medical Council's existing published advice on the principles of good practice. Prior to October 1995 this could be found in the code of *Professional Conduct and Discipline*: *Fitness to Practice*, commonly known as "the Blue Book".[9] This has now been superseded by a pack of four booklets entitled *The Duties of a Doctor*: *Guidance from the General Medical Council*.

The main booklet, *Good Medical Practice*, sets out the basic principles of good practice, enlarged upon in three accompanying booklets on *Confidentiality*, *Advertising* and *HIV and AIDS*: *the Ethical Considerations*. The booklet on HIV and AIDS was itself superseded in September 1997 by the booklet *Serious Communicable Diseases: Guidance for Doctors on the Ethical Issues Raised by HIV and other Serious Communicable Diseases*. There are also other guidance booklets published by the GMC from time to time, one of which – of particular interest to the teleconsultant – is on the making and using of visual and audio recordings of patients.

The replacement of the Blue Book with these new publications represents a conscious effort on the part of the General Medical Council to change its image from that of a "medical courts martial", taking to task doctors who fall short of the required professional standards, towards that of a more caring body which educates doctors in the standards that they must attain and how these may be achieved. This adoption of a broader and more understanding approach towards what constitutes good medical practice – evaluating the conduct of medical professionals not against detailed rules and regulations but by reference to the fundamental ethical principles of medical practice – is also reflected in the introduction during 1997 of new procedures to deal with doctors whose pattern of professional performance is seriously deficient.The emphasis here is on working as far as possible with the doctor's co-operation to assess their practice thoroughly and decide what needs to be done to put right any deficiencies. The General Medical Council (Professional Performance) Rules Order in Council[10] gave effect from 1 July 1997 to the provisions brought into force by the Medical (Professional Performance) Act 1995[11] relating to the powers of the GMC, through its appropriate committees, to investigate cases where there is evidence that a practitioner's general standard of professional performance has been seriously deficient.

Many doctors will, quite rightly, say that this change of emphasis is long overdue. Indeed, as far back as 1986 David Bolt, a surgeon and frequent chairman of the Professional Conduct Committee, stated in a lecture to the Medico-Legal Society that:

> The difficulty that we have in looking at cases is that if what you are looking at is an isolated event in the career of an otherwise estimable doctor, it would seem to me very wrong and stupid that the profession should be seeking to take major action on that account. If, on the other hand, what you are looking at seems to you to be just a particular event in, shall we say, a pattern of practice which is casual and unconcerned and careless and generally inferior and shabby, then the Professional Conduct Committee may feel that this merits more substantial action. It is always very difficult to know what form such action should take. Obviously, if you think that all you are looking at is a failure of understanding of a limited field of medicine, then imposing some kind of condition which would lead to a better understanding of that field upon the doctor's freedom to practice may be justified. But if you are looking at, shall we say, a general standard of practice, it is really terribly difficult. You do not necessarily improve the standard of a doctor's practice by taking him out of the practice altogether. This is why very often, let us say, it is seen by the public that the Professional Conduct Committee acts less strongly than might be justified.[12]

This more positive and flexible approach to medical practice has much to commend it, since the GMC's advice is now based upon what a doctor generally *should* do as opposed to what he specifically *shouldn't* and the Professional Conduct Committee now has more options available to it in dealing with cases of professional misconduct. However, this makes it a great deal more difficult to give cut-and-dried answers to questions about the nature and scope of a teleconsultant's (or even a conventional doctor's) responsibilities, particularly as many of the subjects previously covered by the Blue Book are not now mentioned at all in *The Duties of a Doctor*.

Where *The Duties of a Doctor* is unforthcoming, therefore, the Medical Act 1983 (as amended), the appropriate statutory instruments and the Blue Book (insofar as it represents the accumulated wisdom of the General Medical Council) remain of considerable importance in understanding the role and function of the GMC and its various committees, as well as in understanding its disciplinary powers.

## The powers of the GMC

None of the booklets in the *Duties of a Doctor* series makes any mention of the GMC's Professional Conduct Committee or the sort of circumstances under which a doctor might find himself the subject of an investigation by the Preliminary Proceedings Committee. The main powers of the General Medical Council are set out in section 36 of the Medical Act 1983:

36. (1)  Where a fully registered person—
     (a)  is found by the Professional Conduct Committee to have been convicted in the British Islands of a criminal offence, whether while so registered or not; or
     (b)  is judged by the Professional Conduct Committee to have been guilty of serious professional misconduct, whether while so registered or not;
     the Committee may, if they think fit, direct—

(i)   that his name shall be erased from the register;

(ii)  that his registration in the register shall be suspended (that is to say, shall not have effect) during such period not exceeding twelve months as may be specified in the direction; or

(iii) that his registration shall be conditional on his compliance, during such period not exceeding three years as may be specified in the direction, with such requirements so specified as the Committee thinks fit to impose for the protection of members of the public or in his interests.

Since 1 July 1997 a second part to section 36 has been added to enact the new professional performance rules. This amendment gives the GMC's Professional Conduct Committee an alternative, in what David Bolt described above as "isolated events in an otherwise estimable career" to finding a doctor guilty of serious professional misconduct:

36A.  (1) Where the standard of professional performance of a fully registered person is found by the Committee on Professional Performance to have been *seriously deficient* [emphasis the author's, i.e. Stanberry], the Committee shall direct—

(a) that his registration in the register shall be suspended (that is to say, shall not have effect) during such period not exceeding twelve months as may be specified in the direction; or

(b) that his registration shall be conditional on his compliance, during such period not exceeding three years as may be specified in the direction, with the requirements so specified.

(2) Where a fully registered person, whose registration is subject to conditions imposed under any provision of this section by the Committee on Professional Performance, is judged by the Committee to have failed to comply with any of the requirements imposed on him as conditions of his registration the Committee may, if they think fit, direct that his registration in the register shall be suspended during such period not exceeding twelve months as may be specified in the direction.

(3) Where the Committee on Professional Performance have given a direction for a suspension under any provision of this section the Committee may direct—

(a) that the current period of suspension shall be extended for such further period from the time when it would otherwise expire as may be specified in the direction; or

(b) that the registration of the person whose registration is suspended shall, as from the expiry (or termination...) of the current period of suspension, be conditional on his compliance, during such period not exceeding three years as may be specified in the direction, with such requirements so specified as the Committee think fit to impose for the protection of members of the public or in his interests;

but, subject to subsection (4) below, the Committee shall not extend any period of suspension under this section for more than twelve months at a time.

(4) The Committee on Professional Performance may make a direction extending a period of suspension indefinitely where—

(a) the period of suspension will, on the date on which the direction takes effect, have lasted for at least two years, and

(b) the direction is made not more than two months before the date on which the period of suspension would otherwise expire.

The position and powers of the Preliminary Proceedings Committee and the Professional Conduct Committee as well as the procedure at hearings before them are described in paragraphs 9–30 of the old Blue Book. The Professional Conduct Committee consists of 32 members, of which 11 adjudicate upon a case, elected annually by the Council. Hearings are held in public and doctors appearing before the Committee are usually legally represented. The proceedings of the Committee are governed by the rules of procedure printed by HM Stationery Office as Statutory Instrument 1988 No. 2255.[13]

Cases which will give rise to proceedings of the Committee will henceforth fall into three categories: the criminal conviction of a doctor for an offence other than a minor motoring or other trivial offence, allegations of practice that is seriously deficient, and serious professional misconduct. There is a right of appeal from the Professional Conduct Committee to the Judicial Committee of the Privy Council[14] but the latter will rarely interfere with the findings of the former unless the legal principles or procedures followed by the Committee were clearly incorrect.[15]

## The GMC and criminal offences

Where a doctor is convicted of a criminal offence, which need not be directly connected with the doctor's profession, paragraph 49 of the Blue Book states:

49. The public reputation of the medical professions requires that every member should observe proper standards of personal behaviour, not only in professional activities but at all times. This is the reason why a doctor's conviction of a criminal offence may lead to disciplinary proceedings even if the offence is not directly connected with the doctor's profession. In particular, three areas of personal behaviour can be identified which may occasion disciplinary proceedings:
   – Personal misuse or abuse of alcohol or other drugs
   – Dishonest behaviour
   – Indecent or violent behaviour

The police are under instructions to report to the General Medical Council the convictions of doctors "particularly those involving violence, indecency, dishonesty, drink or drugs".[16]

## The GMC and "serious professional misconduct"

Information or complaints concerning behaviour which could constitute serious deficiencies in medical practice or serious professional misconduct may reach the General Medical Council from a number of possible sources. They may already have been investigated by a committee of inquiry within a hospital or community health service or by family practitioner or medical service committees. Information and complaints may also come from individual doctors or members of the public and in some cases may be received from the Home Office or some other official body or even be brought to light by "investigative" newspaper and television journalism. In all cases the facts alleged must be supported by hard evidence. In many cases evidence in support of a complaint is prepared by the solicitor acting for the complainant although increasingly the GMC is also taking the time and trouble to collect evidence itself.

It was the Medical Act 1969 which introduced the phrase "serious professional misconduct" now contained in section 36(1)(b) of the Medical Act 1983. Before 1969 one would have used the slightly more colourful phrase "infamous conduct in a professional respect" contained in section 29 of the Medical Act 1858 and explained in 1894 by the then Master of the Rolls, Lord Esher, as meaning:

> Not merely whether what a medical man has done would be an infamous thing for anybody else to do, but whether it is infamous for a medical man to do it.[17]

In the 1985 edition of the Blue Book it was stated that in proposing the substitution of the expression "serious professional misconduct" for the phrase "infamous conduct in a professional respect" the General Medical Council intended that the phrases should have the same significance. Yet in *Doughty* v *General Dental Council*[18] Lord Mackay, delivering judgment in the Privy Council, thought that Parliament must have intended to make a change of substance to the law, as well as a change of wording, since in addition to the change from "infamous conduct in a professional respect" to "serious professional misconduct" a lesser penalty of up to 12 months suspension had now been provided for. So it is certainly open to lawyers to argue that any cases on what constituted "infamous conduct in a professional respect" prior to 1969 are no longer relevant in interpreting what is called in modern parlance "serious professional misconduct". So in one respect, at least, it may well be that the law has imputed greater significance to this change of wording than the GMC had intended – imputing a distinction between the two definitions that was never intended.

Ironically however, the dicta of Lord Mackay in *Doughty* should also be of interest to medical professionals because it illustrates very well a distinction that certainly *was* intended by the GMC. In paragraph 38 of the Blue Book it is stated:

> 38. The Council is concerned with errors in diagnosis or treatment, and with the kind of matters which give rise to action in the civil courts for negligence, only when the doctor's conduct in the case has involved such a disregard of professional responsibility to patients or such a neglect of professional duties as to raise a question of serious professional misconduct.... A question of serious professional misconduct may also arise from a complaint or information about the conduct of a doctor which suggests that the welfare of patients has been endangered by a doctor persisting in unsupervised practice of a branch of medicine without having the appropriate knowledge and skill or having the experience which is necessary.

In *Doughty* Lord Mackay has made this same distinction, between "professional misconduct" where a doctor's conduct falls short, by act or omission, of the standard of conduct expected among doctors, and whether or not this falling short would give rise to an actionable case of medical negligence serious enough to warrant the GMC's intervention. It is only if the misconduct falls into this latter category that the medical professional can be found guilty of "serious professional misconduct" and hence be subject to the disciplinary powers of the Council. It is not every negligent act, therefore, that will lead to action by the Professional Conduct Committee. Indeed it is quite possible, in theory at least, for a doctor to be found negligent in a civil action yet not be subjected to any form of admonishment by the GMC.

It would still be open to the GMC, though, to find that the standard of professional performance of a fully registered doctor is seriously deficient and to use the various measures available under the new professional performance regulations to suspend a doctor from practice or to allow him/her to continue to practice on condition that he or she comply with directions from the Professional Conduct Committee. These broader powers having come into force only very recently, however, it remains to be seen how the General Medical Council will use them to protect patients from poor standards in medical practice which, whilst not bad enough to be punished as serious professional misconduct, nonetheless warrant stern but sympathetic interference from the GMC.

### "Serious professional misconduct" and the teleconsultant

So how, then, do we apply *The Duties of a Doctor* booklets or, where they are unhelpful, the Blue Book, to the teleconsultant? And what sort of behaviour, on the part of the teleconsultant, would be "serious professional misconduct"? The Blue Book gave both a positive and a negative point of view. It included a short explanation of what the public is entitled to expect of a registered medical practitioner, and these "positive" points would naturally cover teleconsultancy also. They include:

(a)  the conscientious assessment of the history, examination and, where necessary, diagnostic investigation of a patient;

(b)  competent and considerate professional management; and

(c)  appropriate and prompt action upon evidence suggesting the existence of a condition requiring urgent medical intervention and readiness, where circumstances so warrant, to consult appropriate professional colleagues.

The "negative" points could be found in Part II of the Blue Book which contained the following illustrations of what may constitute serious professional misconduct:

(a)  neglect or disregard of personal responsibilities to patients for their care and treatment;

(b)  abuse of professional privileges or skills such as breaching medical confidentiality, entering into sexual relationships with patients or unlawfully prescribing drugs or undertaking abortions;

(c)  personal behaviour which is derogatory to the reputation of the medical profession such as violence, dishonesty, indecency, drink or drugs; and

(d)  self-promotion, advertising and canvassing.

Paragraph 65 of the Blue Book emphasised that these categories of misconduct were not to be regarded as exhaustive. It was emphasised that any abuse by doctors of any of the privileges and opportunities afforded to them or any grave dereliction of professional duty or serious breach of medical ethics could give rise to a charge of serious professional misconduct. As identified earlier, however, the new guidelines contained in *The Duties of a Doctor* have a much more positive emphasis. There is no "negative" list as such, which would equate with that found in Part II of the Blue Book. However, there is a statement inside the front cover of the folder in which the four booklets are contained – and which is repeated inside the front cover of each of the individual booklets – that it would be helpful to consider in detail:

**The duties of a doctor registered with the General Medical Council**
Patients must be able to trust doctors with their lives and wellbeing. To justify that trust, we as a profession have a duty to maintain a good standard of practice and care and to show respect for human life. In particular as a doctor you must:

- make the care of your patient your first concern;
- treat every patient politely and considerately;
- respect patients' dignity and privacy;
- listen to patients and respect their views;
- give patients information in a way that they can understand;
- respect the rights of patients to be fully involved in decisions about their care;
- keep your professional knowledge and skills up to date;
- recognise the limits of your professional competence;
- be honest and trustworthy;
- respect and protect confidential information;
- make sure that your personal beliefs do not prejudice your patients' care;
- act quickly to protect patients from risk if you have good reason to believe that you or a colleague may not be fit to practise;
- avoid abusing your position as a doctor; and
- work with colleagues in the ways that best serve patients' interests

In all these matters you must never discriminate unfairly against your patients or colleagues. And you must always be prepared to justify your actions to them.

The main booklet *Good Medical Practice – Guidance from the General Medical Council* then begins with a statement common to all the booklets:

> Being registered with the General Medical Council gives you rights and privileges. In return, you must meet the standards of competence, care and conduct set by the GMC.

It goes on to state that the booklet sets out the basic principles of good practice intended not as exhaustive rules, but as guidance only. Emphasis is drawn, early on in the text, to the dangers of a doctor acting outside of the areas of his professional experience. There is certainly a danger that a teleconsultant dealing with situations that require prompt or emergency advice or treatment will be carried away by the prevailing sense of urgency and fail to consult colleagues regarding problems that fall outside of his or her experience or competence. *Good Medical Practice* states at paragraph 4 that in an emergency, a doctor must offer anyone at risk only the treatment that he or she could *reasonably* be expected to provide.

### Teleconsultants in teams

The General Medical Council sets out some guidance for doctors working within teams that will be of particular relevance for teleconsultants working as part of a group of practitioners providing a telemedical service, for example, to merchant shipping, cruise liners or clinics in a remote area. It is stated at paragraphs 25–27 that:

> Health care is increasingly provided by multi-disciplinary teams. You are expected to work constructively within such teams and to respect the skills and contributions of colleagues.
>
> If you are leading a team, you must do your best to make sure that the whole team understands the need to provide a polite and effective service and to treat patient information as confidential.

> If you disagree with your team's decision, you may be able to persuade other
> team members to change their minds. If not, and you believe that the decision
> would harm the patient, tell someone who can take action. As a last resort, take
> action yourself to protect the patient's safety and health.

Is this, effectively, carte blanche to undermine the professional standing of a fellow teleconsultant? This particular paragraph can be criticised, perhaps, for not going into more specific detail as to the circumstances – which must surely be limited – under which a doctor or teleconsultant may interfere with or even reverse a colleague's decision about a patient's clinical care or treatment. Moreover, this is detail that is badly needed: there has been at least one recent case in which a doctor was disciplined by the GMC for failing to inform the proper authorities of a colleague's shortcomings.[19]

This lack of detail seems to extend to other aspects of the new guidelines. For instance, much fuss has been made over the handling of information by non-medical employees who work as part of a health care team within the NHS. The British Medical Association, concerned at the increasing demands being made upon health authorities and NHS trusts to disclose details about lifestyle and history to the providers of life insurance, loans, mortgages, employment, and the like, has called for a statutory code defining the circumstances in which the passing of information to third parties might be justified and clarifying the duties of all people coming into contact with identifiable health information, doctors and non-doctors alike. Yet the General Medical Council has opposed such a move on the grounds that such a code would be inflexible and, moreover, would interfere with the GMC's own jurisdiction concerning breaches of confidentiality.

Now arguably, the renaissance of telemedicine will bring about a huge increase in the incidence of "teams", as opposed to individuals, providing health care. It will be non-medical administrative staff, manning telephones and feeding information into networked computer databases, who will form the backbone of these teams and who will be the first point of contact with patients using a telemedicine service. The British Medical Association feels that in circumstances such as these:

> A statutory code would leave all sections of the health service in a much clearer
> position. Individuals would know which colleagues were covered by the code and
> could feel confident about sharing information.

It firmly believes that flexibility would not be hindered by a detailed and unambiguous code which could be amended in the light of experience. We only have, however, paragraphs 28 and 29 of *Good Medical Practice* which state simply that:

> You may delegate medical care to nurses *and other health care staff* [emphasis
> author's, i.e. Stanberry] who are not registered medical practitioners if you believe
> it is best for the patient. But you must be sure that the person to whom you
> delegate is competent to undertake the procedure or therapy involved. When
> delegating care or treatment, you must always pass on enough information about
> the patient and the treatment needed. You will still be responsible for managing
> the patient's case.
>     You must not enable anyone who is not registered with the GMC to carry out
> tasks that require the knowledge and skills of a doctor.

"Other health care staff" is nowhere defined and the natural conclusion seems to be that the term will therefore cover anyone who is employed as part of a "health care team", regardless of that person's medical qualifications or lack of them. So we seem to be left with a situation in which non-medical staff enjoy the same privileges of access to confidential information as medical practitioners, with none of the attendant strict ethical obligations. Moreover, the BMA believes (and the author would tend to concur) that the "plurality of employers" within the National Health Service and the ease with which administrative staff can transfer posts between different trusts and authorities will hinder any disciplinary procedures that might be brought for misdemeanours discovered only after the employee has left.

## Teleconsultancy and confidentiality

On the thorny subject of confidentiality, *Good Medical Practice* states:

> 16. Patients have a right to expect that you will not pass on any personal information which you learn in the course of your professional duties, unless they agree. If in exceptional circumstances you feel you should pass on information without a patient's consent, or against a patient's wishes, you should read our booklet "Confidentiality" and be prepared to justify your decision.

The principles of confidentiality and the patient's rights of access to their medical records have already been discussed in great depth in chapter 2. The GMC's guidelines do, naturally, make explicit reference to doctors' responsibility for ensuring that confidential information is protected against improper disclosure when it is disposed of, stored, transmitted or received. The guidelines also stress the importance of ensuring that patients are informed whenever information about them is likely to be disclosed to others involved in their health care, and that they should be given the opportunity to withhold permission.

The GMC's booklet *Confidentiality: Guidance from the General Medical Council* provides more detailed guidance, including advice on disclosure within teams that will be helpful to telemedicine services. In addition to making sure that other health workers in a telemedical team understand that any patient information that is given to them is given in confidence, which they must respect, it is also required that doctors make sure that telepatients understand why and when information may be shared between team members and any circumstances in which team members providing non-medical care may be required to disclose information to third parties.

### Making and using visual and audio recordings of patients

The General Medical Council has provided some quite detailed guidelines, separately from *Good Medical Practice*, on the making and using of visual and audio recordings of patients.[20] Naturally, express, informed and fully voluntary consent is required before a patient can be recorded unless, of course, such consent is inherent in the patient co-operating in the procedure in the first place by, for example, consenting to being X-rayed. Hence where disability or immaturity would prevent a patient from giving a valid, informed consent, the agreement of a parent, guardian, close relative or other such proxy will be required. Children below the age of 16 who have the "capacity and understanding" to consent to recording may do so – teleconsultants and conventional doctors should make note, though, of the factors they take into account to justify such a decision. What is interesting for the purposes of teleconsultancy is that in the GMC's guide they define the terms "record" and "recording" to describe video and audio recordings and photographs as well as "other visual images of patients" which would include telemedical images. Any such recording will form a part of the medical record and hence be covered by the GMC's guidance on *Confidentiality* as well as the legal and ethical principles examined in chapters 2 and 3.

There will be limited circumstances where a teleconsultant or conventional doctor feels it prudent to record a patient without first obtaining their consent. The GMC's guidelines give the example of a child who is believed to be the victim of child abuse, but qualifies this proviso with the requirement that before recording a patient without consent, the doctor concerned should discuss their decision with an experienced colleague and be prepared, as in all ethical matters, to justify his or her decision to the patient and, if necessary, others.

Recordings certainly cannot be published or broadcast without the express consent of the subject of the recording first being obtained. Where more than one patient is the subject of a recording then the consent of each will be required, although "anonymised" records may be used for education and research purposes without first having to obtain consent. Consent may, however, be required before such material can be incorporated into a textbook or journal or made accessible to the public in some other way. Where a recording is made for purposes other than the assessment or treatment of a patient, the overwhelming principle seems to be that contained in paragraph 8 of the GMC's guidelines:

> If patients can be identified from the recording, you must ensure that the interests and well-being of patients take precedence over other considerations. This applies in all circumstances, but you should be particularly vigilant if you are involved in recording patients who are mentally ill or disabled, the seriously ill, children or other vulnerable people, for television or other publicly available media.[21]

Where a patient receiving emergency treatment cannot give consent, the consent of a close relative to making a recording of their treatment for training or clinical audit purposes is not necessary. However, should a close relative ask for the recording to be stopped, doctors must respect this decision and their consent, or that of the patient, would certainly be required before such a recording could be used. The guidelines go on to state, at paragraph 19, that:

> When no recording has been planned, but a record of an unexpected development would make a valuable educational tool, you may record patients undergoing treatment. If you cannot get consent at the time because, for example, the patient is anaesthetised, you must ensure the patient is later made aware of the right to object to the use of the recording.[22]

The guidelines also give some specific guidance on conduct before, during and after recording. Before beginning to record a patient teleconsultants must ensure that their patients:

(a) understand the purpose of the recording, who will be allowed to see it – including names if they are known – the circumstances in which it will be shown, whether copies will be made, the arrangements for storage and how long the recording will be kept;

(b) understand that withholding consent, or withdrawing consent during the recording, will not affect the quality of care they receive;

(c)    are given time to read explanatory material and to consider the implications of signing the consent form. Consent forms and explanatory material should not imply that consent is expected. They should be written in language that is easily understood. If necessary, translations should be provided; and

(d)    understand, where a recording is made for a television programme or other publicly available media that, after the filming process has been completed, those who own the recording are not bound to accept withdrawal of consent to use the recorded material. If they wish to restrict the use of material, they should get agreement to this in writing from the owners of the recording before the recording begins.[23]

Insofar as conduct during the recording proper is concerned, the person in control of the recording process must be prepared to stop at any point if the patient asks them to or they reasonably fear that continuing recording will have a harmful effect on the consultation or treatment. Paragraph 13 requires that, after the recording, doctors ensure that:

(a)    patients are asked if they want to vary or withdraw their consent to the use of the recording;

(b)    recordings are used only for the purpose for which the patients have given consent;

(c)    recordings are given the same level of protection as medical records against improper disclosure;

(d)    if a patient withdraws – or fails to confirm – consent, the recording is not used and is erased as soon as possible; and

(e)    patients' instructions about erasure or storage are followed unless you decide the recording includes material which you need to disclose in accordance with the advice in the booklet *Confidentiality*.[24]

## Advertising telemedical services

Since 1993 the General Medical Council has permitted doctors to advertise their services. Paragraph 42 of *Good Medical Practice* states that:

> If you advertise your services your advertisement must be honest. It must not exploit patients' vulnerability or lack of medical knowledge and may provide only factual information.

All doctors' advertisements must follow the detailed guidance in the GMC's booklet *Advertising*. As a general requirement, any advertising of telemedical services should be "legal, decent, honest and truthful" and should conform with the other requirements of the British Code of Advertising Practice. Advertising is given a very broad meaning indeed in the medical context, and covers "the provision of information about doctors and their services, in any form, to the public or other members of the profession". The GMC offers the following specific guidance on advertising by organisations offering medical services:

> The advertisements should not make invidious comparisons with other organisations, either within or outside the National Health Service, or with the services of particular doctors, nor should they claim superiority for the professional services offered or for any doctors connected with the organisation.
>
> Doctors who have any kind of financial or professional relationship with such an organisation, or who use its facilities, are deemed by the GMC to bear some

> responsibility for the organisation's advertising. This also applies to doctors who accept for examination or treatment patients referred by any such organisation. All such doctors must therefore make it their business to acquaint themselves with the nature and content of the organisation's advertising, and must exercise due diligence in an effort to ensure that it conforms to this guidance. Should any question be raised about a doctor's conduct in this respect, it will not be sufficient for any explanation to be based on the doctor's lack of awareness of the nature or content of the organisation's advertising, or lack of ability to exert any influence over it.

The guidance is clearly capable of being applied to private telemedicine services, operating on a subscription or similar basis. The name and qualifications of a doctor who is a director of a telemedicine company are required by paragraph 21 of the GMC's advertising guidelines to be shown on the company's notepaper. Paragraph 21 also requires that:

> Doctors should...take steps to avoid the inclusion, in material published by any company or organisation with which they are associated...of references which draw attention to their attainments in ways likely to promote their professional advantage, whether or not the business of their company is connected with medical practice.

The advertising guidelines will also require that teleconsultants, like conventional doctors, avoid any kind of personal involvement in promoting the services of a telemedical organisation through public speaking, broadcasting, writing articles or signing circulars, and should not permit the organisation's promotional literature to claim superiority for their professional qualifications and experience. Nor are they permitted to allow their personal address or telephone number to be used as an inquiry point on behalf of an organisation.

Would such provisions be fair in a competitive, open market in which many telemedicine services compete for "customers"? The author believes so. For while the present GMC guidelines may appear to tie the hands of medical professionals who have made a conscious decision to limit or even entirely give up their conventional practice in order better to develop and promote telemedicine, the guidance contained in the GMC's booklet on advertising does not, in reality, do any more than apply in a medical context existing principles regarding fairness in advertising.

There are general principles to the effect that all advertisements should be legal, decent, honest and truthful. Such advertisements should be prepared with a sense of responsibility to consumers and society and, most of all, should respect the principle of fair competition. The British Codes of Advertising and Sales Promotion require that advertisers generally avoid making unfair comparisons with the product of a competitor. Although the Code recognises that such comparisons are the fuel of vigorous competition, they do not allow "knocking copy" or indeed any derogatory comments about a competitor's product or service.[25] The British Codes apply to advertisements in all mediums, including newspapers, magazines, brochures, circulars, mailings, catalogues and posters, cinema and video commercials, electronic media, mailing lists, sales promotions and advertisement promotions.[26] Hence if direct comparisons between models of car or brands of washing powder are avoided in general advertising, it seems entirely sensible that the same principles should apply to professional men and women in medical practice.

## Research and development of telemedicine services

This next section relates to doctors involved in either the development or actual "buying in" of telemedicine equipment and services. It is appropriate here to mention the GMC's requirements regarding the medical profession's involvement in the research and development phase of medical services. Paragraph 43 of *Good Medical Practice* requires that where such research involves patients, the doctors concerned must make sure that the research is not contrary to the patient's interests and must confirm that the research protocol has been approved by a properly constituted research ethics committee.

Moreover, any medical practitioner with business interests in a private telemedicine provider must, before taking part in discussions with colleagues in his or her conventional practice about buying goods or services, declare any relevant financial or commercial interest which they or their family might have in the purchase. If they do have a financial or commercial interest in an organisation providing telemedicine or telecare then, just as if they had an interest in a pharmaceutical or other biomedical company, this must not be allowed to affect the way in which they prescribe for or refer their patients. If a practitioner has a financial or commercial interest in an organisation to which they plan to refer a patient, then they must tell the patient about their interest and when treating National Health Service patients they must tell the health care purchaser.

## Reconciling conflicts of interest

The teleconsultant may be forgiven for finding it paradoxical that, while the GMC's ethical guidance to the profession on what might constitute "serious professional misconduct" seems to lack depth and detail, its guidelines for doctors who have business interests outside of their area of practice are both extensive and onerous.

The published guidance expects the very highest standards of ethical and open behaviour from doctors so far as their interests in telemedical or other private companies is concerned. Whether or not this will set some telemedical practitioners on a collision course with the GMC remains to be seen, but many doctors believe that the present guidelines will hinder the development of telemedicine services by practitioners who wish to maintain their links with conventional practice. An open market in health care services will be essential if telemedicine is to flourish and prices are to remain competitive. This will require the right balance of regulation and freedom which has, arguably, already been struck or will soon be struck in relation to the privatisation of many of the former utilities. Finding such a balance may well require the GMC to adopt a more liberal approach to doctors in business than has hitherto been the case.

## Can the GMC's regulations be challenged?

Like other professional regulations, the General Medical Council's rules and guidelines are not "laws" in the strict sense of the word. They can be struck down by the English courts if they are absurd or unreasonable or if, as was stated in *Council of Civil Service Unions* v *Minister for the Civil Service*, they are:

> So outrageous in [their] defiance of logic or accepted moral standards that no sensible person who had applied his mind to the question to be decided could have arrived at it. [27]

But as *Coleman* v *General Medical Council*[28] shows, managing to convince a court that a regulation is outrageous or defies logic is far from easy. In that case the plaintiff doctor wanted to advertise his practice from the point of view of his holistic approach to good health. Under the pre-1993 guidelines, advertising was forbidden and although evidence was presented in the Court of Appeal that the GMC was itself in the process of amending the rules, which of course has since been done, the court nonetheless rejected the argument that the restrictions were unreasonable. Lord Donaldson stated that:

> Parliament has entrusted the resolution of these competing considerations to the General Medical Council and not to the courts. Accordingly, it is quite beside the point to consider whether I would have reached the same conclusion.

The possibility of convincing the courts to interfere with the self-regulation of the medical profession undertaken by the GMC, therefore, would appear to be a very slim one indeed.

## The Royal Colleges

Although the Royal College of Physicians has not yet published any ethical or legal advice regarding telemedicine to its members, it has certainly not hesitated to involve itself in raising awareness of this new speciality among its members. In March 1997 the Royal College hosted a one-day conference entitled "Telemedicine and Beyond" which was opened by the President of the College, Professor Sir Leslie Turnberg, and included clinical presentations and live demonstrations of working examples of telemedicine, how teleconsultants can work together in hospital networks and how telematics can be used to provide emergency medical care and continuing education. The Royal College, it might therefore be expected, will seek to play a continuing role in educating its members about the telemedicine revolution. The adoption of a legal and ethical policy towards the same may well be a corollary of this.

Other Royal Colleges, on the other hand, whilst aware of the emerging telemedicine revolution, have not yet issued formal advice to their members on proper protocols for teleconsultancy and correct ethical conduct in telemedical practice. However, given the plethora of literature and reviews available from them on all aspects of conventional practice, it can be fully expected that once telemedicine is more fully integrated into health care, the Colleges will make it their business to issue detailed guidance to their members and to take a central role in developing the use of telemedicine within their respective specialities.

## Medical Protection Society

The Medical Protection Society (MPS), in common with the Royal Colleges, has not issued any written advice, guidelines or policy statements regarding telemedicine to its members. It has, however, fielded telephone and written enquiries regarding telemedicine, mostly regarding the extent to which doctors can give clinical advice through the Internet. The response of the MPS's medico-legally qualifed advisers to this has been to extrapolate existing guidelines on the extent to which doctors can give clinical advice by telephone. Such a consultation, without the possibility of an actual "laying on of hands" to examine the patient, essentially requires the doctor to ask himself: do I have enough information available to me to make an informed medical judgement? The MPS has stated that if the answer to this question is no then the teleconsultant must refrain from coming to any conclusions, or allowing the patient to believe that they have done so, regarding the possible prognosis. Arrangements must be made to see the patient face-to-face.

Hence any advice given without even the benefit of a telephone conversation, such as through the Internet, must necessarily be only of the most general nature and emphasise the importance of the telepatient seeing their own general practitioner if they are at all concerned about their health. The MPS believes that the difficulty with providing telemedical advice through the Internet will always be the importance of striking a balance between good preventive practice and education on the one hand, and avoiding "scaremongering" on the other – though it does recognise that deciding where this equilibrium properly lies needs to be assessed by comparison with the "reasonable patient" rather than the hypochondriac.

The Medical Protection Society describes the rendering of a medical opinion without the benefit of patient contact as a "level 1" consultation, and speaking to a patient on the telephone as a "level 2" consultation; a live telemedical link-up, then, wherein the examination of the patient and the measurement of his symptoms is carried out by a lay-person such as a ship's medical officer under the instructions of a shore-based doctor, might be described as a "level 3" consultation. At this level the question that a doctor must ask himself becomes not only, "Do I have enough medical information available to me to make an informed judgement?", but also "do I have sufficiently accurate information available to me to make such a judgement?" The MPS advises that the golden rule in such situations should reflect the General Medical Council's requirement that a doctor does not act outside of his or her experience or competence and only administers that advice which he or she might reasonably be expected to give in the circumstances, but with the additional requirement that the [tele]consultant recognises in each and every case the limitations placed upon their diagnostic ability by both the medical information available to them and its reliability. These limitations will vary and be dependent upon the circumstances of each and every clinical case. While the rapid advances in telematics technology will improve both the quantity and quality of this information, telemedical practice requires caution from the professional medic and awareness of what is legally and ethically appropriate in the practice of medicine "from a distance". Dr Gerard Ponting, head of United Kingdom services at the MPS, stated in *GP News* in November 1995 that "it is important that protocols are established for the role of the GP and the role of the specialist in the consultation".[29]

## Medical Defence Union

The Medical Defence Union (MDU), like the MPS, is also aware of the increasing importance of telemedicine, but so far very few complaints or claims have come to its attention. It acknowledges that this situation will no doubt change in the foreseeable future. The MDU has expressed particular concern about doctors treating patients without being able physically to examine them, and about the potential problems of patient confidentiality, identified earlier in this book. Moreover, fears have also been expressed over the clinical risk of the unclear delineation of responsibility that we highlighted in chapter 5. Dr David Morgan, medico-legal adviser to the MDU stated in *GP News* in November 1995 that:

> The GP is effectively making a referral, according to terms of service, as long as the specialist has been given all relevant information such as the patient's history. It is the specialist who cannot perform a physical examination. The GP can however. Whether the responsibility for this is then shifted to the GP we do not know until it has been tested in court.[30]

The Medical Defence Union does not, at present, have any plans to charge a higher subscription to members who practise telemedicine.

## The British Medical Association

The British Medical Association (BMA) is a voluntary, professional association without statutory powers. The BMA can claim much of the credit for the creation of the General Medical Council under the Medical Act 1858, for which it had campaigned since its establishment. Although the BMA lacks the powers of the GMC to determine what was first "infamous conduct" and is now "serious professional misconduct", it does work closely with the GMC, assisting it in its task of applying broad ethical principles to the problems that arise in daily medical practice. Its principle source of guidance and advice on ethical issues is its book *Medical Ethics Today: Its Practice and Philosophy*,[31] while legal issues, including the explanation of relevant case law and legislation, are explored in a companion book *Rights and Responsibilities of Doctors*.[32] Guidance notes are also available from the BMA's Ethics Department.

The BMA originally came into being in 1832 as the Provincial Medical and Surgical Association, having as its aims the "maintenance of the honour and respectability of medicine by defining those elements which ought ever to characterise a liberal profession." It became the British Medical Association in 1856 but it was not until 1902 that a Central Ethical Committee was finally established. The Committee refused, however, to draw up an ethical code and it was not until 1949, and after the persistent supplication of its members, that the Association printed a 16-page pamphlet entitled *Ethics and Members of the Medical Profession*. A proper handbook did not appear until as recently as 1980. This handbook was revised in 1984 but was widely criticised for being over-detailed and inaccessible to doctors seeking a "quick and workable solution for an immediate case".

The present book, first introduced in 1988 and entitled *Philosophy and Practice of Medical Ethics* is now in its fifth edition. It focuses on providing "a practical response to common [ethical] questions". It reflects the findings of a Working Party of the BMA's Medical Ethics Committee which was established in 1990 to review published ethical advice and produce a new, more practically orientated set of guidelines.

To review all of the guidance and recommendations of the BMA on conventional medical practice is beyond the scope of this book, although it would be appropriate to bring attention to the Association's very brief reference to telemedicine, which is almost unique among professional associations:

> Such systems do...raise difficult problems for ensuring patient confidentiality. There are also problems associated with making sure the equipment itself is

always working efficiently, such efficiency being essential if patients are to have safe care. Some of the problems to do with ensuring confidentiality will be addressed by efforts within the European Community aimed at providing common standards for all processing of manual and electronic data.... It is clear that ethical considerations require the implementation of full safeguards for patient confidentiality prior to the introduction of new technology on a routine basis.

Quite what these safeguards might be, the British Medical Association does not specify. The BMA is practically unique, nonetheless, in having made any express reference to telemedicine in its literature at all and it is to be hoped that they will provide further, more detailed guidance, in future editions of their ethical and legal guidelines to medical practitioners.

# The Royal Society of Medicine

The Telemedicine Forum of the Royal Society of Medicine is the United Kingdom's national organisation for telemedicine. It is a non-profit making body concerned with all aspects of telemedicine and telecare. Its membership includes doctors and other health professionals, hospital managers, members of government bodies and those from industry. The Forum hosts an annual international telemedicine and telecare conference as well as smaller seminars and workshops. The Royal Society of Medicine Press publishes a quarterly academic journal, the *Journal of Telemedicine and Telecare*, the only peer-reviewed publication in this country devoted to telemedicine in the primary and secondary care sectors as well as other emerging fields.

## Summary

▶ In the United Kingdom standards in the medical profession are maintained by the General Medical Council, an independent statutory body that maintains a register of doctors, oversees medical education and investigates allegations of serious professional misconduct or serious deficiencies in professional practice.

▶ Although the General Medical Council has not yet issued written guidelines to teleconsultants, the GMC's existing guidance on good medical practice, confidentiality, advertising and HIV and AIDS apply to teleconsultancy in the same way as they apply to conventional medicine. The GMC's guidelines on working in teams and making audio and visual recordings of patients are of particular importance to doctors engaged in telemedicine.

▶ The Royal Colleges have yet to issue detailed guidance on telemedicine, although many are already involved in investigating how telemedicine can be utilised in their various fields.

▶ The Medical Protection Society and Medical Defence Union are also aware of the importance of telemedicine as a growing specialty, although neither has yet had occasion to issue written guidelines to members. Both acknowledge that this may shortly become necessary. Teleconsultancy has not, thus far, been identified as requiring a higher liability insurance premium than other specialties.

▶ The British Medical Association has briefly mentioned telemedicine in its ethical guidance to members but has yet to issue any detailed literature on the subject.

▶ The Royal Society of Medicine is proactive in furthering telemedicine and providing a forum for the discussion of telemedicine and telecare issues. The RSM has set up a Telemedicine Forum which organises an annual international conference and their publishing arm, the Royal Society of Medicine Press, publishes a quarterly academic journal, the *Journal of Telemedicine and Telecare*.

# References

1    Per Mr Justice McNair in *Bolam* v *Friern Hospital Management Committee* [1957] 2 All ER 118 at p. 121, [1957] 1 WLR 582 at p. 586. Applied by the Privy Council in *Chin Keow* v *Government of Malaysia* [1967] 1 WLR 813; by Lord Edmund-Davies in Whitehouse v *Jordan* [1981] 1 All ER 267 at p. 277, [1981] 1 WLR 246 at p. 258 and by Lord Scarman in *Maynard* v *West Midlands Regional Health Authority* [1985] 1 All ER 635.

2    *Sidaway* v *Board of Governors of the Bethlem Royal Hospital and the Maudsley Hospital* [1985] 1 All ER 643.

3    See, for instance, the judgments in *Whitehouse* v *Jordan* [1981] 1 All ER 267 and Maynard v *West Midlands HA* [1985] 1 All ER 635.

4    Newdick C. Common law and the GMC's standards of ethical conduct. *European Journal of Health Law* 1996; 3: 373-381.

5    See further *Cranley* v *Medical Board of Western Australia* (1992) 3 Med LR 94 and *Hucks* v *Cole* (1993) 4 Med LR 393.

6    Section 1 of the Medical Act 1983 states: "(1) There shall continue to be a body corporate known as the General Medical Council (in this Act referred to as "the General Council") having the functions assigned to them by this Act. (2) The General Council shall be consituted as provided by Her Majesty by Order in Council under this section subject to the provisions of Part I of Schedule 1 to this Act. (3) There shall continue to be four committees of the General Council known as the Education Committee, the Preliminary Proceedings Committee, the Professional Conduct Committee and the Health Committee (in this Act referred to as "the statutory committees") constituted in accordance with Part III of Schedule 1 to this Act and having the functions assigned to them by this Act.

7    Section 2 of the Medical Act 1983 states: "(1) There shall continue to be kept by the registrar of the General Medical Council (in this Act referred to as "the Registrar") two registers of medical practitioners registered under this Act containing the names of those registered and the qualifications they are entitled to have registered under this Act. (2) The two registers referred to are "the register of medical practitioners consisting of four lists, namely—(a) the principal list, (b) the overseas list, (c) the visiting overseas doctors list, and (d) the visiting EEC practitioners list, and "the register of medical practitioners with limited registration". (3) Medical practitioners shall be registered as fully registered medical practitioners or provisionally or with limited registration as provided in Parts II and III of this Act and in the appropriate list of the register of medical practitioners or in the register of medical practitioners with limited registration as provided in Part IV of this Act.

8    Section 35 of the Medical Act 1983 states that "The powers of the General Medical Council shall include the power to provide, in such manner as the Council think fit, advice for members of the medical profession on standards of professional conduct or on medical ethics."

9    General Medical Council. *Professional conduct and discipline: fitness to practise*. London: GMC, 1993.

10   SI 1997 No. 1529.

11   Commencement No 3. Order 1997: SI 1997 No. 1315.

12   Bolt D. Dealing with errors of clinical judgment. *Medico-Legal Journal* 1986; 54: 220.

13   General Medical Council Preliminary Proceedings Committee and Professional Conduct Committee (Procedure) Rule Order of Council 1988 (SI 1988 No. 2255).

14   See the Medical Act 1983, S.40 The Judicial Committee of the Privy Council comprises the Lord President of the Council, the Lord Chancellor, the Lords of Appeal in Ordinary and other members of the Privy Council who hold "high judicial office" as defined by ss. 5 and 25 of the Appellate Jurisdiction Act 1876 and s. 5 of the Appellate Jurisdiction Act 1877.

15   See, in this respect, the case of *McCoan* v *General Medical Council* [1964] 3 All ER 143, [1964] 1 WLR 1107 where the Privy Council rejected the appeal of a doctor who had been struck off for having a sexual relationship with one of his patients, Lord Upjohn stating that "Sexual intercourse with a patient

has always been regarded as a most serious breach of the proper relationship between doctor and patient and their Lordships do not see how the finding of the committee on the facts of this case, that the appellant was guilty of infamous conduct in a professional respect can be successfully challenged before their lordships." See also *Tamesby* v *General Medical Council* (20 July 1970, unreported) where Lord Pearson stated that "the decision of the Disciplinary Committee, composed of members of the same profession, must carry weight."

16   See statement by Home Secretary, 14 June 1973, referred to by Adrian Whitfield QC in "The General Medical Council" in J. Leahy Taylor (ed.). *Medical malpractice*. (1980).

17   *Allinson* v *General Council of Medical Education* [1894] 1 QB 750.

18   [1988] AC 164, [1987] 3 All ER 843.

19   Consultant found guilty for failing to act on a colleague. *British Medical Journal* 1994; 308: 1.

20   General Medical Council, *Making and Using Visual and Audio Recordings of Patients*, September 1997. This booklet incorporates the previous documents "Video Recordings of Consultations between Doctors and Patients and of other Medical Procedures for the Purposes of Training and Assessment and Filming Patients for Television Programmes." In the booklet the terms "record" and "recording" are used to describe video and audio recordings, photographs and other visual images of patients. Images taken from pathology slides are not covered by this guidance.

21   Ibid., at p. 5.

22   Ibid., at p. 9.

23   Ibid., at pp. 5-6.

24   Ibid., at pp. 7-8.

25   Advertising Standards Authority's Committee of Advertising Practice, British Codes of Advertising and Sales Promotion (9th ed.) February 1995 at paras 19.1 & 20.1.

26   Commercials are the responsibility of the Independent Television Commission or the Radio Authority. Classified private advertisements, works of art, official notices, private correspondence, regular competitions and flyposting are excluded from the operation of the British Codes. See further: Oughton and Lowery, *Textbook on Consumer Law*. London: Blackstone Press, 1997: 435-440.

27   (1985) AC 374, 410.

28   (1990) 1 Med LR 253.

29   *GP News*, 17 November 1995.

30   See *GP News*, 17 November 1995. For the author's own views about resolving telemedical issues through the courts, see in chapter five, supra.

31   British Medical Association. *Medical ethics today: its practice and philosophy*. London: BMJ Publishing Group, 1993.

32   British Medical Association. *Rights and responsibilities of doctors*. London: BMJ Publishing Group, 1992.

# ▶ 7

# Telemedicine equipment

The question of liability in respect of a faulty medical product was first brought to the public's attention by the thalidomide tragedy of the 1960s. Drug marketing was, as a consequence, subjected to the much tougher regulations contained in the Medicines Act 1968. But although lawsuits in respect of defective drugs are the commonest form of medical product liability action, medical equipment such as intra-uterine devices, pacemakers and artificial joints may also form the basis of a claim and, until quite recently, there was no specific legislation in the United Kingdom controlling the production and sale of such equipment.

Prior to 1994 the safety of medical devices fell within the remit of the Department of Health which operated a system of voluntary registration by manufacturers of certain medical devices used by the National Health Service. This voluntary scheme was operated in parallel with a reporting system whereby the NHS made the Department of Health aware of any "adverse incidents".[1] These purely voluntary arrangements are slowly being replaced during a transitional period, however, by a unified statutory system of European Union Directives, the first of which (the Directive on active implantable medical devices) was implemented in this country on 1 January 1993. Two further Directives on medical devices and in-vitro diagnostic (IVD) medical devices came into force in 1995 and 1997 respectively. The Medical Devices Agency (MDA) was founded in 1994 to ensure that medical equipment and devices used in the United Kingdom meet the required standards of safety, quality and performance set down by these Directives.

The Agency has adopted a definition of "medical device" constructed from the definitions found in the European Union Directives on medical devices. Hence the term includes:

> Any instrument, apparatus, material or other article, whether used alone or in combination, including the software necessary for its proper application, intended by the manufacturer to be used for human beings for the purpose of:
> ▶ diagnosis, prevention, monitoring, treatment or alleviation of disease
> ▶ diagnosis, monitoring, treatment, alleviation of or compensation of an injury or handicap,
> ▶ investigation, replacement or modification of the anatomy or of a physiological process
> ▶ control of contraception
> and which does not achieve its principal intended action in or on the human body by pharmacological, immunological or metabolic means, but which may be assisted in its function by such means.

Hence the sort of telemedical equipment that falls within this definition includes cardiac monitors, CT scanners, diagnostic X-ray equipment and ultrasound imagers. Once the EU Directives are fully in force telemedical devices will have to have a "CE" marking in order to be sold or used in the United Kingdom. But even with the toughest quality controls in place it is still conceivable that a telepatient or teleconsultant may suffer harm during a telemedical consultation not because of the negligence of the medical professional or care provider, but because of the technical failure of telemedicine equipment. Manufacturers of medical devices available in this country must inform the MDA if any of their products present a significant risk of injury to patients or users. The MDA may then require them to remove the device from the market and will advise the European Commission and other members of the common market to take similar action. Additionally, pre-market clinical trials of medical devices intended for clinical investigation cannot be conducted in the United Kingdom until details have been sent to the MDA.

Where an "adverse incident" leads to harm to a telepatient or teleconsultant, liability may be incurred by the designers, developers and/or manufacturers of the faulty equipment, or those responsible for its maintenance. Hence in this chapter we consider the role of the Medical Devices Agency and European Union in setting standards for telemedicine equipment as well as the legal basis of liability for faults in such equipment.

## The Medical Devices Agency

The main function of the Medical Devices Agency, an executive agency of the Department of Health established in September 1994, is to ensure that medical equipment and devices used in the United Kingdom meet required standards of safety, quality and performance. The MDA acts on behalf of the Secretary of State for Health in negotiating and implementing the European Union Directives that control the standardisation and marketing of medical devices within the Common Market and is managed by a chief executive who answers directly to the Secretary of State for the Agency's operation and performance. The Agency also contributes to the establishment of safety and performance standards for medical devices by the British Standards Institution (BSI). The main aims of the MDA, as set out in their framework document, are to:

- operate a system for reporting and investigating adverse incidents;
- issue safety warnings and take safeguard action;
- lead for the United Kingdom in negotiations on medical devices Directives, contributing as necessary to other relevant Directives; and introduce associated UK regulations;
- publicise the provisions of all relevant Directives and provide appropriate guidance to manufacturers and users;
- monitor compliance with the medical devices Directives, taking any necessary enforcement action;
- assess the effectiveness of the UK regulations and their impact on business, taking any necessary action to improve them;
- scrutinise applications from manufacturers for clinical investigations to establish whether the risks to patients outweigh the possible benefits;
- designate and monitor Notified Bodies in the United Kingdom to audit manufacturers, test products and approve the CE marking of relevant medical devices;
- maintain the Manufacturer Registration Scheme until the medical devices Directives are operating fully;
- plan and manage a programme for evaluating medical devices, and disseminate its findings, in accordance with customer needs and public health concerns;

▶ advise the Department of Health (including the NHS Executive) and NHS purchasing agencies on the safety, quality and performance of medical devices, equipment and associated procedures; and

▶ participate in British, European and international Standards work as necessary to support Directives and to safeguard the public health.[2]

The Agency's main customers are the suppliers of health care, principally the NHS trusts, health authorities and social services acting on behalf of patients and users; other purchasers and users of medical devices; the Department of Health and other government departments and agencies; professional bodies; manufacturers; Notified Bodies; the European Commission and the regulatory authorities of other Member States; the European Free Trade Area (EFTA) and the British, European and international Standards-making authorities.

The MDA is split into several sections, the most important of which, for teleconsultants and telepatients, are the Device Technology and Safety Groups 1 and 4 (DTS1 and DTS4) and the Adverse Incident Centre (AIC). The AIC receives reports of adverse incidents from users and manufacturers and co-ordinates their investigation. They also deal with incidents reported under the "vigilance system" put in place by the European Union Directives. The DTS is responsible for the investigation of adverse incidents associated with medical devices and issues Device Bulletins, Hazard and Safety Notices to UK health services where appropriate. The DTS also provides technical advice on devices, including the support and development of the Standards which underpin the EU Directives. DTS1 deals with diagnostic devices and DTS4 with diagnostic imaging, therapy, measurement, electro-surgery and disability devices.

The Medical Devices Agency also carries out device evaluations with the help of specialist centres and provides services including consultancy, reports and review journals which enable users and purchasers to be properly informed about safety, performance and user experience. MDA publications include the *Diagnostic Imaging Review*, which has been published since May 1996; *Diagnostic Imaging Market Reports* and evaluations and reviews of inter alia computed tomography scanners, mobile radiographic X-ray units, magnetic resonance scanners and diagnostic ultrasound units.

## Clinical risk management and the vigilance system

The Medical Devices Agency's Devices Bulletin on *Medical device and equipment management for hospital and community-based organisations*[3] states that its investigations of reports of adverse incidents show that, unless positive steps are taken following an accident, the same adverse incidents happen again and again. The main risks identified are:

(a) inappropriate use;

(b) inadequate training;

(c) poor quality, obsolete or worn-out devices;

(d) mistakes in servicing or lack of servicing;

(e) incompatible ancillary equipment (e.g. leads, probes, infusion sets); and

(f) poor documentation (e.g. service history or manuals missing).

The MDA recommends that device purchasers and providers should develop and implement a device management procedure which aims to ensure that whenever a medical device is used it should be suitable for its intended purpose, properly understood by the professional user and maintained in a safe and reliable condition. One way in which NHS trusts and health authorities can minimise the risk of telemedicine equipment – or indeed any medical device – giving rise to an adverse incident is to take a proactive role in the "vigilance system" set up by the European Union Directives (also known as the "adverse incident reporting" system). The vigilance system aims to minimise the risk to the health and safety of patients, users and others by reducing the likelihood of the same type of serious incident involving medical devices being repeated at different times in the European Community by:

a)  thoroughly evaluating incidents reported by Member States;
b)  disseminating information which can be used to prevent a re-occurrence of the incident or to alleviate the consequences of such incidents; or
c)  if appropriate, modifying the device or taking it off the market.

The European Union's medical devices Directives require that any malfunction of or deterioration in the characteristics and performance of a device, as well as any inaccuracies in the instruction leaflet which might lead to or might have led to the death of a patient or to a deterioration in his or her health should be reported by the manufacturer to the competent authority – in the United Kingdom this would be the MDA. Moreover, any technical or medical reason for the recall of a device from the market by the manufacturer or the issuing of an advisory notice will also have to be reported. These are now legally binding requirements for all devices bearing the "CE" mark.

Initial reports received by competent authorities such as the MDA are treated in the strictest confidence, which is a requirement of the Directive. But following a formal investigation which will usually be carried out by the manufacturer with the active involvement of the competent authority, any information necessary to prevent a repeat of the accident will be disseminated to the other EU competent authorities so that Hazard Notices or Safety Action Bulletins can be issued. If the manufacturer's initial investigation, prior to informing the competent authority, involves altering the device in some way, the competent authority's agreement is required to such alteration.

## The legal duty of the Medical Devices Agency

The legal regime subsisting in this country under which liability for defective products is enforced is examined in detail below. Suffice to say at this juncture that where a competent authority such as the Medical Devices Agency is established with the specific objective of "ensuring that medical devices meet appropriate standards of safety, quality and performance and that they comply with the Directives of the European Union",[4] then it may be possible to find that the Agency itself, as well as a manufacturer of telemedical equipment, owes a duty of care to individual members of the public who are injured or killed as a result of the Agency's failure to carry out their statutory duty. In *Swanson* v *The Queen in Right of Canada*[5] the Federal Court of Appeal held that an agency charged with the regulation of the safety of commercial airliners was liable for negligently permitting an airline to continue unsafe practices. The agency had issued warnings to the airline in question but had failed to take any further enforcement proceedings to require compliance with safety standards.

# The principles of product liability

The basic principle of product liability is that a plaintiff has a cause of action for any detriment caused by a defective product in either contract or tort, depending on whether they are in a contractual relationship with the defendant(s) or whether the latter owes them a duty of care. In English law liability for damage caused by defective products is an amalgam of liability in contract, the tort of negligence and, more recently, statutory provisions. Hence, while the purchaser of a telemedicine system or the subscriber to a telemedical service will be owed a contractual duty, privity will usually exclude a patient from bringing a contractual claim.[6] The landmark case of *Donoghue* v *Stevenson*[7] established that in such circumstances a valid claim can be established independently of any contractual relationship, based on negligence in tort. Despite imposing a very high standard of care in some cases, the English courts have not followed the American example of imposing strict liability in tort for defective products. However, in the 1970s a number of law reform bodies recommended that strict liability for defective products should be introduced and now, following the enactment of the European Union Directive on liability for defective products[8] and its requirement of substantive legal harmonisation with the rest of Europe, the United Kingdom has a form of strict liability under the Consumer Protection Act 1987.

The manufacturer's duty was first expressed by Lord Atkin in the House of Lords in *Donoghue* v *Stevenson* thus:

> A manufacturer of products which he sells in such a form as to show that he intends them to reach the ultimate consumer in the form in which they left him, with no reasonable possibility of intermediate examination, and with the knowledge that the absence of reasonable care in the preparation or putting up of the products will result in injury to the consumer's life or property, owes a duty to the consumer to take that reasonable care.[9]

This duty of care in negligence imposed upon the manufacturers of defective products to the "ultimate consumer" of the product has since been given a broad interpretation. "Products" are not limited to food and drink, but include any item capable of causing damage.[10] Moreover, the "ultimate consumer" will be anyone foreseeably harmed by the defective product, including the user of the product or an employee of the purchaser, someone who handles the product or even a bystander.[11] The range of potential defendants is also wide and includes not only manufacturers but also repairers and assemblers.[12]

Although a supplier of goods, such as a retailer or wholesaler, may be liable if he could reasonably have been expected to inspect or test goods, this duty will not arise in all circumstances. In situations where goods are obtained from "dodgy" suppliers then they ought, of course, to be tested. This would also be the case where the manufacturers themselves recommend that the product be tested.[13] But the mere opportunity for inspection of a product after it has left the hands of the manufacturer will not exculpate that manufacturer.[14] He will be liable even if the possibility of an intermediate examination is not within his contemplation. But if he has given a warning, for example, to test the product before use, this may be sufficient to discharge his duty.[15] So it will be a question of fact in every case whether or not a hospital or NHS trust should insist upon telemedical equipment being carefully tested or examined before use in order to ensure that no harm will occur to the telepatient.[16]

Although it has been held by the courts that where a plaintiff is aware of the danger associated with a product and ignores it the manufacturer cannot then be found liable,[17] a manufacturer who has created a dangerous situation would not be excused merely because someone else has failed to remove the danger. Hence if both a manufacturer and the user are at fault then both will be held responsible and in the case of a negligent failure to inspect or test the product by an intermediary this could be achieved by apportioning liability between the manufacturer and the intermediary under the Civil Liability (Contribution) Act 1978.

However, an explicit and reasonable instruction by a manufacturer that an intermediary should inspect the product will usually discharge their duty. If the end-user misuses a telemedical system in an unforeseeable fashion the architects of the system will not be liable. This is not because of contributory negligence or causation, but because the manufacturer is responsible only for dangers arising from a product's contemplated use. If a fault occurs due to its misuse, a telemedical system cannot be said to be "defective", so there is no breach of duty.[18]

Warnings by the defendant are sometimes treated as part and parcel of the question of intermediate examination but this is not necessarily the case. For example, a warning as to the correct wiring contained in the instructions for installation and use of a telemedicine terminal would not be giving the consumer the opportunity to "examine" the appliance for a defect. The telemedicine terminal is not "defective"; rather it must be used (i.e. wired) in a particular way. An omission to provide proper instructions for use may be negligent, but conversely an adequate "warning" may discharge the manufacturer's duty of care. Similarly, a warning that in its existing condition a product is unsafe may be sufficient to discharge the duty. The standard of care required in each and every case will be whatever is a reasonable degree of care to take in the circumstances.

It is not necessary that a warning be addressed directly to the telepatient where the equipment with which he or she is issued is meant to be used under the supervision of a teleconsultant, general practitioner or nurse. A warning given to the health care professional responsible for supervising the telepatient will be adequate.[19]

## Design defects

If an item of telemedical equipment conforms to its manufacturer's specifications yet, during ordinary use in the manner for which it was intended, causes injury to a telepatient or operator, then the equipment may be intrinsically unsafe. Applying the dicta of Mr Justice Rees in *Vacwell Engineering* v *BDH Chemicals*,[20] it will be the duty of a designer and manufacturer of telemedical equipment to establish and maintain a system under which adequate investigation and research into the scientific literature takes place in order to discover, inter alia, what hazards are known.

Although it seems obvious that manufacturers ought to shoulder a responsibility to exercise reasonable care in the design of a new product, Michael Jones[21] observes that "the courts are generally reluctant...to impose liability for negligent design". This is because for a manufacturer to be liable for a defect it must be one which was foreseeable at the time of the product's design and manufacturing in the light of the extent of existing scientific and technical knowledge.

Indeed, one important question that may arise in connection with the mass production and installation of telemedicine terminals in ocean-going vessels and clinics in remote areas is that of the liability of the manufacturers for what, in some countries, are described as "development defects" or "development risks" by which is meant defects which were impossible to foresee when the product was put into circulation, due to the current level of scientific and technical knowledge. While the European Union Directive on liability for defective products was in its preparatory stages, agreement could not be reached on whether damage due to such defects should be subject to strict liability. Opponents feared that the inclusion of development defects would hamper development and impair the world market competitiveness of European companies engaged in active research into projects such as NIVEMES, MERMAID and HERMES and that, moreover, the costs of insurance cover of this particular risk would be unreasonably high. Supporters found that adequate consumer protection would naturally also include strict liability for development defects. The result was a compromise, expressed in Article 7(e) and Article 15(1)(b), whereby the producer is exempt from liability according to the Directive if he can document that the damage could not be foreseen. However, Member States can uphold, or according to a more detailed procedure introduce liability for development defects under the Directive's strict liability. Furthermore, ten years after the date of notification of the Directive, EU institutions will submit a report on rulings concerning development defects in individual countries for the purpose of repeal of this liability exclusion.

This "development risks defence" has been incorporated into English law by section 4(1)(e) of the Consumer Protection Act 1987, but would not be available to the architects of a telemedical system who had failed to keep up to date with medical and scientific discoveries in health care telematics.[22] Simply operating "at the frontiers of human knowledge" was held, in *IBA v EMI Electronics and BICC Construction*[23] to be insufficient to exculpate the designers of a unique piece of telecommunications hardware, even though the device was the very first of its kind.[24]

Lord Edmund Davies, in the *IBA* case, concluded that "the law requires pioneers to be prudent"[25] and this would be an important message for the ambitious members of the health care telematics community who are impatient to see state-of-the-art telemedical equipment up and running in hospitals, surgeries and clinics throughout the United Kingdom as soon as possible. Although the courts would be reluctant to use the wisdom of hindsight to find the architects of a telemedicine system liable in negligence for harm caused by the system that was not reasonably foreseeable during the research and development phase, this certainly should not be taken as an implied licence to push ahead with development of such a system without a comprehensive evaluation of the risks involved. The risks acceptable in using telemedical equipment will always be dependent upon what a reasonable person would consider acceptable and provided that the risk – benefit ratio is a low one, it is unlikely that negligence will be imputed if and when things do go badly wrong.

### Continuing duty

Liability in the tort of negligence depends upon the reasonable foreseeability of an injury – if at the time that a telemedicine system is put on the market a design defect in the system is unknown, the manufacturers will not be liable for any detrimental consequences for telepatients or consultants arising from the defect. However, if over a period of time it becomes apparent that there is an inherent risk involved in using the equipment then it would clearly be culpably negligent to continue to manufacture, distribute and use the same unmodified version, or at least to do so without attaching an explicit warning.[26]

If a certain type or model of telemedical terminal or such like is already in circulation when the defect is discovered, the manufacturer must take reasonable steps either to warn users of the danger or to recall and replace the defective models.[27] In *Hobbs (Farms) Limited* v *Baxenden Chemical Company Limited*[28] it was stated:

> A manufacturer's duty of care does not end when the goods are sold. A manufacturer who realises that omitting to warn past customers about something which might result in injury to them must take reasonable steps to attempt to warn them, however lacking in negligence he may have been at the time the goods were sold.[29]

This will require the manufacturers of telemedicine equipment and peripherals to keep abreast of scientific developments concerning the safety of their products and to have an effective system for recalling unsafe products. Negligence in implementing the recall procedure may itself be actionable.[30]

## The burden of proof

While the burden of proving negligence rests upon a plaintiff, it is clear that where a defect has arisen in the course of construction it will be virtually impossible for a plaintiff to show by affirmative evidence what went wrong. This difficulty has, however, been recognised. The plaintiff is hence not required to lay his finger on the exact person in a chain of producers who was responsible or to specify what he did wrong. Negligence is found as a matter of inference from the existence of the defects taken in connection with all the known circumstances.[31] Hence if telemedical equipment was defective in its construction and this led to a technical failure during an emergency, the plaintiff end-user in an action against the manufacturers of the equipment could establish negligence by proving the existence of the defect and that this was probably not the result of events that occurred after the product left the manufacturer's possession.[32] By showing how the defect occurred and showing that this was not due to lack of care on their part, the manufacturers may be able to rebut the presumption that any defect in a telemedical system has occurred through their negligence, but this may be difficult. It is both legally and semantically logical that the more indelible the evidence that their manufacturing system is "foolproof", the stronger will be the inference that any defect arose because of the negligence of one of the manufacturer's employees (the so called "human factor"), for whose negligence they may be held vicariously liable.

An end-user who suffers harm from a technical fault with a telemedical system will have greater difficulty in proving negligence where the product is defective in design rather than construction. It is easier to demonstrate that a product was defective if it does not meet the manufacturer's own standards because something has gone wrong during construction or production. Where, however, a product performs as it was designed and intended there is no obvious standard against which to compare it.

Where the designer and manufacturer of telemedical equipment has complied with recognised industry standards this will be useful evidence that they have taken reasonable care and no liability will accrue. But the design may (perish the thought!) be the result of a conscious compromise between cost and safety. Although design defects can be negligent, courts are reluctant to hold defendants liable in such cases.

## Statute law

The stimulus for reform of product liability legislation in the United Kingdom came from European, rather than domestic law. The Strasbourg Convention on Product Liability in regard to Personal Injury and Death 1977, and two draft European Union Directives led finally to the EU Directive on Liability for Defective Products (85/374/EEC) which required Member States to implement its terms within three years. This was accomplished in the United Kingdom by Part I of the Consumer Protection Act 1987 which came into force on 1 March 1988 and applies to damage caused by products which were put into circulation by the producer after that date.[33] The new United Kingdom regulations bringing into force the European Union Directives on medical devices will be enforceable by the Secretary of State as safety regulations under the 1987 Act.

# European law and telemedical equipment

In the Member States of the European Union a great deal of harmonisation of product liability law has been made possible by the European Council Directive on the approximation of the laws, regulations and administrative provisions of the Member States concerning liability for defective products.[34] Over recent years there has also been an increasing tendency, particularly in the United States, to certify medical devices such as telemedical terminals in particular relation to their safety. The Federal Safe Medical Devices Act 1990 (amended in 1992) aimed to improve the regulation of medical devices and provide US-wide standards for equipment, personnel, quality assurance and control, reporting and record keeping.

Similar actions were undertaken in the EU with the enactment of EU Directive 93/42/EEC relating to medical devices.[35] The legal basis of this Directive is Article 100A of the European Union Treaty which stipulates that measures should be adopted for the:

> Approximation of the provisions laid down by law, regulation or administrative action in Member States which have as their objective the establishment and functioning of the internal market.

Such harmonisation guarantees the free movement of medical devices such as telemedicine systems within the internal market. However, because, according to Article 2 of the European Union's Directive on product liability, the definition of "product" is restricted to "movables",[36] liability under the EU Directive as respects telemedical equipment will be restricted to tangible and technical components that may be defective. The move from voluntary controls over some medical devices sold and used in the United Kingdom to a system of mandatory regulation by the Medical Devices Agency will be complete by 13 June 1998 and will require the manufacturers of telemedicine equipment to meet significant new statutory requirements before marketing their products. From this date all devices placed on the market in the United Kingdom, apart from devices intended for clinical investigation and custom-made devices, must carry the "CE" mark.

## The European Union Directive on defective products

Article 6 of the EU Directive stipulates that:

> A product is defective when it does not provide the safety which a person is entitled to expect.[37]

Article 1 of the Directive states that producers are strictly liable for damage caused by a defect in their products. The basis of liability is thus irrespective of any fault on the part of the manufacturer. Historically, such strict liability has not been found to be an unreasonable burden on the producer since manufacturing costs will naturally include the expected costs of damages or insurance premiums, so that in reality all the users of a telemedicine system would bear a proportion of the costs. The rationale for this approach, as touched upon above, is the heavy burden of proving culpability that would rest upon a claimant who does not have any technical or scientific knowledge of how telemedicine works. Article 1 also states the four conditions that must be fulfilled before liability in damages arise. There must be:

(a)   a producer,[38]
(b)   damage,[39]
(c)   a defect,[40] and
(d)   a product.[41]

The products covered by the Directive are defined in Article 2 and are solely industrially manufactured moveables which include not only finished products such as a telemedicine system but component products incorporated into such a system. The distinction vis-à-vis services and products is not clear, however, and no guidelines are provided in the Directive. According to Article 1, liability rests on the "producer" and Articles 3(1) to (3) define exactly what is meant by this. The manufacturer of a finished product such as a telemedicine terminal is its producer. It is he who has put the potentially defective product into circulation and therefore he who has the best possible knowledge of whether the final product is hazardous. Hence he will be liable for foreseeable damage incurred as a consequence of a defect in any component of the product. The producer of any raw materials or components going into the telemedicine equipment will also be liable for damage caused by a defect in those materials or components. The "producer" definition also includes any person who, by putting his name, trademark or other distinguishing feature on the product, presents himself as its producer. According to Article 3(2) any person who imports into the European Community a product for any form of distribution in the course of his business is deemed to be a producer.

Article 5(3) states that a product liability action can be brought at the place where the damage has taken place.[42] If several persons are liable for the same damage, their liability is joint and several, according to Article 5. Article 6 states that a product is defective when it does not provide the safety which can be reasonably expected. The defect can thus be due to a property of the product which it could reasonably and objectively be expected *not* to have, as well as a property which the product lacks but which it should reasonably and objectively be *expected* to have. There is an obligation for the producer(s) of a telemedicine system to state any known risks related to the product. Although the producer won't be liable for damage due to an individual user's subjective susceptibility towards objectively non-hazardous properties, the product can, however, be considered to be defective if the producer has omitted to state such known risks.

Article 12 of the EU Directive prevents the limitation or exclusion of liability by the use of general waivers worded as warnings, although concrete reservations to the effect that the product cannot, for example, be used by persons with certain diseases will probably imply exemption from liability. In Article 6(1) it is stated that an evaluation of whether a product is defective must take place at the time when the product is put into circulation. This means that the safety standards at the time of the launch of the telemedicine system will apply and the fact that safety norms might subsequently be tightened, or better production methods be discovered, does not necessarily imply that the producer of a telemedicine system must revoke all older models. In due course, therefore, the end-user will not always be able to demand the same safety standards of older telemedicine terminals as in the case of the newest ones. Moreover, according to Article 7(b) the producer is exempt from liability if the defect did not exist at the time when the product was put into circulation. The fact that a terminal may in time become worn out and hence not provide the same level of safety or reliability as a brand new terminal does not necessarily imply that it will be considered defective under the terms of the European Union Directive.

Under Article 9 the damage which is covered by the Directive comprises personal injury (including death) and consumer property damage. Compensation for death includes financial claims from the survivors, usually spouse and children. Compensation for personal injury also comprises the costs of medical treatment and recovery and compensation for loss of earnings. However, the Directive does not regulate compensation for non-financial losses such as pain and suffering, which is regulated by the domestic compensation laws of the forum in which an action is brought, and there has been *no* harmonisation of the method of quantifying damages in the different EU Member States. Hence major discrepancies exist between the amounts paid for similar injuries in neighbouring countries. Article 9 also sets out the limited circumstances in which damage to property can be recovered – the damaged property must be an article mainly for private use or consumption. Since a number of items are used in business as well as privately it may often be difficult to distinguish between the two.

## *Exclusion and limitation of liability*

Article 7 states the grounds on which the producer(s) of a telemedicine system may be exempt from liability for damage caused by a defect in the system or a component part of the system. In all cases, though, the producer will be obliged to document that his case fulfils the grounds for liability exemption:

**Article 7**

The producer shall not be liable as a result of this Directive if he proves:—

(a) that he did not put the product into circulation; or

(b) that, having regard to the circumstances, it is probable that the defect which caused the damage did not exist at the time when the product was put into circulation by him or that this defect came into being afterwards; or

(c) that the product was neither manufactured by him for sale or any form of distribution for economic purpose nor manufactured or distributed by him in the course of his business; or

(d) that the defect is due to compliance of the product with mandatory regulations issued by the public authorities; or

(e) that the state of scientific and technical knowledge at the time when he put the product into circulation was not such as to enable the existence of the defect to be discovered; or

(f) in the case of a manufacturer of a component, that the defect is attributable to the design of the product in which the component has been fitted or to the instructions given by the manufacturer of the product.

What will determine whether the component manufacturer will be able to invoke this final provision is presumably the extent to which he could have influenced the design of the component product and his freedom to select certain technical methods in manufacturing. According to Article 8(2) the injured party's own fault can be considered so that the compensation can be reduced or lapse completely if the telepatient himself contributed to the damage by his own negligence, although in the context of telemedical consultation or treatment it is difficult to envisage circumstances where this might occur. Liability is subject to a general limitation period of three years after the injured party gained, or should have gained, knowledge of the damage, the defect and the producer's identity. Article 11 provides for an absolute limitation period of ten years after the product has been put into circulation. The rationale for such a rule is that, since a product such as a telemedicine terminal is subject to wear and tear over a period of time, it becomes increasingly difficult to determine whether the defect existed at the time the product was put into circulation.

Finally, Article 16 provides that a Member State can provide a total maximum limit for product liability of 70 million ECUs (£56 million) for damage resulting from the same defect in identical terminals, since insurance cover would otherwise be prohibitive – though this must be balanced against the need to ensure that the victims of a large-scale product liability catastrophe are not cheated out of proper compensation. Arguably, however, the maximum limit of 70 million ECUs is high enough to function, in practice, as an unlimited liability.

### The EU Directive and product standards
The EU Directive is linked to the consequences of products not performing in the manner which could be expected by the purchaser. Yet there is no relationship stated to exist between liability and the fact that, in the case of products such as a telemedicine system, product performance will be defined in a published technical specification which may be a legally recognised national product standard. To create such a relationship, however, would be to place enormous legal weight upon the technical requirements which are set down in such product standards – and which are the results of considerable compromise between the interested parties (manufacturers, users and law makers) made possible between producer and consumer where most product standards are intended for voluntary use.

Although the European Union Directive does not expressly state that the manufacturer of an item of telemedical equipment will be immune from legal liability for defects in that product where it conforms to the technical specifications set down in a product standard, meeting such a standard (e.g. a BSI standard) will provide convincing evidence that the manufacturer has exercised all due diligence to make the product safe. In such circumstances, a finding of negligence would be near impossible. This reference to standards is supported by parallel EU legislation for the single market where a large range of products are subject to removal of technical trade barriers by Directives which harmonise the essential requirements products must meet to allow free trade between EU Member States. These Directives have been drafted with reference to requirements contained in harmonised European Standards – which are published in each Member State as national standards replacing any previous standards for the products. Thus the essential requirements set down in legislation in general terms by the Directives are defined in specific detail in national standards containing uniform requirements throughout the European Union.

## The EU medical devices Directives

A series of three Directives regulating the safety and marketing of medical devices throughout the European Union started to come into effect from 1 January 1993. For the purposes of the Directives a medical device is defined as:

> Any instrument, apparatus, appliance, material or other article, whether used alone or in combination, including the software necessary for its proper application intended by the manufacturer to be used for human beings for the purpose of:
> ▶ diagnosis, prevention, monitoring, treatment or alleviation of disease;
> ▶ diagnosis, monitoring, treatment or alleviation of or compensation for an injury or handicap;
> ▶ investigation, replacement or modification of the anatomy or of a physiological process;
> ▶ control of conception;
> and which does not achieve its principal intended action in or on the human body by pharmacological, immunological or metabolic means, but which may be assisted in its function by such means.

Prior to the coming into force of the three Directives, each Member State of the European Union controlled the safety and marketing of its medical devices in different ways. The Directives benefit manufacturers by harmonising these controls within a single system instead of requiring them to comply with fifteen different sets of rules. NHS trusts and health authorities can therefore be assured that telemedical equipment manufactured elsewhere in the European Union meets the same standards as regards safety and performance as equipment manufactured in the United Kingdom.

### Active implantable medical devices

The first Directive on medical devices is the active implantable medical devices Directive (90/385/EEC) which covers all powered implants or partial implants that are left in the human body. Heart pacemakers are the most common example of powered implants – about 10,000 are implanted into British patients each year. The Directive was adopted by the European Council on 20 June 1990 and was implemented into English law by the Active Implantable Medical Devices Regulations 1992 (SI 1992 No. 3146) on 1 January 1993. These regulations were amended in 1995 to incorporate the effect of the CE Marking Directive (see SI 1995 No. 1671).

### Medical devices

The second Directive on medical devices will cover most other medical devices from first-aid bandages to hip prostheses. A common position on the Directive was reached by the Council of Ministers on 8 February 1993; it was adopted on 12 July 1993 and entered into force on 1 January 1995 (93/42/EEC). The transitional period during which manufacturers have the choice either to follow the current national controls in force as at 31 December 1994 or to follow the regulatory system established by the Directive will run out on 13 June 1998. The United Kingdom Regulations implementing the Directive were published on 28 November 1994 (see SI 1994 No. 3017).

### In-vitro diagnostic medical devices

The third Directive on in-vitro diagnostic medical devices covers any medical device, reagent, reagent product, kit, instrument, apparatus or system which is intended to be used in-vitro for the examination of substances derived from the human body such as blood grouping reagents, pregnancy testing kits and Hepatitis B test kits and came into force in 1997.

## The "CE" mark and quality management systems

Related to these harmonising Directives is the introduction of the "CE" mark. Once the three European Directives on medical devices are fully implemented, medical devices offered for sale and general use anywhere in the European Union will have to have a "CE" mark[43] which is a statement that the device conforms to the essential requirements concerning safety, quality and performance laid down in the Directives. These requirements vary according to the complexity of the product. Devices are assigned to one of four classes: Class I for low-risk devices, Classes IIa and IIb for medium-risk devices and Class III for high-risk devices.

In Class I the manufacturer declares conformity with the provisions of the Directive, including compliance of the product with all the relevant essential requirements – hence he is legally required to meet those requirements. For Class IIa products this conformity must be supported in all cases with conformity assessment by a Notified Body appointed by the MDA (this will also be required of Class I products where sterility or metrology is an aspect of their manufacture). This assessment may, at the manufacturer's choice, consist of audit of the production quality assurance system, audit of the final inspection and testing or the examination and testing of sample products. Alternatively, the manufacturer could submit the product for an audit of the full quality assurance system or type-testing plus some form of production audit or sample examination that is the requirement for Class IIb products. The Class III controls are equivalent to the controls required under the active implantable medical devices Directive. They are the strictest of all and require the submission of a design dossier as well as submission to all the tests carried out by the Notified Body for a Class IIb product.[44]

Annex IX of the Medical Devices Directive sets out the classification criteria for medical devices. *Prima facie*, most telemedical equipment might be thought to fall within Class I and hence not be subject to conformity assessment since Rule 1 of Annex IX places any non-invasive product in Class I, provided that the other rules do not apply. But active therapeutic devices which administer or exchange energy and active diagnostic devices which supply energy (other than for illumination) which is absorbed by the body or used to monitor a physiological process will fall into Class IIa or – if they are potentially hazardous or intended for critical situations – Class IIb. Moreover, devices which are invasive with regard to body orifices (i.e. not surgically invasive) will always be in Class IIa if they are intended for connection to an active device, regardless of the duration of their continuous use and the degree to which they are inserted in the body. Radiological equipment will generally be in Class IIb.[45]

Hence an important factor in any assessment of a telemedicine system's conformity will be the quality assurance systems provided by the hardware manufacturers during production. These systems are subject to audit by the competent authority such as the MDA and must comply with a series of harmonised standards in the ISO 9000/EN 29000 and EN 46000 series. The ISO 9000/EN 29000 series specifies the components needed in order to set up and manage quality management systems for business. The EN 46000 series defines particular requirements for quality systems relating specifically to medical devices. It embraces all the principles of quality systems management widely used in the manufacture of such devices. It is also supported by other harmonised standards covering such aspects as sterilisation. It can only be used in combination with the ISO 9000/EN 29000 series of standards. These quality system standards are now well established worldwide and in many countries manufacturers are already operating management systems as defined in the requirements of one of the variants ISO 9001/EN 29001, ISO 9002/EN 29002, ISO 9003/EN 29003 and ISO 9004/EN 29004. While there is no evidence at present of a clear link between the operation of a fully registered ISO 9000 quality system and the avoidance of legal liability, the implementation of good practice generally cannot fail to provide significant protection in product liability cases.

## Summary

▶ Responsibility for ensuring that appropriate standards of safety, quality and performance (set by the European Union) are met by telemedicine equipment rests with the Medical Devices Agency (MDA), an executive agency of the Department of Health.

▶ NHS Trusts, health authorities and other telemedicine providers are required to co-operate fully with the MDA in investigating and remedying faulty or dangerous telemedical equipment and in ensuring, through the vigilance system, that accidents involving such equipment are never repeated.

▶ The manufacturer, supplier, retailer and servicer of faulty telemedical equipment which causes harm to a telepatient or user may be liable in damages to the injured party in the law of contract or tort or under Part I of the Consumer Protection Act 1987 (which enacts the EU Directive on product liability) since they will owe a duty of care wherever there is a reasonably foreseeable risk of harm occurring due to their negligence.

▶ The EU Product Safety Directive provides for a general duty to supply safe products (see also Consumer Protection Act 1987, Part II) which will apply to *all* products associated with telemedicine, even outside of the medical devices rules.

▶ Simply operating at the frontiers of human knowledge is insufficient to exculpate the designers and manufacturers of inherently unsafe telemedical equipment from liability.

▶ With very few exceptions all telemedical equipment will, by 13 July 1998, be subject to assessment by a Notified Body appointed by the MDA to ensure conformity with the essential requirements laid down in the relevant European Union Directives. Only devices satisfying such assessment will be awarded the "CE" mark that is a prerequisite for sales in the common market and other European countries.

# References

1    The Medical Devices Agency defines an "adverse incident" as "a hazardous or potentially hazardous occurrence involving medical devices, which have harmed patients, end-users or professional users, or put them at risk". See further MDA. *Medical device and equipment management for hospital and community-based organisations*. January 1998.

2    Medical Devices Agency. *Framework document*. 5 September 1994 at p. 8.

3    Medical Devices Agency. *Medical device and equipment management for hospital and community-based organisations*. January 1998.

4    Medical Devices Agency. *Safeguarding public health*. July 1995.

5    (1991) 80 DLR (4th) 741 (Federal Court of Appeal).

6    Likewise a shipowner or a clinic in a remote area and not its patients will be in a contractual relationship with the supplier of a faulty telemedicine terminal. Though in respect of United Kingdom law see Law Commission Paper No. 242, 1996, *Privity of Contract: Contracts for the Benefit of Third Parties*. See also *Beswick* v *Beswick* [1968] AC 58; *Jackson* v *Horizon Holidays Limited* [1975] 2 All ER 92; *Woodar Investment Development Limited* v *Wimpey Construction (UK) Limited* [1980] 1 All ER 571. Where there is a contractual relationship, however, the terms implied into contracts for the sale and supply of goods and services by the Sale of Goods Act 1979 (as amended) and the Supply of Goods and Services Act 1982 may have been breached. These include terms as to title to sell, description, satisfactory quality and fitness for purpose that are implied into every contract for the sale of goods (though not their hire) and terms relating to the supplier's duty to perform a service with reasonable care and skill, to perform the service within a reasonable time and to charge no more than a reasonable amount.

7    [1932] AC 562.

8    Council Directive 85/374/EEC on the approximation of the laws, regulations and administrative provisions of the Member States concerning liability for defective products, O.J. L210/29 of 7 August 1985.

9    Ibid., at p. 599.

10   Including, inter alia, underpants in *Grant* v *Australian Knitting Mills Limited* [1936] AC 85; motor cars in *Herschtal* v *Stewart & Arden Limited* [1940] 1 KB 155; hair dye in *Watson* v *Buckley, Osborne Garrett & Co. Limited* [1940] 1 All ER 174; lifts in *Haseldine* v *C.A. Daw & Son Limited* [1941] 2 KB 343 and chemicals in *Vacwell Engineering Company Limited* v *BDH Chemicals Limited* [1971] 1 QB 88.

11   *Davie* v *New Merton Board Mills Limited* [1959] AC 604; *Barnett* v *H and J Paker & Co Limited* [1940] 3 All ER 575; *Stennett* v *Hancock* [1939] 2 All ER 578. See also the Employers' Liability (Defective Equipment) Act 1969.

12   *Stennett* v *Hancock; Haseldine* v *C.A. Daw & Son Limited*; *Howard* v *Furness Houlder Argentine Lines Limited* [1936] 2 All ER 781.

13   *Kubach* v *Hollands* [1937] 3 All ER 907; *Watson* v *Buckley, Osborne Garrett & Co* [1940] 1 All ER 174; *Andrews* v *Hopkinson* [1957] 1 QB 229; *Hurley* v *Dyke* [1979] RTR 265.

14   *Herschtal* v *Stewart & Arden Limited* [1940] 1 KB 155; *Griffiths* v *Arch Engineering Co Ltd* [1968] 3 All ER 217.

15   *Haseldine* v *CA Daw & Son Limited* [1941] 2 KB 343; *Holmes* v *Ashford* [1950] 2 All ER 76.

16   *Gallagher* v *N McDowell Ltd* [1961] N I 26, 42. In *Aswan Engineering Establishment Co* v *Lupdine Limited* [1987] 1 All ER 135 it was held that there was no independent requirement for the plaintiff to show that there was no reasonable possibility of intermediate examination. Rather, this was merely a factor, albeit an important one, which a court should consider in determining whether or not the damage sustained was reasonably foreseeable (per Lloyd LJ at pp. 153-4). In *Holmes* v *Ashford* [1950] 2 All ER 76 hair dye manufacturers were exculpated from liability to a customer where the hairdresser failed to follow the manufacturers instructions to test the product prior to use and in *Kubach* v *Hollands* [1937] 3 All ER 907 the manufacturer of a chemical was held not to be liable to a schoolgirl who was injured in an explosion, having warned the retailer to examine and test the chemical before use. The retailer neither tested the chemical nor warned the teacher who bought it to do so.

17   *Farr* v *Butters Bros & Co* [1932] 2 KB 606.

18   *Aswan Engineering Establishment Co* v *Lupdine Ltd* [1987] 1 All ER 135; *Good-Wear Treaders Ltd* v *D & B Holdings Ltd* (1979) 98 DLR (3d) 59.

19   *Holmes* v *Ashford* [1950] 2 All ER 76; *Kubach* v *Hollands* [1937] 3 All ER 907.

20   [1971] 1 QB 88 at p. 99.

21   Jones MA. *Medical Negligence*. London: Sweet & Maxwell, 1991: 302.

22   *Strokes* v *Guest, Keen & Nettlefold (Bolts & Nuts) Ltd* [1968] 1 WLR 1776 at p. 1783; *Cartwright* v *GKN Sankey Ltd* [1972] 2 Lloyd's Rep 242 at p. 259 and *Bolam* v *Friern Hospital Management Committee* [1957] 2 All ER 118 at p. 122.

23  *Independent Broadcasting Authority* v *EMI Electronics Limited and BICC Construction Limited* (1980) 14 Build LR 1.

24  Ibid., at p. 31 where Lord Edmund-Davies stated that it was "no answer simply to say 'it wasn't obvious because it hadn't been considered'. The learned trial judge held that it should have been, and in my judgement he was right in saying so."

25  Ibid., at p. 28.

26  *Wright* v *Dunlop Rubber Co. Limited* (1972) 13 K I R 255.

27  *Walton* v *British Leyland UK Limited* (1978) unreported, cited in Miller, *Product Liability and Safety Encyclopaedia*, Div. III, para. 43.1; *Rivtow Marine Limited* v *Washington Iron Works* (1973) 40 DLR (3d) 530; *Buchan* v *Ortho Pharmaceuticals (Canada) Limited* (1986) 25 DLR (4th) 658, 678.

28  [1992] 1 Lloyd's Rep. 54.

29  Ibid., at p. 62.

30  *Nicholson* v *John Deere Limited* (1986) 34 DLR (4th) 542; *McCain Foods Limited* v *Grand Falls Industries Limited* (1991) 80 DLR (4th) 252.

31  See the dicta of Lord Wright in *Grant* v *Australian Knitting Mills Limited* [1936] AC 85 at p. 101: "[The manufacturing] process was intended to be foolproof. If excess sulphites were left in the garment, that could only be because someone was at fault. The appellant is not required to lay his finger on the exact person in all the chain who was responsible or to specify what he did wrong. Negligence is found as a matter of inference from the existence of the defects taken in connection with all the known circumstances."

32  *Mason* v *Williams & Williams Ltd* [1955] 1 WLR 549.

33  SI 1987/No. 1680 and of the Consumer Protection Act 1987, s. 50(7).

34  Although the Directive does not intend to bring about full harmonisation. What the Directive achieves under Article 13 is to extend or supplement the individual Member States' product liability laws so that the Member States' laws remain in force without change. Gradual but more extensive harmonisation is, however, intended according to the preamble to the Directive.

35  OJ L169/1 of 12 July 1993.

36  Council Directive 85/374/EEC on the approximation of the laws, regulations and administrative provisions of the Member States concerning liability for defective products, O.J. L210/29 of 7 August 1985.

37  OJ L210/29 of 7 August 1985 at p. 31.

38  Article 3.

39  Article 9.

40  Article 6.

41  Article 2.

42  Jurisdictional issues are discussed in detail in chapter 9.

43  The "CE" marking is an indication that the products carrying it satisfy all the relevant essential requirements of the appropriate Directive and can therefore be put on sale anywhere in the Union. The initials "CE" stand for the European Community.

44  A "Notified Body" is a certification organisation which a competent authority, such as the MDA in this country, designates to carry out one or more of the conformity assessment procedures described in the annexes of the European Union's medical devices Directives. The selection criteria contained in the Directives are intended to ensure the impartiality and expertise of prospective Notified Bodies. Indeed, after a Notified Body has been appointed that Body may itself be audited by the MDA to ensure the expected criteria are being met and its status may be withdrawn if they aren't. The active implantable medical devices Directive has designated the British Standards Institution as the Notified Body for the purpose of carrying out conformity assessments under that Directive.

45  See Rules 1–18, Annex IX, European Union Directive on Medical Devices (93/42/EEC) in OJ 12 July 1993 (L169).

# ▶8

# Intellectual property rights and competition law

Intellectual property is a very broad term which describes the commercial value and goodwill associated with literary and artistic works, as well as computer software, inventions, distinctive trade marks and designs. Some lawyers like to distinguish between rights granted to facilitate and reward innovation or creativity and rights granted to protect reputation. The granting of a 20-year monopoly to a person or corporation registering a patent, a 50-year monopoly in copyright or a 15-year monopoly in designs, are examples of the former, while the trade mark system and common law action for passing-off are examples of the latter. Intellectual property in telemedicine equipment exists in both these senses.

But the protection of intellectual property rights in the United Kingdom and the European Community is a complicated area where two principles – the desire to encourage the creation of new inventions and the desire to discourage the monopolisation of a unified single market – regularly come into conflict. Nowhere is this tension more evident than in the complex web of legislation and case law that surrounds intellectual property rights, competition law and the sometimes uneasy relationship between them. The aim of this chapter, therefore, is to provide a broad overview of the major provisions of domestic and European intellectual property and competition law of which the architects of telemedicine equipment and systems should be aware.

## Intellectual property and the European Union

The common market was established by the economic integration of independent European states with the aim of promoting trade competition without legal or financial barriers. Hence, within the European Union "parallel importing", that is the buying of telemedicine equipment in one cheap Member State and transporting it to a more expensive Member State for resale at a profit, is not possible, but the manufacturer of that equipment is allowed to price his products differently in different Member States and also to export his equipment to licensees or distributors in another Member State who will have a far more intimate knowledge of their local or national market. But that licensee or distributor might, themselves, desire the exclusive right to market the equipment in their own territory in order to protect their own investment. So although the division of markets within the European Union through the use of national barriers such as importation quotas and tariffs has been largely abolished by the common market, the EU does still recognise the commercial needs of businessmen to restrain imports of identical products to theirs from other suppliers in order to protect their prices.

In a common market in which a unified intellectual property regime for the entire European Union is envisaged, therefore, certain acts in relation to telemedicine equipment will require the permission of, or a licence from, the holder of the intellectual property rights: manufacture, first sale, resale, importing and exporting and, naturally, use. In a great many cases, however, a property right will expire or be "exhausted" after the first sale by the right-owner, or with his consent; often within the territory or territories, covered by the right. Hence the right is exhausted in the domestic rather than the international market and the exhaustion of a right in the United Kingdom will not prevent the manufacturer of telemedicine equipment from preventing the importation of goods he originally sold abroad, or which were manufactured and sold by a subsidiary of his.

The speed with which such uniformity is reached, though, is entirely at the mercy of political whims. Fully harmonised laws on patents and copyright are still a long way off, but the harmonisation of intellectual property rights that has taken place (for instance, by the creation of a Community Trade Mark) has been largely to prevent them from hindering the free movement of goods between European Union territories. The European Court of Justice and the European Commission have both interpreted provisions in the Treaty of Rome as limiting the extent of national intellectual property rights where these directly conflict with the ideas and philosophies behind the common market. The two principles which have been accorded primacy in this respect are:

(a)  the elimination of restrictions upon the free movement of goods between Member States (Articles 30–36 of the Treaty); and

(b)  the establishment of a system to prevent distortions of competition in inter-State trade (Articles 85–90 of the Treaty).

The principles of freedom to provide services and the right of establishment also have some potential for conflict with intellectual property.

## Free movement of goods

Intellectual property rights aimed at preventing the importing of goods into Member States have been held by the European Court of Justice to be measures of equivalent effect to quantitative restrictions on imports, prohibited by Article 30 of the Treaty of Rome. Unless justified by Article 36 therefore, which permits restrictions on imports if they are made on the grounds of the protection of industrial and commercial property (though not if they are simply arbitrary), the use of intellectual property law to stop the importing of telemedicine equipment into the United Kingdom from elsewhere in the common market will be contrary to EU competition law. Section 2(1) of the European Communities Act 1972 makes it clear that, since this country's accession to the European Economic Community, as it then was, the regulations and Directives of the European Commission and the decisions of the European Court of Justice are binding upon and take precedence over English law.

If all this seems somewhat complicated then perhaps the legal position is best summarised by stating that intellectual property rights in telemedical equipment, be they patents, copyright or trade marks, are only properly exercised when they are used against goods that come from independent competitors and not when used to prevent the free movement from Member State to Member State of telemedical equipment initially sold or licensed by that right owner. The rules on the free movement of goods do not have any application to goods being moved between Member States and non-members; i.e., countries outside of the European Union or the European Economic Area,[1] unless they have direct economic effects within the European Union.

## Competition laws

Article 85 of the Treaty of Rome deals with restrictive practices between enterprises and Article 86 with abuse by one or more firms of their monopolistic position; both principles are essential for the development of the common market in line with market forces. Article 86 declares any conduct which may affect trade between Member States and the object and effect of which is to prevent, restrict or distort competition within the common market to be automatically void unless economically justified. Even if so justified it may only be allowed to subsist for so long as is necessary to contribute to the improvement of the production or distribution of goods, or to technical or economic progress. Article 85 prevents the abuse of a dominant position vis-à-vis the common market that might detrimentally affect trade between the Member States.[2]

# Patents

The Patents Act 1977 has introduced important changes into a hitherto unsophisticated domestic legal regime – mostly designed to accommodate the United Kingdom's accession to several international patent conventions. Since 1 June 1978 it has hence been possible to secure a patent for this country through an application to the British Patent Office; through a bundle of patent applications to the European Patent Office in Munich in common form, of which one may be an application for a European patent; and through an international patent application initiated under the Patent Co-operation Treaty of 1970. In due course a single European Union Patent covering the whole of the Common Market will become available.[3]

Patent applications themselves must relate to an invention, although an invention as such could be a process or a manufactured item.[4] Where a patent is granted to a manufacturer or designer of telemedicine equipment, section 25 of the Act will grant a twenty-year monopoly for the exploitation of this equipment during which no other person or corporation may legally copy or otherwise exploit the unique or innovative ideas and applications contained in the patented equipment. The Patents Act 1977 adopts the European Patent Convention grounds of invalidity for United Kingdom patents whether granted by the British Patents Office or the European Office.

To qualify for the protection of the Patents Act 1977 the equipment will need to satisfy a number of conditions.

### (i) Novelty
Under section 2 of the Patents Act 1977 an invention will be treated as being new if its design has not been previously publicised or used in any way.

### (ii) Inventive step
Under section 3 of the Patents Act an invention must involve an "inventive step" which, so far as the industry is concerned "is not obvious to a person skilled in the art, having regard to any matter which forms part of the state of the art". The state of the art here is the same concept that operates in assessing novelty except that no account is taken of any prior specifications subsequently published.[5]

### (iii) Industrial application

Under section 4 of the Patents Act an invention must be capable of being used in industry (including agriculture). Telemedical equipment, in common with all forms of medical diagnosis or treatment, will not fulfil this criteria unless it is a substantive product. That is, mere methods of surgery, therapy or diagnosis will not suffice.

### (iv) Exclusions

Under sections 1(2) and (3) of the Patents Act a number of possible inventions are denied the protection of the Act, essentially to prevent the discovery of major scientific theories or arithmetical methods being unconscionably withheld from the public at large. Aesthetic creations also fall outside of the operation of the Act, being the reserve of copyright law. Any patent applications can, under this section, be refused on the grounds of public policy where, for instance, the publication or exploitation of the invention would "generally be expected to encourage offensive, immoral or anti-social behaviour".

## Infringing patents in telemedical equipment

In *Centraform* v *Sterling*[6] the European Court of Justice described the privileges which a patent gives in the "specific subject matter", that is to say, the particular kind of commercial or industrial property, such as a telemedicine terminal, for which protection is sought:

> As regards patents, the specific subject matter of the industrial property is the guarantee that the patentee, to reward the creative effort of the inventor, has the exclusive right to use an invention with a view to manufacturing industrial products and putting them into circulation for the first time, either directly or by the grant of licences to third parties, as well as the right to oppose infringements.

Section 60 of the Patent Act 1977 sets out the various acts that will amount to infringement of a patent for an invention such as telemedical equipment if done without the permission of the owner of the patent. A patent is infringed:

(a)  where the invention is a product, another person makes, disposes of, offers to dispose of, uses or imports the product or keeps it whether for disposal or otherwise;

(b)  where the invention is a process, another person uses the process or he offers it for use in the United Kingdom when he knows, or it is obvious to a reasonable person in the circumstances, that its use there without the consent of the proprietor would be an infringement of the patent; or

(c)  where the invention is a process, another person disposes of, offers to dispose of, uses or imports any product obtained directly by means of that process or keeps any such product whether for disposal or otherwise.[7]

A patent in telemedical equipment will also be infringed where another person supplies or offers to supply a non-licence holder or someone else not legally entitled to exploit the equipment with the means to put an essential element of that equipment into effect in the United Kingdom without the permission of the patent's owner, while the patent is still in force.[8] Section 60(5) provides for six exceptions from liability. An act which would otherwise be an infringement of a patent will not be so if, inter alia:

(a)  it is done privately and for non-commercial purposes;

(b)  it is done for experimental purposes relating to telemedicine; or

(c)  it consists of a "spur of the moment" preparation in a pharmacy of a prescription medicine.

Cornish identifies two types of potential patent infringer: a company which through sheer ignorance copies the patentee's own product and the company which, by independent effort tries to find a way round the patent but produces something which is still fairly similar to the patented invention.[9] The precise scope of the claims in the patent specification will therefore be crucial for a manufacturer of telemedical equipment trying to establish whether or not a rival manufacturer can be prevented from manufacturing and selling equipment that they believe infringes their patent.

Within a patent specification "claims" – most often in the form of words but occasionally described with mathematical and chemical symbols and references to drawings – are used to describe the "fence-posts" or the "boundary" that exists around a patent: to delimit the scope of the monopoly claimed. Activities falling within the area or close to it will thus require the patentee's consent, otherwise the patent will be infringed.[10] Drafting a patent specification is a complex art therefore. The draftsman must try to imagine all of the alternative forms for the inventive idea and describe all the possible variations as concisely as possible.

Cornish identifies four dangers that the draftsman of a patent for an item of telemedical equipment would have to deal with. First, specific versions of the invention not mentioned in the specification may be jumped upon by a competitor: a specific description of the item will avoid this. Secondly, the patentee will need to show the Patent Office that there is support in the description for the claims made – the broader the claim, the more support will be required in the description. Thirdly, if the equipment in question is an improvement of a known art as opposed to a completely new breakthrough, the advantage of the new development that gives it the "inventive character" required for it to be patented must be spelled out clearly. Finally, because there are strict limitations placed upon amending an application it is crucial to start with all the information in the description that may later be required.[11]

Hence a rival telemedical product that is similar to a patented product in that it contains all of the features specified in the patent claim but also includes some new features will infringe the patent, even if the new features make it more successful. However, a new product will not infringe a subsisting patent if one or more of the essential elements is left out or replaced with something different which does not fall within the patent specification. The danger for the bona fide inventor of telemedical equipment will always be the rival manufacturer whose products lurk around the very periphery of the claims in the former's patent specification without actually falling within them. Case law illustrates this problem well.

In *Van der Lely* v *Bamfords*[12] there was a claim for a mechanical hayrake whose rear rakewheels could be moved forward, parallel with the front rakewheels. This would enable it to cover wider areas of ground in some operations. The defendant's hayrake had front wheels which moved back, in parallel with the rear wheels producing exactly the same effect. The majority of the House of Lords held that no infringement was committed: the patentee had the opportunity to state all the characteristics of their invention at the time that the patent application was filed; had they wished to cover a mechanism such as the defendant's in their claim then they should have done so expressly.

In *Rodi & Wienenberger* v *Showell*[13] the patent for an expandable watch-strap required by the claim to have two layers of links connected with u-shaped bows was held not to have been infringed by the defendant's product which used two c-shaped bows on each side which essentially amounted to the same thing. By a narrow majority the House of Lords held that no infringement had taken place since some material change in function had been introduced. Though this decision should be viewed circumspectly because of the new approach adopted under the European Patents Convention discussed shortly.

Perhaps the most important dictum on this subject, however, is that of Lord Diplock in the House of Lords case of *Catnic Components Ltd* v *Hill & Smith Ltd*,[14] applied by His Honour, Mr Justice Hoffmann in *Improver Corporation* v *Remington Consumer Products Ltd*[15] (otherwise known as the *Epilady* case) where the inventors of the "Epilady" electric razor which removed body hair by opening and shutting a spring rapidly and hence trapping hairs and pulling them out, challenged the defendants whose "Smooth & Silky" electric razor was substantially similar. The defendants claimed that the "Epilady" used a helical spring whereas their razor used a rubber tube with a series of cuts instead of a spring. Mr Justice Hoffmann, using the test laid down by Lord Diplock, stated that the court must ask itself three questions:

(1) Does the variant have a material effect upon the way the invention works? If yes, the variant is outside the claim. If no—
(2) Would the fact that the variant had no material effect on the way the invention works have been obvious at the date of publication of the patent to a reader skilled in the art. If no, the variant it outside the claim. If yes—
(3) Would the reader skilled in the art nevertheless have understood from the language of the claim that the patentee intended that strict compliance with the primary meaning was an essential requirement of the invention. If yes, the variant is outside the claim.

Hence, reaching the third question, Mr Justice Hoffmann agreed with the defendants that a skilled reader would expect an electric razor, in order to fall within the specifications of the "Epilady", to utilise a spring, spun by an electric motor, to cut hairs rather than a rubber tube cutting almost from one side to the other, rather in the manner of a comb, and they were thus held not to have breached the plaintiff's patent. Interestingly, however, a German court came to the opposite conclusion on the same facts.

The approach of the English court appears, indeed, to be in direct conflict with that contained in Article 69 of the European Patents Convention which states:

**Article 69**
**Extent of Protection**
(1) The extent of the protection conferred by a European patent or a European patent application shall be determined by the terms of the claims. Nevertheless, the description and drawings shall be used to interpret the claims.
(2) For the period up to the grant of the European patent, the extent of the protection conferred by the European patent application shall be determined by the latest filed claims contained in the publication under Article 93. However, the European patent as granted or as amended on opposition proceedings shall determine retroactively the protection conferred by the European patent application, insofar as such protection is not thereby excluded.

Although the European Patent Convention has not been adopted by the Community as such, all the Member States and some others have joined. And in a Protocol on the Interpretation of Article 69 of the Convention it has been stated that:

> Article 69 should not be interpreted in the sense that the extent of the protection conferred by a European patent is to be understood as that defined by the strict, literal meaning of the wording used in the claims, the description and drawings being employed only for the purpose of resolving an ambiguity found in the claims. Neither should it be interpreted in the sense that the claims serve only as a guideline and that the actual protection conferred may extend to what, from a consideration of the description and drawings by a person skilled in the art, the patentee has contemplated. On the contrary, it is to be interpreted as defining a position between these two extremes which combines a fair protection for the patentee with a reasonable degree of certainty for third parties.

There is clearly a conflict between the third limb of the *Catnic/Epilady* test used by Mr Justice Hoffmann (requiring the wording of the claim to be the "decisive basis of protection") and the requirement of the Protocol to have reference simply to "what the patentee has contemplated". In *PLG Research* v *Ardon International*[16] the Court of Appeal thought that the English common law test should be consigned to oblivion and only the Protocol used. But this case flies in the face of the general trend, which has been to use the *Catnic/Epilady* test, advocated in three fairly recent cases: *Kastner* v *Rizla*,[17] *Assidoman* v *Mead*[18] and *Beloit* v *Valmet*.[19]

## Exhaustion of rights

Where a British manufacturer of telemedicine equipment markets that equipment overseas he will be able to stop the importation of those goods back into the United Kingdom only if a clear and express embargo against doing so was attached to the patent right.[20] Where, however, the overseas sale is made by a licence under the foreign patent, the equipment cannot enter the United Kingdom unless there is an express or implied licence from the British patentee.[21]

This principle, however, is affected by the Treaty of Rome and the European Union's policies on the free movement of goods whereby such a condition upon exporting equipment into other Member States would infringe EU competition rules. Moreover, if and when the Community Patents Convention 1975 comes into effect it will introduce a specific doctrine of exhaustion of patent rights affecting both Community and national patents within the European Union. Under the Convention, once a piece of telemedical equipment is put on the market in any part of the EU by the patentee or with their permission, the rights conferred by the patent or other national patents within the EU will no longer extend to the equipment unless European Union law admits of some specific exception.

## Licensing patents in telemedicine equipment

It has been said that a licence gives a person "what he is strong enough to demand or canny enough to include".[22] An exclusive licence to market an item of telemedical equipment gives the licensee the right to sue anyone (including the licensor) who sells the patented product within the licensee's territory and also prevents the licensor from granting any other licences to that product for that territory. So for instance, where Company A manufactures and sells telemedicine equipment in the United States of America, they may grant an exclusive licence to Company B to sell that equipment anywhere else in the world other than the USA or they might grant Company B, along with Companies C, D, E, F and G the exclusive licence to sell the equipment in their individual countries. Where, however, a licence agreement is at odds with the doctrine of free movement of goods within the European Union, specific contractual undertakings by the licensees to respect each others' territoriality will be necessary, but even then may contravene competition laws: such is the ongoing tension between property rights and free trade within the European Union.

The constantly present danger, however, is that Company A might grossly underestimate the success of an invention, the patent of which was licensed to Company B or others for a modest lump sum, and hence be left without the possibility of varying the agreement. Indeed, one cannot help but wonder now and again if this might already have happened in the field of telemedicine equipment, although of course it would be in nobody's interest to publicise such an event. Even if it has not happened already, it may only be a matter of time before a licensor catastrophically misunderstands the state of the market. Hence we can usefully examine the sort of factors that, from a purely commercial point of view, Companies A and B would each need to bear in mind in reaching a licence agreement that correctly anticipates the vagaries of the telemedicine marketplace, bearing in mind that some commercial strategies may conflict with EU competition law and policy.

### (i) "Know-how"

Where the licensor is granting not just the rights to manufacture telemedicine equipment but also the right to work a certain system of production and selling, then any knowledge of how to exploit the equipment to its maximum potential gained by the licensor during the research, development and launch of the product will need to be locked into the agreement. This knowledge may well be contained in a manual or disseminated in seminars and workshops held between staff of the licence granting and licence receiving companies and even the secondment of technical and other staff to the licensee.

The wise licensor, however, will insist on a preliminary agreement that anything revealed during the course of negotiations will be kept secret. It is beyond the scope of this chapter to describe in detail the law of confidence as it affects intellectual property. Suffice it to say that much of the licensor's "know-how" may be subject to the laws of confidence. Indeed, the principle that a licensee should keep something secret if he has promised he will has been given the full backing of the English courts.[23]

### (ii) Other forms of intellectual property

Intellectual property rights other than patent rights may need to be included in a licence. This might include, for instance, the right to use the licensor's registered or unregistered designs or trade marks, particularly where there is already a substantial reputation attached to those designs or marks that will benefit sale of the equipment in the licensee's territory.

### (iii) Exclusivity

Licence agreements are by no means always exclusive, although at present it can be expected that licences to exploit telemedicine equipment will remain so due to the present, fairly unevolved state of the British and European telemedicine marketplace. As telemedicine services move more and more into the mainstream of healthcare provision, however, it may well be that the market will grow to allow several suppliers of similar products to co-exist and compete. In the future, therefore, the exclusivity of a licence may well become of less importance. Until then, however, a prudent licensee will seek as much support as possible from the licensor and if he is unable to give this, he should expect an exclusive licence in order to offset his investment in plant, labour, sales outlets, advertising and the provision of spare-parts and servicing.

Section 130(1) of the Patents Act describes exclusive licensees as those whose rights exclude all others, including the proprietor. Where both have rights the licence is a "sole" licence. While exclusive licences give a great deal of protection and independence to licensees since they are enabled to sue infringers in their own name under section 67 of the Act, a non-exclusive licensee may well develop an understandable paranoia that his rivals are obtaining identical or similar licences for less, or even gratis.

### (iv) Duration

The ending of a licence, particularly a know-how licence, would be catastrophic to the licensor if at that point all obligations of confidence owed to him by the licensee vanished. Hence it will be necessary to incorporate into any agreement a continuing obligation of confidentiality which may be coupled with the expectation that relevant documents are returned.[24] A "strong" licensor, i.e. a company with a "must have" telemedicine product, may well require continued royalty payments beyond the expiry of the licence or indeed the originating patent.

### (v) New information

Telemedicine equipment will, naturally, be subject to further development and the sharing of new information between licensee and licensor will be essential if new procedures and techniques in teleconsulting are to be exploited and developed to the benefit of both the parties to the patent and telepatients generally. The prudent licensor should get a "grant-back" agreement out of his licensee so that any new patents or allied rights acquired by that licensee and arising from the licensed telemedical equipment will at least be the subject of a license agreement in the opposite direction or at best assigned back to the original inventor of that equipment. Which of these two options is chosen will very much come down to the enthusiasm of the parties for the licence granted and their commitment to an ongoing business relationship. Both will be happy if they feel they are getting as much out of the arrangement as they are putting in, but if they are not, they may be reluctant to reveal new discoveries or innovations or may, on the other hand, be unwilling to give more than a superficial commitment to making such discoveries.

### (vi) Monogamy

Given that the market in telemedical equipment will soon develop significantly when health authorities and NHS trusts begin a more wholesale investment in telemedicine systems, licensor "brides" may be justifiably nervous at the prospect of entering into an open marriage with a licensee "groom" who has a number of successful and flirtatious relationships with other manufacturers and suppliers of non-patented products. The sensible licensor should therefore insist upon their potential mate acquiring non-patented goods or start-up materials from them alone and even upon the licensee selling their products exclusively through the former's distribution channels.[25]

### (vii) Diligence

Unless, for whatever reason, a licence is to be free, the licensee will be required to pay either a lump sum or a royalty on each article of patented telemedicine equipment bought or sold, usually calculated as a proportion of the net selling price, or indeed both. But royalties in telemedicine equipment, as in any other product, will be meaningless unless there is a cross-undertaking by the licensee to use their "best endeavours" to exploit the invention.

Likewise, a cross-undertaking that the licensee will not use the intimate knowledge of the patent or know-how that he acquires through working it to challenge its validity during the currency of the licence or require the payment of royalties is also usual although such a "no challenge" clause may well fall foul of the dictum of His Honour, Mr Justice Clauson in *VD Ltd* v *Boston*[26] where a similar "no challenge" clause was held to be an unreasonable restraint of trade and hence contrary to public policy.

## Patent licences and competition law

There is of course the scope for restrictive licences to have a significant impact on trade within the European Union by creating the basis for anti-competitive liaisons. Such agreements, therefore, are subject to regulation by the European Court of Justice, which has taken quite a severe line,[27] and by the European Commission in its Block Exemption on Patent Licences of 1984 and the Block Exemption on Know-How Licences of 1988, now amalgamated into a single Block Exemption for Technology Transfer[28] which contains a "White List" of permitted clauses which would otherwise contravene Article 85 of the Treaty of Rome and a "Black List" of unpermitted clauses such as non-essential tie-ins, exclusive grant-backs and inequitable post-patent obligations. The Commission itself can also issue individual exemptions.

## Remedies

Infringement proceedings can be brought by a manufacturer of telemedical equipment in the High court or before the comptroller of patents (who heads the Patents Office) with appeal permitted to the court. Five possible remedies are available in the High Court, although only the first two are available from the comptroller.

### (i) Declaration

That the patent is valid and has been infringed.

### (ii) Damages

While damages for breach of contract will seek to put the plaintiff in the position that he would have been in had the contract been carried out, and damages in tort seek to put the victim back to his position before the tort, damages in intellectual property often do not fall within these two distinct classes and it is therefore difficult to define strict rules under which a court will provide damages. The measure of damages may hence be based on what the plaintiff would have charged for a licence or upon a royalty for each infringement: much will depend upon the degree of competitiveness that exists in the market place for that particular product. So far as non-competitive infringements are concerned, the courts have held that a reasonable royalty for non-competing use will be awarded upon a principle "of price or of hire" to avoid the rights being exploited with impunity by an unscrupulous defendant.

### (iii) Account of profits
This is an investigation of the accounts of the defendant to discover what profit he has made from his wrongful exploitation of another's intellectual property rights. An account of profits is usually viewed as an alternative rather than an accompaniment to damages and is particularly advantageous where the defendant has been making profits that the plaintiff would not have made himself.

### (iv) Injunction
An injunction is an order of the court directing a party to litigation to do or refrain from doing an act. To disobey an injunction is a contempt of court punishable by fine, imprisonment or seizure of assets. Interlocutory injunctions ordering a defendant not to continue or to begin a course of conduct until the trial of the issue is a quick and fairly cheap way of obtaining temporary relief against a business competitor and is often treated as settling an issue in any event. The granting of such an injunction is at the discretion of the court, however, and usually requires a cross-undertaking to make good any damage suffered by any defendant from the injunction, should the plaintiff fail at a full trial of the issues.

### (v) Order
To deliver up or destroy an infringing article. Often a defendant might be required to carry out the destruction "under oath", but if they cannot be trusted to do so then the court will order delivery up of infringing articles or documents to them.

## Patents in the 1990s
The Banks Committee of 1970 examined the patent system and agreed with the Sim Committee of 1945–47 that the system has four distinct advantages:

> First, that it encourages research and invention; second that it induces an inventor to disclose his discoveries instead of keeping them as a trade secret; third, that it offers a reward for the expense of developing inventions to the stage at which they are commercially practicable; and fourth, that it provides an inducement to invest capital in new lines of production which might not appear if many competing producers embarked on them simultaneously.29

But because this inducement involves the granting of a monopoly within a competitive market place, with the attendant dangers of thus destroying competition and being able to dictate supply and pricing, it has come in for heavy criticism over the years: not least because it might encourage many companies to divert research and development funds away from non-patentable but nonetheless worthy projects into less beneficial but ultimately protectable (i.e. patentable) products. Some EU countries grant "utility patents" which employ a less strict test of novelty but inevitably provide less protection. The European Commission is proposing extending this concept throughout the EU. However, a study into the economic effect of the UK patents system on manufacturing industry[30] concluded that, on balance, its benefits far outweighed its burdens and hence the better view may well be that, provided the potential excesses of the present system can be properly checked by United Kingdom and European Union competition law, the system remains a good one.

# Copyright

Copyright law aims to protect artistic, aesthetic and literary works by granting authors and their publishers long periods of legal protection against any reproducing of their work without their permission. Unlike with patents though, there is little that can be done to prevent a copyright holder abusing any monopoly he might hold although, because a copyright owner will usually face stiff competition from owners of rival copyrights, such abuse is rare. Copyright protection in the European Union lasts for the lifetime of the author plus 70 years thereafter. Authors, and their successors in title, can sue anyone copying their work without their permission.

In the United Kingdom computer programs are classed as literary works. Section 3 of the Copyright, Designs and Patents Act 1988 states:

**3 Literary, dramatic and musical works**

(1) In this Part—

"literary work" means any work, other than a dramatic or musical work, which is written, spoken or sung, and accordingly includes—

(a) a table or compilation

(b) a computer program, and

(c) preparatory design material for a computer program;

"dramatic work" includes a work of dance or mime; and "musical work" means a work consisting of music, exclusive of any words or actions intended to be sung, spoken or performed with the music.

(2) Copyright does not subsist in a literary, dramatic or musical work unless and until it is recorded, in writing or otherwise; and references in this Part to the time at which such a work is made are to the time at which it is so recorded.

(3) It is immaterial for the purposes of subsection (2) whether the work is recorded by or with the permission of the author; and where it is not recorded by the author, nothing in that subsection affects the question whether copyright subsists in the record as distinct from the work recorded.

For the purposes of the Act "writing" is stated in section 178 to include any form of notation or code, whether by hand or otherwise and regardless of the method by which, or medium in or on which, it is recorded. Hence it is copyright law that has for some time been the most satisfactory method of protecting intellectual property rights in computer programs and databases. Not all countries, however, have accepted without question that computer programs, many of which are never expressed on paper, should be treated in the same way as a literary work.[31] In the United Kingdom the Copyright (Computer Software) Amendment Act 1985 extended the Copyright Act 1956 to computer programs and the protection of computer programs by copyright law was reaffirmed in sections 50A, B and C of the Copyright, Designs and Patents Act 1988. This Act has itself been amended since 1988 to include the European Union's software Directive which harmonises the domestic copyright laws of all the Member States.[32]

## The European software Directive

Article 3(1) of the European Union's software Directive requires that, in order to fall within the terms of the Directive, a computer program must be its author's own intellectual creation. Where there are joint authors copyright protection will be afforded for seventy years after the death of the longest living author and where the software is created by an employee whilst in employment, first ownership will go to the employer unless a contract between the two provides otherwise. The software Directive grants to the copyright holder the exclusive right to reproduce the computer program in question, in part or in whole and any loading, displaying, running, transmission or storage of the program can only be carried out with the permission of the copyright holder. Copyright also covers any selective, altered, summarised and otherwise varied versions of a work, where the version still involves substantial reproduction of the original.

But computer programming is a complex area where the line between the creation of similar, competitive programs and the unacceptable copying of an existing one is extremely difficult to draw. If the "look and feel" of a program is substantially recreated in another program the copyright may have been infringed in the same way that copying the *detailed* plot (but not the broader premise) of a novel may well infringe the copyright in that novel, regardless of whether or not the language employed is new and original. In this context Article 1(2) of the software Directive states that:

> Ideas and principles which underlie any element of a computer program, including those which underlie its interfaces, are not protected.

Although not actually incorporated into the United Kingdom regulations, this Article merely reiterates the longstanding assumption in English copyright law that protection goes only to the expression of an idea and not to the idea itself, a principle stated most famously by His Honour Mr Justice Peterson in *University of London Press* v *University Tutorial Press*:[33]

> The word "original" does not in this connection mean that the work must be the expression of original or inventive thought. Copyright Acts are not concerned with the originality of ideas, but with the expression of thought, and, in the case of "literary work", with the expression of thought in print or writing. The originality which is required relates to the expression of the thought. But the Act does not require that the expression must be in an original or novel form, but that the work must not be copied from another work – that it should originate from the author.

The originality referred to by Mr Justice Peterson operates as a *de minimis* requirement that excludes from copyright instances where the author has not expended a sufficient degree of skill, selection, judgement, labour or experience to justify the substantial protection afforded by it. It is in this respect that the approach of the courts in America and Britain shows marked differences. In the United States two completely different conclusions were reached in the cases of *Whelan* v *Jaslow*[34] and *Computer Associates* v *Altai*.[35] In the former case it was held that "line-by-line" copying was not required for the copyright in a program designed to organise the business of dental laboratories to have been breached by a similar program.

All that was necessary were significant similarities of "structure" since:

> The purpose or function of a utilitarian work would be the work's idea, and everything that is not necessary to that purpose or function would be part of the expression of the idea.

But in the latter case of *Computer Associates* the court adopted a complex and thorough approach by examining the way in which the program designer had written the program. In doing so the court was trying to differentiate between those elements of the program taken from the public domain and those elements which, if the program was to work properly, could only be expressed in a particular way. Only the elements falling into the public domain were protectable if that which remained was essential to carry out the task required of the program and the court found that, on the facts, the defendants in *Computer Associates* had not taken this protectable element. In subsequent British cases such as *John Richardson Computers* v *Flanders*[36] and *Ibcos Computers* v *Barclays Mercantile*[37] on the other hand, although some attention has been paid to the *Computer Associates* approach, the courts have tended to avoid the method used in that case of finding a "core of protectable expression". Instead they have favoured the approach of considering whether or not a substantial duplication of the copyright work as a whole has taken place – whether "line-by-line" or by copying structures, routines or elements into another computing language.

These judgments leave us with a minefield of legal methodology to navigate if we are to make any safe prediction about the approach of the courts to a case involving an alleged breach of copyright in computer software designed to operate a telemedicine system. The guiding principle, however, is a clear one – the courts will always examine whether or not a defendant has produced his own original work as opposed to having merely tried to disguise the use of a plaintiff's work unless, of course, there is only one way in which to accomplish a particular step in a computer program. Difficulties may arise where an ex-employee of the plaintiff software company, now working for the defendant company, reproduces some of his ideas that were originally incorporated into one of the plaintiff's products, into a program newly launched onto the market by the defendants. In such a case, unless the employee has exploited a "trade secret" in breach of the law of confidence or the goodwill existing between his original employer and that employer's customers, the courts would be unlikely to interfere with the ex-employee's right to use his skill and knowledge to the advantage of his new employers, the defendants.

## Exceptions to the software Directive

Article 5(2) of the software Directive, as incorporated in section 50A of the Copyright, Designs and Patents Act 1988 allows the creation of back-up copies by a lawful user and any term or condition appearing in a contract which purports to prohibit or restrict the making of back-up copies will be void. However, the correction of errors in a program through copying and adaption may be prohibited under section 50C and in such circumstances the lawful user of a telemedicine system whose software contains "bugs" will be required to return it to the manufacturer or supplier rather than attempting to remedy the problem themselves. Section 50B of the 1988 Act states that:

(1) It is not an infringement of copyright for a lawful user of a copy of a computer program expressed in a low level language—

    (a) to convert it into a version expressed in a higher level language, or

    (b) incidentally in the course of so converting the program, to copy it,

    (that is, to "decompile" it), provided that the conditions in subsection (2) are met.

(2) The conditions are that—

    (a) it is necessary to decompile the program to obtain the information necessary to create an independent program which can be operated with the program decompiled or with another program ("the permitted objective"); and

    (b) the information so obtained is not used for any purpose other than the permitted objective.

(3) In particular, the conditions in subsection (2) are not met if the lawful user—

    (a) has readily available to him the information necessary to achieve the permitted objective;

    (b) does not confine the decompiling to such acts as are necessary to achieve the permitted objective;

    (c) supplies the information obtained by the decompiling to any person to whom it is not necessary to supply it in order to achieve the permitted objective; or

    (d) uses the information to create a program which is substantially similar in its expression to the program decompiled or to do any act restricted by copyright.

(4) Where an act is permitted under this section, it is irrelevant whether or not there exists any term or condition in an agreement which purports to prohibit or restrict the act (such terms being by virtue of section 296A, void).

This section broadly enacts Article 6 of the software Directive but differs in two important respects. First of all, the software Directive does not make any mention of the level of languages used and secondly, the 1988 Act gives a much clearer definition of the types of interoperable program that can form the "permitted objective" for the purposes of decompilation. Section 296A, to which section 50B(4) refers, enacts Article 5(3) and Recital 19 of the software Directive and renders void any term or condition in a contract which prohibits the use of any device or means to observe, study or test the functioning of the program in order to understand the ideas and principles which underlie any element of it.

### Screen displays

The monopolisation of the global marketplace by Apple and Microsoft (more especially the latter) has made it inevitable that most commercial applications will have the same "look and feel" in the context of their user interface, or in layman's terms, the layout of the information that appears on the computer screen itself. Indeed, almost all users of telemedicine equipment and databases in the United Kingdom and the rest of Europe would reasonably expect such systems to be controlled by programs operating in the ubiquitous "windows" environment that has become the worldwide standard and with which anyone who uses a personal computer on a day to day basis is familiar.

Hence, rival software companies who are competing to create patient databases and other software for use with telemedicine systems will, before they have even started, be resigned to the fact that their finished products are all going to look and function in broadly the same manner, in the windows operating environment that we are all used to. Not unexpectedly, this topic is much litigated in the United States, where the *Computer Associates*[38] test of filtering out elements of the software which were "functional, unoriginal or indispensable in the circumstances" was used in the case of *Apple* v *Microsoft*[39] to find that there was no breach of copyright where the latter had copied features of Apple's software screen display, such as overlapping windows, menus and icons. Likewise, in *Lotus Development* v *Borland International*[40] the plaintiffs, Lotus, were not able to protect the menu command hierarchy of its "1-2-3" spreadsheet against the defendants who had replicated it with their own program. The US courts rightly felt that, due to the prevalence of the windows operating environment, rival software companies should not be prevented from creating programs designed to operate within that environment.

The British courts, as has already been noted however, are not equipped with the legal methodology necessary to come to a similar conclusion. Although the question has not yet arisen for judgment in a United Kingdom court, it would be difficult to conclude that a new program which operates under windows does not infringe the copyrights in other, similar windows programs. But as Cornish points out, it would be open to an English court to find that the assertion of copyright in a user interface such as windows is anti-competitive and an abuse of dominant position under Article 86 of the Treaty of Rome. Alternatively, an English court may simply discount functional similarities when deciding whether there has been a taking of an expression of an idea (as opposed to an idea) and in assessing whether or not that taking is substantial enough for a breach of copyright to have taken place.[41]

## Telemedicine databases

The European Union Directive on the legal protection of databases which came into force on 1 January 1998 defines a database as a collection of independent works, data or other materials arranged in a systematic or methodical way and individually accessible by electronic or other means.[42] It provides for the copyright protection of databases (rather than their contents) where intellectual judgment of some sort has been exercised by the author in choosing the contents, and a separate right that lasts for 15 years from the completion of the database (or alternatively, 15 years from its becoming available to the public) to prevent extraction or re-utilisation of the contents of the database.[43] To qualify for the protection under the latter right the database must be the product of substantial investment.[44] However, quite how the provisions of this Directive will be applied, particularly to the telepatient databases of telemedicine and telecare services, only time will tell.

## Multimedia applications

At present, with no cases reported or specific legislation created dealing with multimedia applications such as telemedical encyclopaedias on CD-ROM, it is difficult to predict how the law will react to disputes involving copyright in a mixture of media: written text, graphic images, moving images, spoken words, music and other sounds. But the remarkable way in which copyright has survived the introduction of photography, sound recording, broadcasting and computer programming is surely excellent evidence that it will continue to provide protection to the new forms of expression created at the turn of the millennium, including multimedia programs that are, essentially, an amalgam of individual components, each of which is subject to copyright protection. Where an author uses skill, selectivity, judgment and experience to combine different media to produce a sophisticated work there should be no problem in granting such a "compilation" copyright protection. Indeed, in New Zealand a "compilation" has been defined as a form of literary work. There a literary work can include compilations of works and/or other data of any kind – "work" covering the same broad range of matter as our own Copyright, Designs and Patents Act.

# Trade marks, designs and other forms of intellectual property

Finally, brief mention should be made of trade marks, industrial designs and other aspects of the goodwill associated with the "look and feel" of a product. Trade mark protection may last as long as goods or services are provided with that mark attached to them. The holder of a trade mark, such as a well known telemedicine equipment manufacturer, can take legal action against anyone who tries to exploit the mark and the goodwill associated with it in an attempt to mislead consumers into thinking that their products emanate from the proper holder of the trade mark. Moreover, distinctive shapes and designs designed to be eye-catching can be protected from the point of view of the association that is created between a particular shape, configuration, pattern or ornament that is applied to the product and the popularity of that product, and, in the UK, functional aspects of shape can be protected by an unregistered design right.[45]

It is not difficult to think of products whose name can be associated with particular forms of advertising and which are well regarded as offering excellent value or as being of high quality - just think of the Coca-Cola symbol and the distinctive contour design of the famous glass bottle. Telemedicine companies seeking to exploit the goodwill associated with the distinctive shape of a rival's well regarded product or the trade marks applied to it, by substantially copying the same, can be prevented from doing so under the laws relating to industrial designs, trade marks and passing off.

## Summary

▶ A number of types of intellectual property right exist that can be used to reward the creative effort of the inventor and protect both the intellectual and commercial investment that has been made in developing telemedicine technology.

▶ A patent will give the manufacturer of telemedical equipment, provided it meets the required standards of novelty, inventiveness and industrial application, the exclusive right to use and exploit that equipment for a twenty-year period. During that time no other person or company can legally copy or exploit the ideas contained in the patented equipment. It is therefore strategically important that in drafting a patent application all the possible alternative forms for the inventive idea are described carefully.

▶ The manufacturer of a patented item of telemedical equipment may grant licences in that equipment permitting others to exploit the patent in other territories. Contractual

▶ undertakings may be required between the licensees however, by which they promise to respect each other's territoriality and not to attempt to import telemedical equipment from one state in which it is cheap into another state in which it is expensive.

▶ In seeking to combine a fair degree of protection for the patentee with a reasonable degree of freedom for third parties to trade in the patented telemedical equipment, the principles of intellectual property law inevitably come into conflict with European competition laws.

▶ The computer programs used to operate telemedical systems are classified as literary works under the Copyright, Designs and Patents Act 1988 and can therefore be protected by copyright law for the lifetime of their creator plus seventy years, provided they are original works upon which the creator has expended a sufficient degree of skill and labour. In certain cases technical effects achieved in computer programs can be patented.

▶ The European software Directive prevents the substantial duplication of a computer program's method of operation and expression but not the broad idea or principle behind it. The Directive grants the copyright holder the exclusive right to reproduce the computer program in question, in part or in whole, and any loading, displaying, running, transmission or storage of the program can only be carried out with the permission of the copyright holder.

▶ The power of a telemedicine equipment manufacturer to prevent a former employee from using the skill and knowledge gained during his employment with them to the benefit of a rival manufacturer is strictly limited to preventing breach of confidence, the disclosure of trade secrets or the damaging of the goodwill existing between that manufacturer and his clients.

▶ The laws relating to trade marks, design rights and passing off can also be used to protect intellectual property rights in telemedicine equipment.

## References

1   The only European states which are not a part of the European Union are Switzerland, Iceland, Norway and Leichtenstein. However, the latter three are members of the European Free Trade Association (EFTA) which, together with the European Union (EU) form the European Economic Area (EEA) within which the EU principles of free movement and competition apply equally to the EEA, albeit that their application is somewhat more sophisticated.

2   The Competition Bill 1998 will introduce domestic competition Rules into the UK.

3   See in this respect the Community Patent Convention 1976, as revised in 1985 and 1996.

4   Patents Act 1977, s. 1.

5   Evaluating what is and what is not an "inventive step" is perhaps the single most important cause of uncertainty and dispute in patent applications. Lord Justice Oliver in *Windsurfing International* v *Tabur Marine* [1985] RPC 59 approached the issue by describing four "stages": (1) the court must identify the inventive concept embodied in the patent; (2) it must assume the mantle of the normally skilled but unimaginative addressee in the art at that date, and impute to him what was, at that date, common general knowledge in the art in question; (3) it must identify what, if any, differences exist between the matters cited as being "known or used" and the alleged invention; and (4) it must ask itself whether, viewed without any knowledge of the alleged invention, those differences constituted steps which would have been obvious to the skilled man or whether they required any degree of invention.

6   [1974] ECR 1147, Case 15/74.

7    Patents Act 1977, s. 60(1).
8    Ibid., s. 60(2). By sub-section (3), however, this provision does not apply to the supply or offer of a staple commercial product unless the supply or the offer is made for the purpose of inducing the person supplied or, as the case may be, the person to whom the offer is made to do an act which constitutes an infringement of the patent by virtue of sub-section (1).
9    Cornish WR. *Intellectual property*. (3rd ed.) London: Sweet and Maxwell, 1996: 207.
10   Though the Protocol to Article 69 of the European Patent Convention requires a significant degree of latitude in this respect.
11   Cornish WR. *Intellectual property*. (3rd ed.) London: Sweet and Maxwell, 1996: 225.
12   [1963] RPC 61 (HL). See also *Birmingham Sound Reproducers* v *Collaro* [1956] RPC 232 at 245 (CA).
13   [1969] RPC 367 (HL).
14   [1982] RPC 183, [1983] CLY 2776.
15   [1989] RPC 69.
16   [1993] CLY 3041.
17   [1995] RPC 585.
18   [1995] RPC 321.
19   [1995] RPC 705.
20   See the cases of *Betts* v *Willmott* (1871) LR 6 Ch 239; *Smithkline* v *Salim* [1989] FSR 407 (High Court of Malaysia).
21   *SA des Glaces* v *Tilghmann* (1883) 25 ChD 1 (CA); *Beecham* v *International Products* [1968] RPC 129; *Minnesota Mining* v *Geerpres* [1973] FSR 113.
22   See Cornish WR. *Intellectual property*. (3rd ed.) London: Sweet and Maxwell, 1996: 238.
23   See further Gurry, *Breach of confidence* (1984). See also the cases of *Stephenson Jordan* v *McDonald and Evans* (1951) 68 RPC 190; *Thomas* v *Mould* [1968] 1 All ER 963 and *Interfirm Comparison* v *Law Society of New South Wales* [1975] RPC 137.
24   Where this is not expressly provided for it is often implied: *Regina Glass Fibre* v *Schuller* [1972] RPC 229 (CA) and *Torrington* v *Smith* [1966] RPC 285.
25   Interestingly, however, the creation of "ties" and exclusions of competitive technology have been cut down at times as being abuses of monopoly: see the Patents Act 1977, s. 44.
26   (1935) 52 RPC 303 at p. 331. See also *Mouchel* v *Cubitt* (1907) 24 RPC 194 at 200.
27   As evidenced in cases such as *AOIP* v *Beyrard* [1976] 1 CMLR D14 and *Vaessen* v *Moris* [1979] FSR 259.
28   Regulation 1996/240.
29   *The British Patent System*, Cmnd 4407 (1970) at para. 41, repeating the words of the Sims Committee, Cmds. 6618, 6789, 7206 (1945-47).
30   Taylor and Silbertson, *The Economic Impact of Patents* (1973).
31   In *Computer Edge* v *Apple Computer* [1986] FSR 537 the High Court of Australia took the view that when a computer program takes on electronic form it becomes a means of operating a machine and is hence no longer appropriate subject-matter for copyright protection, thus adopting the dicta of Lord Justice Davey in *Hollingrake* v *Truswell* [1894] 3 Ch 420 who stated that "a literary work is intended to afford either information and instruction, or pleasure, in the form of literary enjoyment". See also *Exxon* v *Exxon* [1982] RPC 69. In countries that require a degree of originality for works to receive copyright protection a computer program that involves what Cornish describes as merely "humdrum writing skills" may not be afforded protection. See in this respect the decision of the German Supreme Court in *Inkasso-Program* [1986] EIPR 185. See further Cornish WR. *Intellectual property*. (3rd ed.) London: Sweet & Maxwell, 1996: 443.
32   See now the Copyright (Computer Programs) Regulations 1992 (SI 1992 No. 3233).
33   [1916] 2 Ch 601 at p. 608.
34   [1987] FSR 1.
35   (1992) 982 F 2d 693.
36   [1993] FSR 497.
37   [1994] FSR 275.
38   Supra, ref. 30.
39   (1994) 35 F 3d 1435.
40   (1995) 49 F 3rd 807.
41   Cornish WR. *Intellectual property*. (3rd ed.) London: Sweet & Maxwell, 1996: 455.
42   See article 3(1).
43.  See Article 10(1), (2).
44.  See Recital 19.
45   See *Coulthard* v *Bentley* [1997] EIPR 1.

# ▶9

# Jurisdictional problems

In the United States of America the existence of 50 different states has made jurisdictional considerations one of the key barriers to the implementation of telemedicine there. The problem, essentially, is that in the United States a physician who practises medicine must be licensed to practise in the state in which they are working. The Medical Practice Acts of each state have been created to protect the citizens of that state from unlicensed individuals.[1] Likewise, malpractice insurance covers a physician only in the state in which he practises. So a teleconsultant providing telemedicine services across state borders may well run the risk not only of "practising bare", that is practising without any form of liability insurance, but also of practising illegally.

Such a scenario creates nightmares for insurers and lawyers alike. For the lawyers the problem is identifying in which state to sue a negligent teleconsultant. Since different states may have different laws, the problem of "forum shopping" arises – choosing to commence an action in the state whose legal system is most sympathetic to patients or is known to award higher damages. Similarly, lawyers involved in defending a telemedical malpractice suit will have a vested interest in preferring the state whose legal system is more "doctor friendly", if such a choice is available. For the insurers there are difficult choices to make in finding and instructing defence lawyers in the out-of-state location who are competent to perform the discovery and investigation regarding the events surrounding the malpractice allegation. Moreover, it will be inherently more expensive and time-consuming to defend an action in another state.

On a slightly larger scale, conducting telemedical consultations across national borders (that is, speaking to and observing telepatients or teleconsultants in one country from a hospital or clinic in another) raises the interesting and complex question – which country's law applies to the cross-border communication? Telemedical advice provided in one country will in many cases be received in another country, indeed this is the very beauty of telemedicine. But whilst common sense dictates that, where a tort is committed by a lay-person in a remote clinic or by a ship's medical officer alone, then both the negligence and the resultant damage will have occurred in the same place, it is less clear what the position will be where the negligent act is the bad advice of a teleconsultant doctor given from a different country or "jurisdiction" to that in which the harm to the telepatient actually occurs. In such a situation, which system of law should apply to determine the defendant's liability?

In this chapter we examine the principles of jurisdiction and choice of law that must be considered in deciding in which jurisdiction to bring an action for medical malpractice against a teleconsultant, a product liability claim against the manufacturers or distributors of a faulty telemedicine system or an action for breach of copyright or patent.[2]

# The American experience

In the United States it is assumed that anyone diagnosing, treating or prescribing for a patient in the state in which the patient is located is practising medicine in that state.[3] The Federation of State Medical Boards (FSMB) is presently examining various methods of legalising telemedicine consultations across state lines and has published a model Act on regulating the practice of telemedicine or medicine by other means across these borders. Model legislation has also been drafted which would grant teleconsultants a special licence to practise telemedicine. If adopted, such an Act would allow teleconsultants to engage in telemedical consultations in any state without having to first obtain a full licence to practise in that state.[4]

However, there is every possibility that quite the opposite requirement (i.e. that teleconsultants be fully licensed in any state in which they wish to practise) may evolve following the adoption by the House of Delegates of the American Medical Association of a policy to this effect at their annual meeting in Chicago in June 1996. The rationale for such a policy is that this would be the only way to enable states closely to control standards in the practice of telemedicine. Some states have already adopted such an approach. In Kansas, Regulation §2382 (1994) has been enacted requiring any doctor treating, prescribing, practising or diagnosing a condition in a patient located in Kansas to have a Kansas state medical licence. Similar, vaguer requirements have also become the law in South Dakota.

Physicians wishing to treat telepatients in California from outside of that state are required to submit to a special registration procedure for out-of-state physicians and surgeons and must meet the legal requirements of medical practice in California or run the risk of being found guilty of unprofessional conduct.[5] The state of Texas passed legislation in 1995 requiring physicians practising in Texas to be state-licensed, and clearly states that "electronic mediums" of consultation such as telemedicine will require a full licence if undertaken by out-of-state physicians.[6] Likewise, Florida passed telemedicine laws in 1995. Under the Florida Senate Bill 498 which came into effect on 1 July 1995 an out-of-state teleconsultant will not require a licence to practise in Florida provided that the treating physician is Florida licensed and the teleconsultant is transmitting and receiving electronic images only.

The debate over the licensing of doctors to practise across state lines is fairly well evolved in the United States therefore. But what is their approach to "forum shopping" and choice of law where a malpractice claim is in fact brought?

The correct approach is a combination of two classic American legal methods: the principle of *forum non conveniens* – that a legal action should be brought in the jurisdiction that is, in all the circumstances, the most convenient and fair for all the parties concerned, and the "Due Process Clause" of the US Constitution (the Fourteenth Amendment).[7] The latter principle would operate to require a defendant teleconsultant who reaps the benefits of operating within a particular state by treating telepatients there, to be prepared to submit to the legal system of that state. The case of *Compuserve* v *Patterson*[8] illustrates this principle clearly.

The defendant claimed to own rights in software which the plaintiffs, Compuserve, claimed to have developed themselves and they therefore sought a declaration to this effect in the Ohio courts, since Compuserve was itself based in Ohio. But the defendant was resident in Texas and the court held that, since sales of his product in Ohio were minimal (twelve orders worth about $1,000), he could not be said to have "personally availed himself" within that state. So there will evidently need to be a more substantial connection with a state before a defendant teleconsultant can be said to have "purposefully availed himself of the privilege of acting in the forum" and this can properly be expected to be a question of fact which will depend upon the circumstances of each case, with the *number* and – since we are speaking here of a country with a system of private health insurance – the *value* of telemedical consultations being a pivotal issue. But although the basic constitutional requirement in the United States is that a defendant must have sufficient contact with a forum state before he can be sued there, the case of *Burger King* v *Rudzewicz*[9] shows that the Supreme Court has been prepared to hold that when operating by "wire and mail", if one's efforts are "purposely directed" at another state, there will be jurisdiction there. So the better view is perhaps that, as far as the USA is concerned, the correct forum or jurisdiction for a lawsuit involving telemedicine will be that of the state into which the telemedicine service is directed and in which, in most cases, the teleconsultant will be subject to supervision by the appropriate licensing body. This is a view which is supported by the learned Judge Hand's dicta in *United States* v *Aluminum Co of America (Alcoa)*:[10]

> It is settled law...that any state may impose liabilities, even upon persons not within its allegiance, for conduct outside its borders which has consequences within its borders which the State reprehends; and these liabilities other States will ordinarily recognise.

Landau[11] reports that this idea has been reformulated over the years into a requirement that a state will consider a case against an out-of-state teleconsultant where the effects of the telemedicine service are intended and where the effects of the alleged malpractice are direct, substantial and foreseeable.

## Civil jurisdiction and judgment in the English forum

The law in the United Kingdom is slightly different from that in the United States. If there is a dispute as to jurisdiction under English law then proceedings are usually stayed and moved to another forum where "the interests of the parties and the ends of justice" would be better served by hearing the case there.[12] In deciding whether or not to stay a case an English court will consider which country's jurisdiction is the "natural forum" for hearing the dispute; i.e. the forum with which the dispute has the most real and substantial connection. Other factors to be taken into account include:

(a) the availability of witnesses;

(b) convenience;

(c) expense; and

(d) the residence of the parties.

Where the defendant manufacturer or teleconsulting doctor is domiciled in a State within the European Union, jurisdiction is governed in English law by the Civil Jurisdiction and Judgments Act 1982 which implements the Brussels Convention on Jurisdiction and Judgments. Where the defendant is domiciled in a country party to the Lugano Convention (which governs the former EFTA states) jurisdiction is governed by the Civil Jurisdiction and Judgments Act 1991. The two acts are, broadly speaking, identical. Under the two Conventions a plaintiff may issue proceedings against a European Union defendant in the defendant's country of domicile: known as the "primary jurisdiction".[13]

Where the action concerns a "harmful event" such as a tort, a trade mark infringement, a breach of confidentiality, a copyright infringement or some other civil wrong, then the action can be brought in the "place where the harmful event occurred": the "alternative jurisdiction".[14] The Conventions are of little assistance for present purposes, however, as in the cases of *Shevill* v *Press Alliance SA*,[15] *Handdalswekerij Bier* v *Mines de Potasse d'Alsace*[16] and *Minister Investments* v *Hyundai*[17] the European Court of Justice has interpreted "harmful event" to encompass either the place where the wrongdoing occurred *or* the place where the resulting damage ensued! So these cases seem to indicate that the European Court of Justice has largely treated the "primary" and "alternative" jurisdictions provided for by the Brussels and Lugano Conventions as being of equal status.

If the defendant manufacturer or teleconsultant is domiciled in a country party to neither the Brussels nor the Lugano Conventions then a writ may still be served on him or her simply by virtue of their presence in England. If the claim had little or no connection with England, however, the defendant could apply for a stay of proceedings on the grounds of *forum non conveniens*.[18] Such an application may well succeed where neither the people involved in a telemedical malpractice action nor the place where the malpractice is alleged to have occurred have any real connection with the United Kingdom. Moreover, a defendant may also be able to prevent a medical malpractice claim from continuing abroad.[19]

## Computer hacking from abroad

In *R* v *Tomsett*[20] the defendant attempted to divert funds from New York to his bank account in Geneva by the use of a telex from London. The Court of Appeal held that, had Tomsett succeeded, the theft would have taken place in New York and the English courts would have been powerless. In response to such an obvious inadequacy in the law, the Computer Misuse Act 1990 brought into force, in sections 4–9, a requirement of some tangible link with the United Kingdom in order to commence a prosecution here. That is, the hacking must either be directed at a computer in the UK or be performed using a computer located in the UK.

## Telemedical malpractice at sea

### (i) Malpractice on a British ship or in British waters

If negligent medical advice or a negligent act took place or subsequent damage was sustained following a teleconsultation on board a British ship on the high seas or a foreign ship sailing through British territorial waters such that for the purposes of the Rules of the Supreme Court, Order 11, rule 1(i)(f) the tort was "committed in England", then leave may be sought to serve the writ abroad. It would not be necessary to establish that all the relevant harm was caused to the telepatient within the jurisdiction or by acts occurring within the jurisdiction and this would be of some benefit to a seafarer or passenger who believes themselves to have been harmed by the negligence of *both* the teleconsultant doctor and the ship's medical officer. In the case of *Metall und Rohstoff AG* v *Donaldson Lufkin & Jenrette Inc*[21] Lord Justice Slade stated that a judge should:

> Look at the tort alleged in a common-sense way and ask whether the damage has resulted from substantial and efficacious acts committed within the jurisdiction.

An application under Order 11 of the Rules of the Supreme Court would, however, require the plaintiff telepatient to show that England is the appropriate and proper forum for the resolution of the dispute between the parties.[22]

### (ii) Malpractice on a foreign ship or in foreign waters

It is a matter of public policy that, if possible, any state which grants its nationality and flag to a ship should be able to have effective jurisdiction over that ship in technical and social matters. Registration, under international law, is recognised as the ultimate "root" test of a ship's nationality. Article 90 of the United Nations Convention on the Law of the Sea 1982, which is materially the same as Article 4 of the Geneva Convention on the High Seas of 1958, states that:

> Every State, whether coastal or land-locked, has the right to sail ships flying its flag on the high seas.

Because the high seas are not subject to the jurisdiction of a sovereign state it is essential that ships sailing on them are subject to the control of such a state which is provided for by Article 5(1) of the Geneva Convention and Article 91(1) of the UN Convention:

> Every State shall fix the conditions for the grant of its nationality to ships, for the registration of ships in its territory, and for the right to fly its flag. Ships have the nationality of the State whose flag they are entitled to fly.

Hence where a tort is committed on board a ship on the high seas the governing principle is that established in the case of *Phillips* v *Eyre*[23] and the *locus delicti* is that of the ship's flag.[24] In that case it was held that in order to found a suit in England for a wrong alleged to have been committed abroad, two conditions must be fulfilled:

(a)  the wrong must be of such a character that it would have been actionable if committed in England; and

(b)  the act must not have been justifiable by the law of the place where it was done.

   Where an act complained of takes place on board a ship anchored in or sailing through the territorial or national waters of another country and the act is lawful in the country in whose territorial or national waters the ship in question is present, such act, although it would have been wrongful if committed within the English jurisdiction, cannot be made a ground of an action in an English court. The law in this respect has been slightly modified, however, by the case of *Boys* v *Chaplin*[25] where it was held that the relevant wrong must be civilly actionable both in England and in the place where the tort occurred before the English courts would accept jurisdiction. Hence the *locus delicti* in such a case is the country in whose waters the ship is present and not the country of registration whose flag the ship is flying.[26]

### (iii) Application of English Admiralty jurisdiction

The conventional view is that English Admiralty law is applicable where the harm caused is external to the ship, as in a collision. Section 20(2)(f) of the Supreme Court Act 1981 provides jurisdiction over:

> Any claim for loss of life or personal injury sustained in consequence of any defect in a ship or in her apparel or equipment, or in consequence of the wrongful act, neglect or default of—
>
> (i) the owners, charterers or persons in possession or control of the ship; or
> (ii) the master or crew of a ship, or any other person for whose wrongful acts, neglects or defaults the owners, charterers, or persons in possession or control of a ship are responsible,
>
> being an act, neglect or default in the navigation or management of a ship, in the loading, carriage or discharge of goods on, in or from the ship, or in the embarkation, carriage or disembarkation of persons on, in or from the ship;"

In the event of a seafarer's personal injuries falling within the above section, English Admiralty law would be applicable and the nationality of the parties and the law of the ship's flag would not be material.[27] While common sense would seem to dictate that any harm caused to a seafarer through the negligence of a teleconsulting doctor or ship's medical officer, not being an "act, neglect or default in the navigation or management of a ship" would not come within this jurisdiction, a recent Australian case may represent an inroad into this narrow interpretation.

In *Yulianto & Ors* v *The Ship "Glory Cape"*[28] the Supreme Court of Western Australia decided that a ship can be arrested and security sought for a claim by a crew member for personal injury resulting from mistreatment since such a claim can found an action in Admiralty law. In this case there had been a long-standing dispute between the Indonesian crew members of the vessel and its Korean master. The dispute came to a head at the port of Dampier, Western Australia, with the Indonesian crew refusing to sail with the vessel. The dissident crew were persuaded to stay on board by an undertaking that the vessel would move to anchorage but not sail while the dispute was being sorted out with the assistance of the International Transport Federation. In breach of that undertaking, the master took steps to sail undetected and at night. The dissident crew, on discovering this, resolved to leave the vessel in a life raft but found the rafts locked with steel cables. It appeared that their attempt to depart from the vessel had been anticipated. Other crew, led by the First Officer, and armed with steel bars, confronted the dissidents. Blows were exchanged before the dissidents fell or jumped overboard. They were rescued by shore-based authorities five hours later, suffering from exposure and various injuries relating to the assault on board the vessel. One of them died.

The dissident crew as plaintiffs then issued a writ *in rem*, arrested the vessel and negotiated security in exchange for allowing the vessel to sail. The owners sought to set aside the writ of summons on the basis that the court lacked jurisdiction to hear the matter because it did not fall within the provisions of the Admiralty Act 1988. Section 4(3) of that Act mirrors section 20(2)(f) of the Supreme Court Act 1981 and the plaintiffs argued that their claim was a claim for "personal injuries sustained as a consequence of a defect in the ship or in the apparel or equipment of the ship". Alternatively, they said that it was a claim arising out of the act of the owner, master or crew for whom the owner was vicariously liable, being an act or omission in the management of the ship pursuant to section 4(3)(d).

His Honour Mr Justice Murray decided that the immobilisation of the life rafts was a contributing cause to the injuries and that constituted a claim for personal injury as a consequence of a defect in the equipment of the ship. He also considered that the acts of the master and other crew were wrongful and were acts for which the owners of the ship and their employer would be held vicariously liable. He cited in particular the master's decision to set sail in breach of his undertaking, the acts of the crew members under the command of the first officer who assaulted the plaintiffs and put them in such fear of their lives that they jumped or fell overboard, the act of immobilising the life rafts, the omission of the master to undertake a proper search and rescue operation and the delay in reporting the men overboard to shore-based authorities. Ultimately, Mr Justice Murray concluded that the acts in question were directly part of the management of the ship and that the Admiralty Act accordingly conferred jurisdiction.

Hence personal injuries suffered by a seafarer as a result of mistreatment on board a vessel may well be grounds for arresting the vessel pursuant to the Admiralty Act 1988. This case could be the beginning of a body of law that will provide a significant weapon against crew abuse. *Yulianto & Ors* will also be authority for the proposition that a claim arising out of a culpable defect in a telemedicine system installed on board an ocean-going vessel would also clearly come within the Admiralty jurisdiction of the High Court, that system being a part of the ship's "apparel or equipment" pursuant to section 4(3) of the Australian Admiralty Act or section 20(2)(f) of the Supreme Court Act 1981.

## Judgment of a foreign court

Section 34 of the Civil Jurisdiction and Judgments Act 1982 states:

> No proceedings may be brought by a person in England and Wales or Northern Ireland on a cause of action in respect of which a judgment has been given in his favour in proceedings between the same parties, or their privies, in a court in another part of the United Kingdom or in a court of an overseas country, unless that judgment is not enforceable or entitled to recognition in England or Wales or, as the case may be, in Northern Ireland.

Where there are separate causes of action against different defendants for the same damage, for instance, where there is a claim against both a teleconsulting doctor and a lay-person, a judgment obtained against one of them in a foreign court, even though satisfied, is not a bar to proceedings against the other for the same *damnum* in courts of this country, save that the damages eventually awarded to the plaintiff telepatient must be reduced by the amount by which they have been *pro tanto* satisfied by the foreign judgment.[29]

## Limitation periods

A question that very often arises in medical malpractice claims is the effect of foreign limitation periods on actionability there. Previously, the law distinguished between extinction of remedy and extinction of right but the present position is to be found in the Foreign Limitation Periods Act 1984. This provides that the English court shall apply the relevant foreign law as to limitation of actions generally rather than the English law relating to limitation. If an action is time-barred there, it is time-barred here although the Act does reserve to the English courts discretion to ignore foreign law if it conflicts with public policy or would cause undue hardship to a plaintiff telepatient.

## Finding our way out of the maze

The complexity and uncertainty created by the above maze of common law, convention and statute may, it is hoped, be either safely navigated or avoided by one of two approaches.

### (i) The Private International Law (Miscellaneous Provisions) Act 1995

The first solution would be to invoke Part III of the Private International Law (Miscellaneous Provisions) Act 1995 which received the Royal Assent in November 1995. This Act is designed to facilitate civil actions by foreigners in the English courts, by allowing them to sue for wrongful acts, under their own laws, if this is substantially more appropriate. The Act provides that the applicable law is the law of the country in which the events constituting the tort or delict in question occur. The place where the negligent act is committed will, therefore, become the jurisdiction whose law governs a claim for medical malpractice or product liability. Where the negligence of the teleconsulting doctor *and* a lay-person in another jurisdiction both contribute to the harm befalling a telepatient and occur in different jurisdictions, the applicable law is taken as being that of the jurisdiction where the telepatient was when he or she sustained the injury. However, there is one special provision in that, where it appears in all the circumstances that from a comparison of:

(a) the significance of the factors which connect a tort with the country whose law would be the applicable law under the general rule, and

(b) the significance of any factors connecting the tort with another country, that is substantially more appropriate

then the general rule is displaced and the applicable law will be the law of that other country. Factors to be taken into account as connecting an act of malpractice of a teleconsultant or instructed lay-person with another country will include their respective nationalities, the nationality of the telepatient involved, if on board a ship then the nationality of the ship and the status of the waters they are sailing in, as well as the circumstances and consequences of such an event.[30]

### (ii) Jurisdiction clauses

The second possible solution would be for the telemedicine service and accompanying equipment to be provided to users in foreign jurisdictions under a contract which provided that any claim for product liability or medical malpractice arising from treatment or advice given through the system was to be referred to the jurisdiction of a particular court or tribunal. It is quite common for a contract to provide that all disputes will be referred to the jurisdiction of an English or a foreign court or to an independent arbitration tribunal. In these circumstances the named court would stay proceedings brought in that country in breach of contract unless, of course, the plaintiff telepatient established that it would be just and proper to allow them to continue. The approach in cases where there is a jurisdiction clause is essentially that where the parties have voluntarily agreed to a choice of forum clause, they should be bound by it, unless there are strong reasons why this should not be so.[31]

## Summary

▶ The difficulties experienced in the United States of America concerning jurisdictional issues arising from licensing and insuring teleconsultants to practise "out-of-state" should serve as a warning to British and European teleconsultants that these issues can be complex and difficult to resolve.

▶ In the United Kingdom, the Brussels and Lugano Conventions governing choice of law state that a plaintiff telepatient may sue a defendant in either that defendant's country of domicile or in the country where the harm took place. These are known as the "primary" and "alternative" jurisdictions though in practice they tend to be given equal precedence by the European Court of Justice.

▶ Where the Brussels and Lugano Conventions do not apply a writ may be served on the defendant if he is present in the United Kingdom but a stay of proceedings will usually be granted if the matters in dispute have little or no connection with the UK.

▶ Under the Computer Misuse Act 1990 computer hackers can be prosecuted in the United Kingdom where their crime was either directed at a computer in the UK or was performed using a computer in the UK against a telemedicine system located in another country.

▶ Harmful events taking place on board British registered vessels or in British territorial waters are treated as if they had occurred within Britain proper, provided that is the appropriate place to hear the dispute.

▶ Harmful events taking place on board a foreign flagged vessel or in the territorial waters of a foreign state will be subject to the laws of that foreign flag or state. The English courts will not accept jurisdiction over such an event unless the harm would have been actionable in the courts of the foreign state as well as the British courts.

▶ The complexities of private international law can be avoided by bringing a claim in the British courts to which the law of the country in which the harmful event took place is applied, under the Private International Law (Miscellaneous Provisions) Act 1995 or by expressly agreeing upon which legal system will be used in the event of a dispute (a "jurisdiction clause") in a contract for the provision of telemedical services.

## References

1   See further, PIAA. *Telemedicine: an overview of applications and barriers – a malpractice industry perspective*. Rockville: Physician Insurers Association of America, 1996.
2   For a full account see *Clerk & Lindsell* on *Torts*; *Dicey & Morris* on *The Conflict of Laws*; Morris, *The Conflicts of Laws* or Cheshire and North, *Private International Law*.
3   Granade JD, Phyllis F, Sanders MD, Jay H. Implementing telemedicine nationwide: analysing the legal issues. *Defence Counsel Journal* 1; 63: 72.
4   Mjoseth J. Model Act would create special licences for physicians practising telemedicine. *BNA Health Law Reporter* 1995; 4: 1645.
5   California SB 2098. Signed by the Governor on 24 September 1996.
6   See Granade JD, Phyllis F. Implementing telemedicine on a national basis – a legal analysis of the licensure issues. *Federation Bulletin* 1996; 83: 7.

7   As illustrated in cases such as *International Shoe Co* v *State of Washington* (1945) 326 US 310 at p. 316 and *Southern Machine Co* v *Mohasco Industries Inc* (1968) 401 F 2d 374 at p. 381. See further on this topic Landau J. The effect of multi-media communication on jurisdiction and enforcement. *Communications Law* 1996; 1: 58.

8   Case no C2-94-91, USDC, Ohio (1994).

9   471 US 462 (1985).

10  (1945) 148 F 2d 416.

11  Landau J. The effect of multi-media communication on jurisdiction and enforcement. *Communications Law* 1996; 1: 60. See also *United States* v *General Electric Co* (1949) 82 F Supp 753 DNJ.

12  *Spiliada Maritime Corp* v *Consulex Ltd* [1987] AC 460; *The "Abidin Daver"* [1984] AC 398 and *Trendtex Trading Corp* v *Credit Suisse* [1982] AC 679.

13  See Article 2 of the Brussels and Lugano Conventions.

14  Article 5(3) of the Brussels and Lugano Conventions.

15  [1995] All ER 289.

16  Case 21/76, [1976] ECR 1735.

17  [1988] 2 Lloyd's Rep 621.

18  *Spiliada Maritime Corp* v *Cansulex Limited* (supra).

19  *SNI Aerospatiale* v *Lee Kui Jak* [1987] 3 All ER 510 (HL).

20  [1985] Crim LR 369.

21  [1990] 1 QB 391 (CA).

22  *Spiliada Maritime Corp* v *Cansulex Limited* (supra); *Arab Monetary Fund* v *Hashim* (No.3) [1991] 2 AC 114.

23  (1870) LR 6 QB 1 at p. 28-29.

24  *Canadian National Steamship Co*.v *Watson* [1939] 1 DLR 273.

25  [1971] AC 356.

26  *The "Arum"* [1921] P 12. See also *Sayers* v *International Drilling Co NV* [1971] 1 WLR 1176; [1971] 3 All ER 163 (CA) applying Dutch law to an injury on a Dutch drilling rig in Nigerian waters.

27  *The "Esso Malaysia"* [1975] QB 198; [1974] 2 All ER 705.

28  (1995) 134 ALR 92.

29  *Kohnke* v *Karger* [1951] 2 KB 670.

30  See sections 11 & 12, Private International Law (Miscellaneous Provisions) Act 1995.

31  *The "Eleftheria"* [1969] 1 Lloyd's Rep 237; *Aratra Potato Company Ltd and Morello International Ltd* v *Owners of the El Amira* [1980] 1 Lloyd's Rep 390.

# ▶ 10
# Regulating telemedicine in the future

In leading text on medical law Kennedy and Grubb[1] argue that litigation between patients and doctors has long been recognised as a less than satisfactory means of regulating the doctor–patient relationship and dealing with a patient's unhappiness over treatment – a view we examined and concurred with in chapter 5. But despite the arguments of many well-regarded doctors and lawyers, the system of tort litigation continues to be the means by which patients must seek compensation from NHS trusts, health authorities or telemedicine services.

For many patients, this means that recompense is often simply not available. Indeed, many potential classes of telepatient, such as a merchant seafarer, an elderly person or someone living in a remote area, would find it very difficult if not impossible to avail themselves of a country's civil legal system without the practical and financial assistance of a powerful trade union or an altruistic attorney. Even with that assistance, gaining access to medical records, finding expert witnesses and proving causation would be a colossal task. Indeed, a Council of Europe colloquy on the civil liability of physicians, held in Lyons in June 1975, reported that most of the doctors and lawyers there agreed that information should be more readily available to a patient's legal advisers.[2]

A situation where the telepatient is unable to complain about the standard of his or her care, however, would be contrary to the whole spirit in which telemedicine has been conceived. The telehealth care system must develop in a way which is professionally and ethically regulated to the very highest standards. Telemedicine is, after all, about improving the quality of health care and the quality of people's lives, as well as reducing the cost of providing that health care where possible. Seafarers and people living in remote rural areas have to endure greater hardships than perhaps any other class of telepatients; they have higher mortality rates from accidents and serious illnesses than those in suburban areas, and greater problems with alcoholism and depression. Telemedicine and telecare will help to mitigate much of the hardship that comes with living and working in environments where up to now, standards of medical care and health education have been poor, and of course will improve the quality of life still further for those of us who need the care of specialists from time to time. But if telemedicine is to improve healthcare so radically, it is as well to ensure from the outset that it is properly regulated, with all the necessary safeguards in place.

In practice this means, as we have seen earlier, not only undertaking comprehensive clinical risk assessments from the outset but also providing clear guidelines and protocols on practice and procedure. Such guidelines or protocols could well look something like the "Clinical Risk Points" proposed by Darkins in his paper *The management of clinical risk in telemedicine applications*:

> ▶ Any telemedicine application should be viewed in terms of its health care context, the clinical process it is enabling, and whether it is appropriate to apply telemedicine to that process.
> ▶ The appropriate use of telemedicine should be as a tool to enable the transfer of clinical information which, by being transferred, will reduce the clinical risks.

► Because managing clinical services involves knowing where clinical decisions are being made, it is important to ensure that telemedicine activity is recorded as part of the routine clinical and investigative data sets that will be kept for clinical audit and health service costing purposes.

► There may be areas of health care delivery where the telemedicine solution becomes the treatment of choice. In this event, *not* to provide telemedicine may be unethical and may expose a service to high levels of clinical risk.

► If a service is based on the use of telemedicine, it is important to ensure that the technical specifications are adequate, that the system is sufficiently reliable, and that there are adequate back-up provisions in the case of system failure.[3]

## Malpractice insurance through existing subscriptions

The insurance subscriptions paid by doctors working at hospitals in a telemedicine network should be viewed in the context of those paid by other professions. Although it is difficult to make comparisons between the risks involved in providing telemedical care and those involved in giving other forms of professional advice, it should certainly be possible to give such advice a "risk-rating" and hence arrive at a premium for liability insurance that expresses this risk and can be included in the premiums paid in respect of the insurance of conventional medical practice. The risk could therefore be expressed simply as part of the overall cost of providing medical care and perhaps be subsidised, at least in the early stages, by the telemedicine industry itself. The danger here, however, is that telemedicine might be given a comparatively high differential insurance premium which will act as a disincentive for doctors and hospitals considering entering the telemedical field. Moreover, there is the possibility, as with all state-of-the-art technologies in development, that the cost of manufacturer's liability insurance will be prohibitively expensive, this expense being passed on (in the absence of subsidisation) to the ultimate purchasers of a telemedicine system. Unless government is prepared to bear a major share of the additional burden of providing telemedical care, therefore, changing this particular aspect of health care financial management might be highly detrimental to the development and expansion of telemedicine in the United Kingdom.

Of course, that is not to say that telemedicine might, in the final analysis, incur no additional premium at all. Neither the Medical Defence Union nor the Medical Protection Society have any plans, at present, to charge higher premiums of those involved in teleconsultancy. Dr Lori Bartholemew, Director of Loss Prevention and Research at the Physician Insurers Association of America (PIAA), believes that telemedicine, in common with any other new technology or procedure, requires up-to-date equipment and training in order to obtain positive outcomes in the largest majority of cases. So where this is achieved the potential benefits to patients that telemedicine has to offer should far outweigh the risks.

But one area that does concern the PIAA as well as their counterparts in the United Kingdom's Medical Protection Society is the practice of medicine on the Internet. Both Dr Lori Bartholemew at the PIAA and Dr Gerard Ponting of the MPS believe that far too many physicians are turning this sort of activity into a business venture. Because, as we saw in chapter 5, a doctor owes a duty of care to any person to whom he has held himself out as being available to provide medical care, there *is* a doctor–patient relationship formed via an Internet consultation. In a letter to the author Dr Bartholomew has stated:

> I don't believe the disclaimer statements that exist will protect them [doctors practising medicine on the Internet] from a liability action if an untoward outcome occurs to a patient. Liability carriers need to know the extent of the activities of practitioners on the Internet. If an action does occur, I believe that the first phone call that a practitioner will make is to their liability carrier for coverage. Suddenly, carriers will be faced with the possibility of defending international claims and the like and will be at a disadvantage in their defence. Carriers need to know the extent to which this exposure exists.

So the possibility that, in an otherwise all-embracing insurance policy provided to a doctor engaged in teleconsultancy, the provision of medical advice via the Internet will be specifically excluded from cover, is a very real one.

## Independent tribunals

This insurance solution looks only at providing for the outcome of a negligence action – an action which, as we have already considered, should seldom be brought. The fact remains, though, that there should be an accessible procedure for dealing with an aggrieved telepatient, or their next of kin, without resort to litigation. Such a procedure could take the form of an independent tribunal to which all users and providers of telemedical care must expressly agree to submit malpractice and product liability claims. The tribunal would need to be independent of the personnel and companies involved in telemedicine, accessible and cheap to operate.

We have also identified the need for literature to be made available to the telepatient explaining how telemedicine works, as well as the need to obtain the advance consents of the telepatient to the various processes requiring such consent (i.e. the transmission and receipt of medical records and the giving of treatment). Ideally the telepatient could also be made aware at this time, and in the same manner, of the means by which a complaint might be brought if he or she believes they have been poorly treated, in conjunction with the "Information Charter" proposed in chapter 4. Similar forums exist in other contexts, e.g. the Association of British Travel Agents (ABTA) for disappointed holidaymakers bringing claims against travel agents. Although medical negligence claims and claims against travel companies differ fundamentally in many respects, the speed and efficiency that such a tribunal would bring to telemedicine claims – perhaps with the potential to deal with many of these entirely on paper without the need for a formal hearing – would greatly benefit manufacturers, teleconsultants, medical officers and telepatients alike.

## No-fault compensation schemes

The term "no-fault" compensation refers, strictly, to any scheme which abandons the rule that an injured telepatient must show that the teleconsulting doctor was negligent in order to obtain redress. However, there is a distinction between those schemes which still require patients to identify an individual responsible for their condition and those which don't. The former, examples of which are seen in Sweden and New Zealand, share with the negligence system the advantage of being able to make constructive use of the desire of injured patients to obtain redress. Adverse outcomes can be attributed to individual doctors and, at least potentially, used as a basis for promoting high standards. Those schemes, on the other hand, that break the link between the patient "victim" and the agent(s) of their injuries must find alternative ways of achieving this objective, although it is questionable whether in the case of the telepatient, as distinct from other classes of patient, this would be a high priority, for the reasons given below.

In many of the countries in which telepatients will be treated there is no welfare state. Hence whilst in the United Kingdom the attribution of "fault" to an individual has some value to the injured patient in their desire to see justice done, but achieves less in terms of putting right something done badly, in other jurisdictions such as the United States of America, compensation is essential if the patient is to put right what was carried out improperly or negligently in the first instance. The importance of a successful outcome to the telepatient may often be rooted more in the practicalities of being fit to work than in the desire for attrition.

The extent to which the differences between these two types of "no fault" scheme cause problems will depend on the ability of individual teleconsultants to avoid accidents. If a hospital in a telemedicine network adopts the pragmatic attitude that an accident is better understood as a result of organisational or technological failures, rather than personal mistakes, then that attribution of responsibility to an individual doctor or manufacturer is otiose. All that is required is adequate information to demonstrate that the telepatient's injury arose from medical treatment together with a means of referring that information to the appropriate manager or component in the NHS trust or health authority. Information on claims for compensation might then be fed back to the teams of doctors responsible for providing telemedical services at the local level and be used in general reviews of the telemedicine or telecare service to alert all service providers of common problems.

## Improving health care through telemedicine

Where the alleged negligence is that of, say, a ship's medical officer – essentially the negligence of one employee towards another – the shipowner or demise charterer of the ship will be vicariously liable for that harm and a claim would ideally proceed in an almost identical manner to any conventional claim brought for injury in the workplace. Where the harm results from a failure to comply with statutory provisions there will be a breach of statutory duty from which strict liability will arise. Likewise, where a nurse practitioner or lay-person causes harm there may be an NHS trust or health authority that can be approached and which will be vicariously liable for the acts or omissions of their employees, according to the legal principles examined in chapter 5.

Once again, however, one can query the extent to which the involvement of a lay-person such as a ship's medical officer (who is often little more than a glorified first-aider) in the provision of medical care according to instructions administered through a telemedicine system will create a new and distinct risk for which a separate insurance "risk-rating" must be applied and, in the final analysis, a greater premium paid. Would this constitute an unacceptable risk for most telemedicine service providers, or the purchasers of such a service? Would they simply "self-insure" and pass the risk on through their rates? Alternatively, would they cut costs elsewhere, for instance by reducing wages? The installation of telemedicine terminals on board ocean-going vessels, in remote areas and at other sites where non-professional medics will be administering medical care on the basis of instructions received through the telemedicine service, will undoubtedly need to be accompanied by comprehensive regulations and procedures to ensure the equipment is correctly and competently used. The great danger the European Union faces is that there are plenty of shipowners in business, to whom telemedicine terminals might in due course be supplied, who frequently cut corners in many aspects of the running of their ships. They may fail to implement many of the system's requirements and make no provision whatsoever for the training of medical officers – not only in the proper use of telemedicine terminals, but also in the minor surgical and medical techniques they must know to be able to get the best from such a service. Moreover, the regular maintenance of telemedical equipment may also, in time, be overlooked. Clearly if the "risk-rating" for telemedical consulting is to be kept as low as possible, great emphasis will need to be placed on both initial and "refresher" training courses for personnel, as well as on the continuing serviceability and operability of installed hardware. The decline in the importance of the ship's medical officer must be halted, and his unique role as the facilitator of telecare, re-asserted. Nurses and other non-doctors would likewise need the benefit of proper, comprehensive training and frequent revision of their skills.

## Standards in the design and delivery of telemedicine services

Quality management system standards have taken on a great deal of importance in the manufacture and supply of medical equipment since the European Union's medical devices Directives came into force. There is a presumption of compliance with the essential requirements of the Directives necessary for telemedical equipment manufactured in the EU to receive the "CE" mark and hence be marketed within the Union, where quality management systems are used which comply with the relevant harmonised standards. Where standards in the ISO 9000/EN 29000 and EN 46000 series are used, the Notified Body appointed by the Medical Devices Agency must presume that the items manufactured comply with the requirements of the Directives.

The EN 29000 series of standards specifies the components needed in order to set up and manage a quality system, regardless of the product or production technology. Standard EN 29000 is the basis for the entire series since it deals with the general philosophy underlying quality systems standards. Standard EN 29001 deals with the most complete quality system, the components of which cover all aspects including design/development, production, installation and servicing. Standard EN 29002 covers production and installation. Standard EN 29003 deals with final inspection and testing and Standard EN 29004 is intended to assist managers in designing, developing and setting up the quality system most suited to the company.

The EN 46000 series of standards defines particular requirements for quality systems relating specifically to medical devices. It embraces all the principles of quality systems management widely used in the manufacture of such devices. It is also supported by other harmonised standards covering such aspects as sterilisation. It can only be used in combination with the EN 29000 series of standards.

## The view from here

If there is one lesson that teleconsultants could learn thus far from what lawyers have done for the medical profession then, ironically, it would be to keep them out of telemedicine as much as possible. We should perhaps qualify this by saying that we consider the involvement of lawyers in medicine and health care to be essential. But it is the manner of that involvement which concerns us. A potted history of modern medical litigation shows that lawyers are more than willing to get involved in what might be called the negative aspects of medico-legal practice: medical malpractice litigation. On the other hand, the numbers of lawyers involved in the positive tasks of assisting trusts with clinical risk assessment and management are few, and those assisting the telemedicine community, even fewer. It is the medical profession that, by and large, sets the standards that must be attained by medical practitioners, not the lawyers. And it is the telemedical profession that, by and large, *should* set the standards that must be attained by telemedical practitioners.

There is a belief among some members of the legal, medical and telemedical professions that the answers to questions about the legal and ethical aspects of telemedicine will only become clear as these issues are litigated. Litigation does indeed provide authoritative answers – particularly where complex issues are argued right the way up to the House of Lords. But so much more can be accomplished by examining existing medical practice and clinical risks carefully.

The coming years will see the integration of this decade's numerous telemedicine research and development projects into the mainstream of health care, and there will be a continuing need for comprehensive, informed and focused information on the evolving legal and ethical issues in telemedical practice. We hope this book, informed by the views and experiences of teleconsultants and health managers themselves, has begun to address that need.

## References

1　Kennedy I, Grubb A. *Medical law: text with materials*. (2nd ed.) London: Butterworths, 1994: 508.
2　See further *Report of the Royal commission on Civil Liability and Compensation for Personal Injury*. Cmnd 7054, 1978.
3　Darkins A. The management of clinical risk in telemedicine applications. *Journal of Telemedicine and Telecare* 1995; 2: 179-184.

# ▶ Glossary

**Anatomy** the bodily structure of the human body and the study of the same.

**Biopsy** the examination of tissue removed from the body to discover the presence, cause or extent of a disease.

**Cardiac** of or relating to the heart.

**Cardiology** the section of medical science concerned with the function and diseases of the heart.

**Common law** that part of the law of England formulated, developed and administered by the law courts.

**Compression** the reduction in volume of a computer program or set of instructions or of a computer generated display, usually for the purposes of its transmission.

**Computed tomography (CT)** a computer assisted scanning technique which displays details of a cross-section through the body.

**Computer virus** a hidden code within a computer program intended to corrupt a system or destroy data stored in it.

**Contract** an agreement enforceable at law. An essential feature of a contract is a promise by one party to another to do or forebear from doing certain specified acts. The offer of a promise becomes a promise by acceptance. Contract is that species of agreement whereby legal obligation is constituted and defined between the parties to it.

**Copyright** the exclusive right of reproducing or otherwise multiplying copies of a published literary, dramatic or musical work and of preventing others from doing the same.

**Coronary ischaemia** the narrowing of the arteries which supply the heart muscles with blood until they are unable to transport sufficient blood for the muscles to function efficiently. If the narrowing occurs slowly, then the individual will show signs of a failing heart such as pains on exertion. If it occurs suddenly, in a major artery, then the victim collapses in acute pain and distress. This is sometimes known as a "heart attack".

**Damnum** Latin legal expression meaning "harm" or "damage".

**Decompression** the return to normal size of a compressed computer program or image.

**De minimis non curat lex** a Latin legal expression meaning "the law does not concern itself with trivialities".

**Dermatology** the study of the diagnosis and treatment of the skin and its disorders.

**Diagnosis** the identification of a disease by means of a patient's symptoms, and the opinion arrived at as to the nature of that disease.

**Dicta** the observations of a Judge contained in his judgment of a case. *Obiter dicta* is a saying on a legal question suggested by a case but not actually requiring a decision. The *ratio decidendi* is the reason or ground of a decision.

**Duodenum** the first part of the small intestine immediately beyond the stomach.

**Electrocardiogram (ECG)** a record traced by an electrocardiograph, an instrument which records the electric currents generated by a person's heartbeat.

**Endocrinology** the study of the endocrine system, the substances (hormones) it secretes and its disorders.

**ENT** refers to the medical and surgical speciality of studying and treating the diseases which affect the ear, nose and throat.

**Equity**   the body of rules based on fairness and natural justice which supplement the rules and procedures of the common law.

**Ex parte**   an application in a judicial proceeding made by a person who is either interested in a case but not a party to it or by one party in the absence of another.

**Fiduciary**   the relationship of one person to another where the former is bound to exercise rights and powers in good faith for the benefit of the latter; e.g. as between a solicitor and his client.

**Fluoroscopy**   the use of X-ray images viewed on a fluorescent screen without taking and developing X-ray photographs, often used to study patient physiology such as heartbeat and respiration.

**Forum**   a place where disputes may be tried; a court. Usually used to refer to the particular court or courts having jurisdiction in a matter.

**Gastric**   of or pertaining to the stomach.

**Gastroenterology**   the branch of medicine which deals with disorders of the stomach and intestine.

**Gynaecology**   the science of the physiological functions and diseases affecting the female reproductive system.

**Histology**   the study of the microscopic structure of tissues.

**Histopathology**   the study of changes in tissues caused by disease.

**Hyperglycaemia**   an excess of glucose in the bloodstream, often associated with diabetes.

**Hypoglycaemia**   a deficiency of glucose in the bloodstream.

**ISDN**   Integrated Services Digital Network, a type of digital telecommunication service allowing the integrated transmission of voice data and still pictures.

**Jurisdiction**   the district or limits within which the judgments or orders of a court can be enforced or executed.

**Legislation**   the process of making laws or the product of that process, usually used to refer to written law.

**Litigation**   the conduct and process of legal action.

**Locus delicti**   a Latin legal expression meaning "the law governing the matter".

**Logic bomb**   a set of instructions secretly incorporated into a program so that if a particular logical condition is satisfied they will be carried out, usually with harmful effects.

**Magnetic resonance imaging (MRI)**   a form of medical imaging using the nuclear magnetic resonance of protons in the body.

**Malpractice**   improper or inadequate medical treatment that fails to match the standards of skill and care that are reasonably expected from a qualified health care practitioner – usually a doctor or dentist.

**Medico-legal**   of or pertaining to both medicine and law.

**Morbidity rate**   the number of diseases or injuries received per 1000 persons over a given year.

**Mortality rate**   the number of deaths per 1000 persons over a given year.

**Myoskeletal**   of or pertaining to the muscles and bones.

**Neurosurgery**   surgery performed on the brain or the spinal column.

**Nuclear medicine**   the use of electromagnetic radiation in body imaging for diagnosis.

**Obstetrics**   the branch of medicine and surgery concerned with childbirth and midwifery.

**Oncology**   the study and treatment of cancer.

**Orthopaedics**   the branch of medicine dealing with the treatment of disorders of the bones and joints and the correction of deformities.

**Paediatrics**   the branch of medicine dealing with children and their diseases.

**Patent**   the right to the exclusive use and benefit of a new invention capable of industrial application.

**Pathology**   the science of bodily diseases and their symptoms.

**Per**   as stated by.

**Prognosis**   a forecast of the course of a disease.

**Pro tanto**   Latin legal expression meaning "for so much" or "to that extent".

**Psychiatry**   the study and treatment of mental illness and disease.

**PSTN**   Public Switched Telephone Network.

**Radiology**   the scientific study of X-rays and other high-energy radiation, especially for medical purposes.

**Research and development**   work directed towards the innovation, introduction and improvement of products and processes.

**Res ipsa loquitur**   a Latin legal expression meaning "the thing speaks for itself".

**Respiration**   the act or an instance of breathing in and out.

**Statute**   an Act of Parliament, particularly a public Act.

**Thermography**   the taking or use of images produced by infra-red radiation from a human or animal body.

**Time bomb**   a program or set of instructions incorporated into a computer designed to be commenced at a pre-set time, usually with harmful effects.

**Tort**   an act which causes harm to a natural or legal person (i.e. a corporation), whether intentionally or not, being the breach of a duty arising out of a personal relation and which is either contrary to law, or an omission of a specific legal duty.

**Trade mark**   a distinctive mark or device affixed to or accompanying an article intended for sale for the purpose of indicating that it is manufactured, selected or sold by a particular person or firm.

**Ulcer**   an open sore on an external or internal surface of the body.

**Ultrasound**   the use of sound waves above the frequency of human hearing to investigate the structure and function of the body and its organs.

**Urology**   the scientific study of the urinary system.

**Videoconferencing**   the use of television sets linked by telephone lines to enable a group of people to communicate with each other in sound and vision.

# ▶ Selected bibliography

## Telemedicine

Cross M. Healthsmart 2010: *A Tale of Life, Death and Health Care in the Information Age*. London: Kable, 1997.
NHS Estates: *Telemedicine: Health Guidance Note*. London: The Stationery Office, 1997.
Royal Society of Medicine Press Ltd. *Journal of Telemedicine and Telecare*. 1995-1998.

## Confidentiality, rights of access, consent and malpractice

Brazier M. *Medicine, Patients and the Law*. 2nd edn. London: Penguin, 1992.
British Medical Association. *Medical Ethics Today: its Practice and Philosophy*. London: BMJ Publishing Group, 1996.
British Medical Association. *Rights and Responsibilities of Doctors*. London: BMJ Publishing Group, 1992.
General Medical Council. *The Duties of a Doctor*: guidance from the General Medical Council. London: GMC, 1995.
Kennedy I, Grubb A. *Medical Law: Text with Materials*. 2nd edn. London: Butterworths, 1994.
Knight, B. *Legal Aspects of Medical Practice*. 5th edn. Edinburgh: Churchill Livingstone, 1992.
Jones M, Morris A. *Statutes on Medical Law*. London: Blackstone Press, 1994.

## Data protection, security and European law

Bainbridge DI. *Introduction to Computer Law*. 2nd edn. London: Pitman Publishing, 1993.
Barber B, Treacher A, Louwerse CP. *Medical Telematics: Legal and Technical Aspects*. Amsterdam: IOS Press, 1996.
Reed C. *Computer Law*. 3rd edn. London: Blackstone Press, 1996.
Commission of the European Communities (ed). *Data Protection and Confidentiality in Health Informatics: Handling Health Data in Europe in the Future*. Amsterdam: IOS Press, 1991.
Van Goor JN, Christensen JP (eds). *Advances in Medical Informatics: Results of the AIM Exploratory Action*. Amsterdam: IOS Press, 1992.

## Medical equipment and product liability

Powers M, Harris N. *Medical Negligence*. 2nd edn. London: Butterworths, 1994.
Jones M. *Medical Negligence*. London: Sweet & Maxwell, 1991.
Jones M. *Medical Negligence*. First Supplement to the First Edition. London: Sweet & Maxwell, 1994.

## Intellectual property rights and competition law

Cornish WR. *Intellectual Property*. 3rd edn. London: Sweet and Maxwell, 1996.

Korah V. An *Introductory Guide to EC Competition Law and Practice*. 6th edn. Oxford: Hart Publishing, 1997.

Phillips J, ed. *Butterworths Intellectual Property Handbook*. 3rd edn. London: Butterworths, 1997.

## Jurisdiction

Dicey, AV. *Dicey and Morris on the Conflict of Laws*. 12th edn. London: Sweet & Maxwell, 1993.

Cheshire, GC. *Cheshire and North's Private International Law*. 12th edn. London: Butterworths, 1992.

# ▶ Index